Jeremiah

A Study in Ancient Hebrew Rhetoric

Jeremiah

A Study in
Ancient Hebrew Rhetoric

Second Edition

Jack R. Lundbom

Winona Lake, Indiana
EISENBRAUNS
1997

Library of Congress Cataloging in Publication Data

Lundbom, Jack R.
  Jeremiah : a study in ancient Hebrew rhetoric / Jack R. Lundbom —
2nd ed.
      p.   cm.
  Originally presented as the author's thesis—Graduate Theological
Union, Berkeley, 1973.
  Includes bibliographical references and indexes.
  ISBN 1-57506-016-7 (pbk. : alk. paper)
  1. Bible. O.T. Jeremiah—Language, Style.   2. Bible. O.T. Jeremiah—
Criticism, interpretation, etc.   I. Title.
BS1525.2.L86   1997
224'.2066—dc21   96-53337
                                                              CIP

To
James Muilenburg
Scholar, Teacher, Friend

Contents

Preface

The present study was presented as a dissertation to the San Francisco Theological Seminary and the Graduate Theological Union in the spring of 1973, and is here made available to a wider reading audience in essentially the form in which it was presented. The research upon which the study is built has a longer history, however, more like ten years from start to finish. During this time many have contributed to the final product and I now happily give them the credit which it is rightly theirs to receive.

My interest in structure predates any work in Jeremiah. While doing my B.D. work at North Park Theological Seminary I was introduced to a book by Nils W. Lund entitled *Chiasmus in the New Testament*. Lund taught at North Park from 1922–1953 and was its dean from 1925–1949. He was also a family friend, but unfortunately one I was never able to know as scholar and teacher. I nevertheless developed a quick kinship with him during my seminary days and his particular interest in "chiasmus" became mine as well.

The book of Jeremiah was opened up to me by William L. Holladay, another scholar for whom I have the highest regard. It was my privilege to study with Professor Holladay during 1964–1965 at the Near East School of Theology in Beirut. Already by then a scholar of Jeremiah, his interest in structure and style—not to mention his expertise in the biblical languages—was sufficient to push me further along a course I had already chosen. Together we set to work on Jeremiah and our labors, especially in the poetry, were more than amply rewarded. The reader will have no difficulty in seeing the extent to which he has put me in his debt. Professor Holladay, although not a member of my doctoral committee, has been supportive of my work all along the way. He encouraged the dissertation's publication and has rendered help in proofreading a portion of the final manuscript.

My doctoral work was done primarily under the direction of James Muilenburg. Professor Muilenburg had already distinguished himself as a scholar and teacher at Union Theological Seminary in New York, but in his later years at San Anselmo was still vigorous and much beloved by students, all of whom drank freely from his deep well of knowledge and were able to profit immeasurably from a mind that had now come to maturity. I am grateful to have been one of those students. Seminars in Deuteronomy and Jeremiah contributed to my research, not least of all in helping me to clarify my methodology. Dr. Muilenburg was chairman of my doctoral committee until his retirement in 1971. Because of failing health he was able to read only part of the dissertation in first draft. Nevertheless I continued to write as if he were still listening. Now it is to him I dedicate what is finally done. I owe him far more. Wilhelm Wuellner chaired my committee following Dr. Muilenburg's departure and handled the final stages of dissertation preparation and the oral defense exceedingly well.

The other scholar with whom I worked closely in my doctoral studies was David Noel Freedman. Professor Freedman is another outstanding Old Testament scholar who contributed much to the present work. His probing questions brought about a necessary refinement of my thinking, and his insistence that biblical scholarship employ a rigorous historical and scientific methodology helped bring a measure of objectivity to my work when I may otherwise have relied too much on strict intuition. I also received from him a better understanding of Hebrew poetry. Dr. Freedman supported the dissertation from the beginning and became its primary support in the final stages. He carefully read two drafts and made comments that improved the work greatly over what it might otherwise have been.

Others joined my committee at various points along the way and I owe each of them a word of thanks. Professor Edwin M. Good of Stanford and Professor Norman K. Gottwald were members of the dissertation committee in addition to being readers of the dissertation. Each in his own way contributed to the final product. I also wish to thank Professors Thomas Conley and William J. Brandt of the Rhetoric Department at the University of California, Berkeley, for their interest in my work. I profited from their insistence that a rhetorical study of Jeremiah be related to studies in rhetorical criticism currently being done outside biblical studies. The result is thus a work which is essentially inter-disciplinary. Professor Brandt kindly supplied me with a portion of the manuscript for his forthcoming book *The Rhetoric of Poetry*. This was much appreciated. I must convey thanks also to Professor Leonard Nathan of the Rhetoric Department at UCB for allowing me the use of his article on Vedic poetry prior to publication.

I was privileged to have Professor Norbert Lohfink, who in 1973 was visiting the GTU from Germany, as reader and guest at my oral defense. He proved to be a stimulating critic, and he is one with whom I hope an ongoing dialogue can be maintained.

The San Francisco Theological Seminary graciously afforded me the place to do my study and I thank them for this. Their library was a great asset, and so also was the personal assistance rendered by Head Librarian David Green and Louise Beck. Both aided me in locating materials which might otherwise have remained inaccessible.

To George MacRae of Harvard Divinity School and the Society of Biblical Literature, my thanks for their decision to include this in the new Dissertation Series. Dr. MacRae has provided every possible assistance in the preparation of the dissertation for publication. I have also been fortunate indeed to have a most capable typist, Miss Dorothy Riehm, who with remarkable ease has prepared the camera-ready copy for Scholars' Press.

To Dean George Peck and the Andover Newton Theological School, my thanks for a generous grant of money with which to pay the cost incurred in preparing the dissertation for publication. This too was greatly appreciated.

Finally, my work on Jeremiah has taken me away from my good wife and children, and they are to be thanked for patience and understanding beyond measure. For a long time now they have wondered when the end would finally come. A good family—no less than a good teacher or a good friend—is indeed a gift from God, and it is to him ultimately that thanks must be given, even as it is to him in the end that all glory must be given for whatever good might come of a human effort such as this.

Jack R. Lundbom
Newton Centre, Massachusetts
Easter, March 30, 1975

Preface to the Second Edition

The present work is a dissertation written more than 20 years ago, republished here essentially as it appeared in the Society of Biblical Literature Dissertation Series in 1975. I have not attempted to revise the text even though I might express some things differently now than I did then and could cite additional works that support this point or that. I have resisted as well the urge to improve the style in places where it could be improved. The thesis presented is one I would still defend, and the conclusions reached have not changed substantially, even though my forthcoming *Jeremiah I* in the Anchor Bible series will show more charity toward other lines of research, most notably form criticism. This is as it should be.

I have used the occasion of republication to add an introductory essay that traces the history of rhetorical criticism in America, discusses the enterprise as a method, and examines its use in the book of Jeremiah. The essay was originally given as a lecture on March 18, 1991, to faculty and students of the Åbo Akademi in Åbo (Turku), Finland. My thanks to Professor Karl-Johan Illman for his kind invitation to visit Åbo Akademi, the Swedish university of Finland, and for the warm hospitality he and colleagues displayed on that occasion, making the visit a memorable one. I wish also to acknowledge receipt of a generous grant from the American-Scandinavian Foundation, which supported research and writing of the essay.

Republication has also afforded me the opportunity of updating and expanding the original bibliography. Even then, it is nowhere near being exhaustive. It was possible 20 years ago to compile a reasonably complete bibliography on rhetorical criticism. Today one can no longer do so. The present bibliography will simply give the reader some indication of how studies in rhetorical criticism have multiplied in the intervening period. Included mainly are works on the Old Testament and on non-

biblical texts. A growing number of works are applying rhetorical criticism to the study of the New Testament, a few of
which are also included.

References to pages in the first edition are followed by
double brackets containing the appropriate page numbers in
the second edition.

Jack R. Lundbom
University of California, San Diego
October, 1996

Abbreviations

AB	The Anchor Bible (ed. W. F. Albright and David Noel Freedman)
ABD	*The Anchor Bible Dictionary* (ed. David Noel Freedman; New York, 1992)
ABR	*Australian Biblical Review*
AcOr	*Acta Orientalia* (Copenhagen)
AJP	*American Journal of Philology*
AJSLL	*American Journal of Semitic Languages and Literatures* (continued by *Journal of Near Eastern Studies*)
ANE	Ancient Near East
ANQ	*Andover Newton Quarterly*
AramB	The Aramaic Bible
ATD	Das Alte Testament Deutsch
AThR	*Anglican Theological Review*
AUSS	*Andrews University Seminary Studies*
AV	The Authorized King James Version (1611)
BA	*Biblical Archaeologist*
BASOR	*Bulletin of the American Schools of Oriental Research*
BBR	*Bulletin for Biblical Research*
BDB	*A Hebrew and English Lexicon of the Old Testament* (ed. F. Brown, S. R. Driver, and C. A. Briggs; Oxford, 1962)
BeitM	*Beit Mikra*
BH³	*Biblia Hebraica* (3d edition; ed. R. Kittel)
BHS	*Biblia Hebraica Stuttgartensia* (ed. K. Elliger and W. Rudolph; Liber Jeremiae prepared by W. Rudolph; Stuttgart, 1970)
BHT	Beiträge zur historischen Theologie
BiInt	*Biblical Interpretation*
BiOr	*Bibliotheca Orientalis*
BiRes	*Biblical Research*
BiTr	*The Bible Translator*
BJRL	*Bulletin of the John Rylands University Library of Manchester*
BSOAS	*Bulletin of the School of Oriental and African Studies*
BTB	*Biblical Theology Bulletin*

BWAT	Beiträge zur Wissenschaft vom Alten Testament
BZAW	Beihefte zur Zeitschrift für die Alttestamentliche Wissenschaft
CB	The New Century Bible (ed. W. F. Adene)
CBQ	*Catholic Biblical Quarterly*
CBQMS	Catholic Biblical Quarterly Monograph Series
CBSC	The Cambridge Bible for Schools and Colleges (OT ed. A. F. Kirkpatrick)
CCC	*College Composition and Communication*
CJ	*Classical Journal*
ComLit	*Comparative Literature*
CP	*Classical Philology*
CQ	*Classical Quarterly*
CroQ	*Crozer Quarterly*
CTM	*Concordia Theological Monthly*
DLZ	*Deutsche Literaturzeitung*
DS	*Dansk Studier*
EJ	*Encyclopaedia Judaica* (ed. C. Roth and G. Wigoder; Jerusalem, 1971–73)
EncB	*Encyclopaedia Britannica*
EncBib	*Encyclopaedia Biblica* (ed. T. K. Cheyne and J. Sutherland Black; New York, 1913)
ET	*Expository Times*
GRBS	*Greek, Roman, and Byzantine Studies*
HAR	*Hebrew Annual Review*
HAT	Handbuch zum Alten Testament (ed. Otto Eissfeldt)
HDB	*A Dictionary of the Bible* (ed. James Hastings; New York, 1902)
HDivB	*Harvard Divinity Bulletin*
HebRev	*Hebrew Review*
HibJ	*Hibbert Journal*
HKAT	Handkommentar zum Alten Testament (ed. D. W. Nowack)
HOS	Harvard Oriental Series
HSCP	Harvard Studies in Classical Philology
HSM	Harvard Semitic Monographs
HThR	*Harvard Theological Review*
HUCA	*Hebrew Union College Annual*
IB	*The Interpreter's Bible* (ed. George Buttrick)
ICC	The International Critical Commentary (ed. S. R. Driver, A. Plummer, and C. A. Briggs)

IDB	*The Interpreter's Dictionary of the Bible* (ed. George Buttrick; New York, 1962)
IDB Supp	*The Interpreter's Dictionary of the Bible, Supplementary Volume* (ed. Keith Crimm; Nashville, 1976)
Int	*Interpretation*
ITC	International Theological Commentary
JANES	*Journal of the Ancient Near Eastern Society of Columbia University*
JAOS	*Journal of the American Oriental Society*
JB	*The Jerusalem Bible* (Garden City, N.Y., 1966)
JBL	*Journal of Biblical Literature*
JCS	*Journal of Cuneiform Studies*
JHS	*Journal of Hellenic Studies*
JJS	*Journal of Jewish Studies*
JMEOS	*Journal of the Manchester Egyptian and Oriental Society*
JNABI	*Journal of the National Association of Biblical Instructors* (continued by *Journal of Bible and Religion* and currently *Journal of the American Academy of Religion*)
JNES	*Journal of Near Eastern Studies*
JNSL	*Journal of Northwest Semitic Languages*
JPOS	*Journal of the Palestine Oriental Society*
JQR	*Jewish Quarterly Review*
JR	*Journal of Religion*
JSOT	*Journal for the Study of the Old Testament*
JSS	*Journal of Semitic Studies*
JThS	*Journal of Theological Studies*
JTT	*Journal of Translation and Textlinguistics*
KAT	Kommentar zum Alten Testament (ed. E. Sellin)
KBH	W. L. Holladay, *A Concise Hebrew and Aramaic Lexicon of the Old Testament*, based on *Lexicon in Veteris Testamenti Libros*, by Ludwig Koehler and Walter Baumgartner (Grand Rapids, Mich., 1971)
KHC	Kurzer Hand-Commentar zum Alten Testament
LB	*Linguistica Biblica*
LCL	Loeb Classical Library
LQ	*The Lutheran Quarterly*
LXX	Septuagint, according to *Septuaginta II* (8th edition; ed. Alfred Rahlfs; Stuttgart, 1965)
Ms(s)	Manuscript(s)
MT	Masoretic Text, according to BH³ or BHS
NCBC	The New Century Bible Commentary

NEB	New English Bible (Oxford and Cambridge, 1970)
NICOT	The New International Commentary on the Old Testament
NKZ	*Neue kirchliche Zeitschrift*
NLH	*New Literary History*
NT	*Novum Testamentum*
NTS	*New Testament Studies*
OS	*Oudtestamentische Studiën*
OT	Old Testament
OTL	Old Testament Library
OTM	Old Testament Message
PBA	*Proceedings of the British Academy*
PhRh	*Philosophy and Rhetoric*
PIBA	*Proceedings of the Irish Biblical Association*
PMLA	*Publications of the Modern Language Association of America*
PresO	*Presbyterian Outlook*
QJS	*Quarterly Journal of Speech*
RB	*Revue biblique*
RevBib	*Revista bíblica* (Buenos Aires)
*RGG*²	*Die Religion in Geschichte und Gegenwart* (2d edition)
RIDA	*Revue internationale des droits de l'antiquité*
RQ	*Revue de Qumrân*
RSR	*Recherches de science religieuse*
RSV	Revised Standard Version (New York, 1953)
SBLDS	Society of Biblical Literature Dissertation Series
SBLMS	Society of Biblical Literature Monograph Series
SBU	*Svensk Bibliskt Uppslagsverk I–II* (ed. Ivan Engnell; 2d ed.; Stockholm, 1962–63)
ScrHier	*Scripta hierosolymitana*
SEÅ	*Svensk exegetisk årsbok*
SJOT	*Scandinavian Journal of the Old Testament*
SJT	*Southwestern Journal of Theology*
SpeMo	*Speech Monographs*
ST	*Speech Teacher*
STh	*Studia theologica*
STK	*Svensk teologisk kvartalskrift*
TAik	*Teologinen aikakauskirja*
TAPA	*Transactions and Proceedings of the American Philological Association*
TS	*Theological Studies*

UF	*Ugarit-Forschungen*
UUÅ	Uppsala universitetsårsskrift
VT	*Vetus Testamentum*
VTSupp	Supplements to Vetus Testamentum
WBC	Word Biblical Commentary
WMANT	Wissenschaftliche Monographien zum Alten und Neuen Testament
ZAW	*Zeitschrift für die Alttestamentliche Wissenschaft*
ZDA	*Zeitschrift für deutsches Altertum*
ZNW	*Zeitschrift für die Neutestamentliche Wissenschaft*

Rhetorical Criticism
History, Method and Use in
the Book of Jeremiah

Rhetorical criticism as a non-prescriptive, analytical method for the study of discourse, ancient and modern, oral and written, in prose and in poetry, was born roughly 75 years ago on American soil, where it also developed in subsequent years (1) among non-biblical scholars working in the university and (2) among biblical scholars working largely outside the university. For most of its history neither group has had much direct contact with the other.

Rhetorical Criticism in the American Universities

The beginnings of rhetorical criticism belong to a revival of classical rhetoric that took place in American colleges and universities between 1900 and 1925, a time, ironically enough, when an older rhetoric movement in many of the same institutions had only recently died out. Key figures in this revival included Fred Newton Scott of the University of Michigan, Charles Sears Baldwin of Yale, and after 1914, of Columbia University and Barnard College, James M. O'Neill of Dartmouth and later the University of Wisconsin, and James Albert Winans of Cornell and later Dartmouth.[1] It was with faculty in

---

1. Carroll C. Arnold, "Rhetoric in America since 1900," in *Re-establishing the Speech Profession: The First Fifty Years* (eds. Robert T. Oliver and Marvin G. Bauer; [Mineola, N.Y.]: Speech Association of the Eastern States, 1959), 3–7; Wayne C. Booth, "The Revival of Rhetoric," in *New Rhetorics* (ed. Martin Steinmann Jr.; New York: Scribner's, 1967), 1–15; Robert J. Connors, *et al.*, "The Revival of Rhetoric in America," in *Essays on Classical Rhetoric and Modern Discourse* (eds. Robert J. Connors, *et al.*; Carbondale, Ill.: Southern Illinois University Press, 1984), 1–15; Donald C.

the Department of Speech at Cornell—notably Everett Lee Hunt, Hoyt Hudson, and Herbert Wichelns—that graduate work in rhetoric was first undertaken in America, and rhetorical criticism as we know it today in the American universities was born.[2]

Classical rhetoric had experienced an earlier revival in the mid-18th century, when, for the first time, the works of Cicero and Quintilian became widely available and new textbooks on rhetorical theory and practice were written. When John Quincy Adams became the first Boylston Professor of Rhetoric at Harvard in 1806, rhetoric as an academic discipline was broadly conceived, although still essentially *prescriptive* in nature. The subject was taught to produce skilled public speakers.[3]

A century later things had changed dramatically. A shift from oral to written discourse had occurred in the universities, with the result that departments of rhetoric were now largely departments of English. Gone were the oral examinations, student debate societies, recitations, and public disputations associated with college commencement. In 1874, Harvard added written exams for its applicants, and two years later, in 1876, a new Chair of English Literature was created for James Francis Child, occupant of the Boylston Chair of Rhetoric.

The 19th century also witnessed a specialization of disciplines that truncated rhetoric to the point that it became associated primarily with *belles-lettres*. Its emphasis was now largely on correctness, style, and the aesthetic appreciation of literature. Style and delivery (*elocutio* and *pronunciatio*) formed the core of rhetorical instruction at Harvard, as it was even before the classical revival of the 18th century. Style, that darling of the Renaissance, dominated rhetorical instruction in other American colleges and universities through the end of the 19th

---

Stewart, "The Status of Composition and Rhetoric in American Colleges, 1880–1902: An MLA Perspective," *College English* 47 (1985), 734–46.

2. Everett Lee Hunt, "Herbert A. Wichelns and the Cornell Tradition of Rhetoric as a Humane Study," in *The Rhetorical Idiom* (ed. Donald C. Bryant; Ithaca, N.Y.: Cornell University Press, 1958), 1–4; Edward P. Corbett, "The Cornell School of Rhetoric," in *Selected Essays of Edward P. J. Corbett* (ed. Robert J. Connors; Dallas: Southern Methodist University, 1989), 290–304.

3. Connors, *et al.*, "The Revival of Rhetoric in America," 1–2.

century,[4] with the result that by 1900 rhetoric found itself in sharp decline.

Yet in 1903 Fred Scott created a Department of Rhetoric at the University of Michigan. A renewal of classical scholarship had begun, more critical in nature than what preceded, and it was helped along by individuals such as Charles Sears Baldwin, who in 1914 contributed an important essay on rhetoric to Monroe's *Encyclopaedia of Education*. This essay was a fresh inquiry into the nature of classical rhetorical theory.[5] A decade later Baldwin published his *Ancient Rhetoric and Poetic*.[6]

The year 1914 was pivotal. In this year a group of speech professors decided to break away from the National Council of Teachers of English and form the National Association of Academic Teachers of Public Speaking (later the Speech Communication Association). This new association, led by James Winans and James O'Neill, began campaigning immediately for separate departments of rhetoric and public speaking in the universities. Many such departments were thus formed between 1915 and 1920.

The Department of Speech and Drama at Cornell never became a Department of Rhetoric in name; nevertheless, Cornell in the 1920s was the center of this new interest in classical rhetoric and became the place where rhetorical criticism was born. The history of the so-called "Cornell School of Rhetoric" is well known, beginning with the celebrated graduate seminar on classical rhetoric offered by Alexander Drummond and Everett Hunt in 1920, said to have been "the first significant graduate seminar in classical rhetoric offered at a major American university in the twentieth century."[7] Hoyt Hudson defined graduate course work for the study of rhetoric,[8] and Hunt, in addition to his graduate seminar, offered an undergraduate

---

4. Ibid., 2–4.
5. Arnold, "Rhetoric in America since 1900," 5.
6. (Gloucester, Mass.: Peter Smith, 1959).
7. Corbett, "The Cornell School of Rhetoric," 295–96.
8. Hoyt H. Hudson, "The Field of Rhetoric," *QJS* 9 (1923), 167–80 [= Raymond F. Howes (ed.), *Historical Studies of Rhetoric and Rhetoricians* (Ithaca, N.Y.: Cornell University Press, 1961), 3–15]; cf. Cornell Faculty in the Department of Public Speaking, "Some Subjects for Graduate Study Suggested by Members of the Department of Public Speaking of Cornell University," *QJS* 9 (1923), 147–53.

course in argumentation where rhetorical discourse from both classical and modern periods was studied. Finally, it was Herbert Wichelns' highly influential essay, "The Literary Criticism of Oratory,"[9] which defined "rhetorical criticism" and mapped out its agenda.[10] These three individuals on the Cornell faculty, Hunt, Hudson, and Wichelns, all understood rhetoric in its broad classical sense, and for each of them rhetoric was a humane discipline, not a science.

Wichelns' essay transcended its own title by making a distinction between literary and rhetorical criticism that is now classic. Literary criticism, he said, is out to find the permanent value in a literary work; it looks at the work's thought and eloquence to see what gives it enduring quality over the ages—its "perennial freshness." Rhetorical criticism,

> on the other hand, is not concerned with permanence, nor yet with beauty. It is concerned with effect. It regards a speech as a communication to a specific audience, and holds its business to be the analysis and appreciation of the orator's method of imparting his ideas to his hearers.[11]

Wichelns was after a speech's persuasive quality, for which reason he said rhetorical criticism "is concerned with effect." This revived a central idea from Aristotle (*Rhetoric* I ii 1). But the key term is really *audience*, and by audience Wichelns meant the original audience, not the subsequent reader.[12] It was left to later rhetorical critics to expand the term to include subsequent readers.[13] What was important in Wichelns' program, however,

---

9. *Studies in Rhetoric and Public Speaking in Honor of James Albert Winans* (ed. A. M. Drummond; New York: The Century Co., 1925), 181–216 [= Bryant, *The Rhetorical Idiom*, 5–42]. For a briefer version, see Wichelns, "Some Differences between Literary Criticism and Rhetorical Criticism," in *Historical Studies of Rhetoric and Rhetoricians* (ed. Raymond F. Howes; Ithaca, N.Y.: Cornell University Press, 1961), 217–24.

10. Corbett, "The Cornell School of Rhetoric"; Mark S. Klyn, "Toward a Pluralistic Rhetorical Criticism," in *Essays on Rhetorical Criticism* (ed. Thomas R. Nilsen; New York: Random House, 1968), 154; Charles J. Stewart, "Historical Survey: Rhetorical Criticism in Twentieth Century America," in *Explorations in Rhetorical Criticism* (eds. G. P. Mohrmann, *et al.*; University Park, Penn.: Pennsylvania State University Press, 1973), 2–6.

11. Wichelns, "The Literary Criticism of Oratory," 209.

12. Ibid., 201.

13. Edwin Black, *Rhetorical Criticism* (New York: Macmillan Co., 1965), 11; Chaim Perelman and L. Olbrechts-Tyteca, *The New Rhetoric* (trans. John

was the renewed emphasis on the classical triumvirate of speaker, text, and audience, a delineation again going back to Aristotle (*Rhetoric* I iii 1). Today these combine into or else are supplemented by what is called the "rhetorical situation." Lloyd Bitzer says the rhetorical situation is "the context in which speakers or writers create rhetorical discourse."[14]

We may now sum up the main characteristics of rhetorical criticism as it emerged in the early 20th-century revival of rhetoric within American colleges and universities—a revival some call the "new rhetoric(s),"[15] although New Rhetoric derives from the French (*La nouvelle rhétorique*) and is associated largely with the argumentative rhetoric of Chaim Perelman.[16]

(1) Rhetorical criticism is first of all a modern, analytical discipline. In classical times, in the Renaissance, and up through the end of the nineteenth century, rhetoric was studied for its prescriptive value; its aim was to train people for effective public speaking. Rhetorical criticism analyzes discourse—ancient and modern, written and oral, in poetry and in prose—asking questions about structure, style, intention, impact upon the audience, and how these together create a rhetorical situation.

(2) Rhetorical criticism builds upon the broad classical tradition, which is to say its concern is not simply with style (*elocutio*), but with structure (*dispositio*) and all the other classical components of suasive discourse.

Wilkinson and Purcell Weaver; Notre Dame, Ind.: University of Notre Dame Press, 1969), 7.

14. Lloyd F. Bitzer, "The Rhetorical Situation," *PhRh* 1 (1968), 1 [= Walter R. Fisher (ed.), *A Tradition in Transition* (East Lansing, Mich.: Michigan State University Press, 1974), 247–48]; cf. Perelman and Olbrechts-Tyteca, *The New Rhetoric*, 412, 460–65, 491.

15. Corbett, "Rhetoric and Teachers of Rhetoric," *QJS* 51 (1965), 376–80; Bryant, "Rhetoric: Its Function and Its Scope *Rediviva*," in Donald C. Bryant, *Rhetorical Dimensions in Criticism* (Baton Rouge: Louisiana State University Press, 1973), 9–10 [= W. R. Fisher, *A Tradition in Transition*, 235–36].

16. Perelman, "The New Rhetoric: A Theory of Practical Reasoning," in *The Great Ideas Today 1970* (trans. E. Griffin-Collart and O. Bird; eds. Robert M. Hutchins and Mortimer J. Adler; Chicago: Encyclopaedia Britannica, 1970), 273–312; idem, "The New Rhetoric and the Rhetoricians: Remembrances and Comments," *QJS* 70 (1984), 188–96; and with L. Olbrechts-Tyteca, *The New Rhetoric*.

(3) Rhetorical criticism goes beyond the simple identifying and cataloguing of figures; it wants to know how figures *function* in discourse.

(4) Finally, rhetorical criticism focuses on the "audience," which sets it off most clearly from earlier forms of literary criticism, and is doubtless responsible for the shift to "reader-response" and other more recent forms of literary criticism. Rhetorical criticism studies a text with an eye to discerning its impact on single and multiple audiences, beginning with the original audience and extending up to current audiences made up of hearers or readers, individuals or members of a group.

Since the 1920s, the study of rhetoric has continued among so-called "neo-Aristotelians" at the University of Chicago during the 1940s and 1950s; at Michigan State University and the University of Iowa where the Communication Skills Movement originated during the 1940s and 1950s, then at other midwestern state universities; and at the University of California at Berkeley through the turbulent 1960s and 1970s, to name some of the more prominent centers in America.

Rhetoric today is a respected academic discipline, although few schools have, as The University of California at Berkeley does, a department of rhetoric with a graduate program. In some universities, however, graduate programs in rhetoric can be found in departments of English. Harvard and Princeton, despite well-known rhetoric faculty and many years of undergraduate teaching in rhetoric, have never had graduate programs in rhetoric.[17]

The division that existed earlier between English and Speech / Rhetoric faculties has all but disappeared, and since the mid-1960s, rhetoric has been well represented in a number of interdisciplinary programs.[18] In the universities we are even beginning to see signs of an emerging synthesis between classical rhetorical theory and the study of the Bible, for example, among such people as George Kennedy of the University of North Carolina at Chapel Hill[19] and Hans Dieter Betz currently

---

17. Corbett, "The Cornell School of Rhetoric, 302.

18. Connors, *et al.*, "The Revival of Rhetoric in America," 11–13.

19. See, e.g., *Classical Rhetoric and Its Christian and Secular Tradition from Ancient to Modern Times* (Chapel Hill, N.C.: University of North Carolina Press, 1980); and *New Testament Interpretation through Rhetorical Criticism* (Chapel Hill, N.C.: University of North Carolina Press, 1984).

at the University of Chicago. Betz, who does not come out of the American rhetorical movement, has been studying Paul against the Socratic tradition.[20] These beginnings could be helped along by more interdisciplinary programs and by joint seminary-university programs, such as the one that developed and flourished for a time between the University of California and Graduate Theological Union in Berkeley.

Mention should also be made of other studies in the American universities, many of them in Departments of Classics, which have been rhetorical despite their not being so named. A turn-of-the-century work on chiasmus in classical writers was done by R. B. Steele,[21] and structural works of a more expansive sort appeared later on the Homeric epics and Herodotus by J. L. Myres, George E. Duckworth, Cedric Whitman, and others,[22] and on Pindar,[23] Euripides,[24] Propertius,[25] Horace,[26] Vergil,[27]

---

20. See, e.g., *Der Apostel Paulus und die Sokratische Tradition* (BHT 45; Tübingen: J. C. B. Mohr [Paul Siebeck], 1972); idem, *Galatians* (Hermeneia; Philadelphia: Fortress Press, 1979); idem, *2 Corinthians 8 and 9* (Hermeneia; Philadelphia: Fortress Press, 1985).

21. "Anaphora and Chiasmus in Livy," *TAPA* 32 (1901), 154–85; "Chiasmus in the Epistles of Cicero, Seneca, Pliny and Fronto," in *Studies in Honor of Basil L. Gildersleeve* (Baltimore: Johns Hopkins University Press, 1902), 339–52.

22. J. L. Myres, "The Last Book of the 'Illiad,'" *JHS* 52 (1932), 264–96; idem, "The Structure of Stichomythia in Attic Tragedy," *PBA* 34 (1948), 199–231; idem, "The Pattern of the Odyssey," *JHS* 72 (1952), 1–19; idem, *Herodotus: Father of History* (Oxford: Clarendon Press, 1953); George E. Duckworth, *Foreshadowing and Suspense in the Epics of Homer, Apollonius and Vergil* (Princeton: Princeton University Press, 1933); Cedric Whitman, *Homer and the Heroic Tradition* (Cambridge, Mass.: Harvard University Press, 1958); Henry Immerwahr, *Form and Thought in Herodotus* (Cleveland: Western Reserve University Press, 1966); Stephen Bertman, "Structural Symmetry at the End of the *Odyssey*," *GRBS* 9 (1968), 115–23.

23. Gilbert Norwood, *Pindar* (Berkeley: University of California Press, 1945).

24. T. V. Buttrey, "Accident and Design in Euripides' 'Medea,'" *AJP* 79 (1958), 1–17.

25. O. Skutsch, "The Structure of the Propertian 'Monobiblos,'" *CP* 58 (1963), 238–39; William R. Nethercut, "Notes on the Structure of Propertius Book IV," *AJP* 89 (1968), 449–64.

26. R. W. Carrubba, "The Technique of the Double Structure in Horace," *Mnemosyne* Series 4, 20 (1967), 68–75.

27. Gilbert Norwood, "Vergil, *GEORGICS* iv, 453–527," *CJ* 36 (1940–41), 354–55; Duckworth, *Structural Patterns and Proportions in Vergil's Aeneid* (Ann Arbor: University of Michigan Press, 1962).

and Plutarch[28] by various scholars. Mark Rose has shown in an important study[29] that the Shakespearean plays, before acts came into being, were structured by design, not plot, and as a result were symmetrical. Literature has thus been compared to balancing movements in Beethoven and Mozart[30] and to artwork on ancient pottery (Myres; Whitman).

James Muilenburg and Rhetorical Criticism

Rhetorical criticism had its beginning in Old Testament (OT) with James Muilenburg, whose celebrated Presidential Address to the 1968 Meeting of the Society of Biblical Literature in Berkeley, "Form Criticism and Beyond," laid out the method.[31] Muilenburg defined *rhetorical criticism* in this address as understanding and exhibiting in Hebrew poetry and prose "the structural patterns that are employed for the fashioning of a literary unit . . . and . . . the many and various devices by which the predications are formulated and ordered into a unified whole."[32]

The rhetorical critic, said Muilenburg, should seek to discover "the texture and fabric of the writer's thought" by undertaking "a responsible and proper articulation of the words in their linguistic patterns and in their precise formulations."[33] Muilenburg wanted to go beyond form criticism because the emphasis there was too much on the typical features of a genre and not enough on those features that made the biblical passage unique. He said, "The passage must be read and heard precisely as it is spoken."[34]

In this lecture Muilenburg named a method he had been using for 45 years or more, and in this sense "rhetorical criticism" was not new. The name was new. Yet, only for the first time was Muilenburg able to distance himself sufficiently from his work to explain precisely what he had been doing. Rhetori-

---

28. T. F. Carney, "Plutarch's Style in the *Marius*," *JHS* 80 (1960), 27.
29. *Shakespearean Design* (Cambridge, Mass.: Belknap/Harvard University Press, 1972).
30. George Thomson, "Notes on *Prometheus Vinctus*," *CQ* 23 (1929), 158.
31. *JBL* 88 (1969), 1–18.
32. Ibid., 8.
33. Ibid., 7.
34. Ibid., 5.

cal study in the literary tradition of Robert Lowth and R. G. Moulton, and the stylistics of E. König and more recently Luis Alonso-Schökel, was for him a supplement to form criticism.[35] Muilenburg's combined use of these two critical methodologies, form criticism and the yet-to-be-named rhetorical criticism, reached a brilliant climax in his II Isaiah commentary in the *Interpreter's Bible*.[36]

Others besides Alonso-Schökel at Rome's Pontifical Biblical Institute were doing structural work on the biblical text without calling it rhetorical *per se*; for example, William Moran and Norbert Lohfink[37] in their studies on Deuteronomy were carrying on the tradition of earlier Scripture scholars A. Condamin, Cardinal A. Bea, and H. Galbiati.[38] There was also the important research of Nils W. Lund done during the 1930s and early 1940s at the University of Chicago.[39] These scholars isolated in the biblical text keyword, motif, and speaker distributions that

---

35. Robert Lowth, *Lectures on the Sacred Poetry of the Hebrews* (trans. G. Gregory; Boston: Joseph T. Buckingham, 1815); idem, *Isaiah: Preliminary Dissertation and Notes* (10th ed.; London: T. T. & J. Tegg, 1833); Richard G. Moulton, *The Literary Study of the Bible* (New York: D. C. Heath and Co., 1895); E. König, *Stilistik, Rhetorik, Poetik in Bezug auf die biblische Literatur* (Leipzig: Dieterich'sche Verlagsbuchhandlung, 1900); idem, "Style of Scripture," in *HDB Extra Volume* (1904), 156–69; and Luis Alonso-Schökel, *Estudios de poética hebrea* (Barcelona: Juan Flors, 1963); idem, *A Manual of Hebrew Poetics* (Rome: Pontifical Biblical Institute, 1988).

36. Vol. 5 (ed. George A. Buttrick; New York: Abingdon Press, 1956), 381–773.

37. Moran's class notes at the Pontifical Biblical Institute, *Adnotationes in libri Deuteronomii capita selecta* (Rome: Pontifical Biblical Institute, 1963), and Lohfink's class notes, *Lectures in Deuteronomy* (trans. S. McEvenue; Pontifical Biblical Institute, 1968), had limited circulation among their students. See also Moran, "Deuteronomy," in *A New Catholic Commentary on Holy Scripture* (ed. Reginald C. Fuller; Camden, N.J.: Thomas Nelson and Sons, 1969), 256–76; and Lohfink, "Darstellungskunst und Theologie in Dtn 1,6–3,29," *Biblica* 41 (1960), 123 n. 2 [= Lohfink, *Studien zum Deuteronomium und zur deuteronomistischen Literatur I* (Stuttgart: Verlag Katholisches Bibelwerk, 1990), 32–33 n. 70]; idem, *Das Hauptgebot* (Rome: Pontifical Biblical Institute, 1963).

38. The two important works by Condamin were *Le Livre de Jérémie* (Paris: Librairie Victor Lecoffre, 1920); and *Poèmes de la Bible* (2d ed; Paris: Gabriel Beauchesne et ses Fils, 1933).

39. Lund's major work was *Chiasmus in the New Testament* (Chapel Hill, N.C.: University of North Carolina Press, 1942; reprint: Peabody, Mass.: Hendrickson Publishers, 1992).

formed inclusios and large chiasmi (Moran and Lohfink called the latter "concentric inclusions"). Lund in his study of chiasmus built as Muilenburg did on the English tradition, in his case on the works of John Jebb and Thomas Boys.[40]

The rhetorical criticism of Muilenburg was at once broader and narrower than the rhetorical criticism of Wichelns and those working in the universities. It was broader by virtue of its being an adjunct to form criticism, from which it gained much of its vitality. Form criticism took for granted the oral provenance of OT literature, also seeking out "life situations" (*Sitze im Leben*) in which the biblical passages were originally "at home." Hermann Gunkel, the founder of form criticism (*Gattungskritik*), was an eclectic scholar of the first order, making form criticism broad in scope from the very beginning. Muilenburg met Gunkel while he was in Germany in 1929–1930 and became the person chiefly responsible for introducing Gunkel's method to America.[41]

Compared with the rhetorical criticism practiced in the universities, however, the Muilenburg program appears somewhat narrow.[42] It does not, for example, evaluate discourse over against its "audience," unless one takes *Sitz im Leben* to include audience. Nor does it deal much with classical concerns associated with a speaker's ability to persuade, that is, intent, stance, strategies, ethos moves, etc. Most of the effort is expended doing close work on the biblical text—engaging in "a responsible and proper articulation of the words in their linguistic patterns and in their precise formulations." Rhetorical criticism in the Muilenburg tradition is therefore perceived by many as being little more than an exercise in textual description—perceptive and sensitive description, to be sure, especially when the master was at work—but textual description all the same.

There are reasons for this limited agenda, besides the obvious one that rhetorical criticism gained its dynamism from form

---

40. John Jebb, *Sacred Literature* (London: T. Cadell and W. Davies, 1820); Thomas Boys, *A Key to the Book of Psalms* (London: L. B. Seeley and Son, 1825).

41. Muilenburg, "The Gains of Form Criticism in Old Testament Studies," *ET* 71 (1959–60), 229–33.

42. See, e.g., Michael V. Fox, "The Rhetoric of Ezekiel's Vision of the Valley of the Bones," *HUCA* 51 (1980), 1–4, and C. Clifton Black, "Rhetorical Criticism and Biblical Interpretation," *ET* 100 (1989), 254, 256.

criticism and was largely adjunct to it. To cite the prophetic material, in which one finds precisely the sort of discourse a rhetorical critic would be most eager to study, conditions for doing rhetorical criticism of the broad type could hardly be worse. Little or no background information is available. We lack biographical material on the speaker, and relevant historical data on the speech, such as date, what the occasion was, or who the audience happened to be, is scanty at best, usually unavailable. There is only the speech, and to make matters worse, speeches are placed end to end in the biblical text, making delimitation difficult, if not impossible. Interpolations are common. In some instances, part of a speech appears to be missing. Ancient methods of composition were quite different from modern methods, and we are still learning about the ancient methods and what sort of logic lay behind them.

In the book of Jeremiah, where conditions are good, perhaps the best, speeches embedded in the prose of chapters 18–45 do contain bits of historical information, less often speaker and audience data. Only in rare cases (for example, 26:1–19; 29) does one find all three. The bulk of the speeches—which are poetry and appear grouped together in chapters 1–20, 22–23, 30–31, and 46–51—typically lack a historical context and contain few clues about audience, occasion, and intent. We are therefore left inferring a rhetorical situation from the text itself. Muilenburg was aware of this problem.[43]

So while it is true that the book of Jeremiah contains a relatively large amount of background material—substantially more than any other prophetic book—solid correlations to the book's oracles, confessions, and other prophetic utterances remain few. It is no wonder, then, that biblical scholars say nothing or else talk sparingly about the prophet's intent, stance, strategy, or argumentation in a given speech, not to mention what the audience response might have been.

We can sum up the Muilenburg agenda for rhetorical criticism as follows:

(1) One must first define the limits of the literary unit. Where does the unit begin and where does it end? This is priority one. Delimiting the unit is essential for grasping the author's "intent and meaning." Muilenburg finds that once the literary unit has

---

43. Muilenburg, "Form Criticism and Beyond," 6.

been delimited, major motifs stated at the beginning are seen to find resolution at the end. Keywords make inclusios. He says, "No rhetorical feature is more conspicuous and frequent among the poets and narrators of ancient Israel than the proclivity to bring successive predications to their culmination."[44]

(2) Second, one must perceive the structure of the literary unit or, in Muilenburg's words, "discern the configuration of its component parts." This means close analysis of poetic bicola and tricola where particular attention is paid to keywords, figures of speech, and particles appearing in "strategic collocations" or in "crucial or climactic contexts." Repetitions are all-important, and one must be alerted also to the use of chiasmus. Muilenburg says, "rhetorical devices . . . are employed for marking, on the one hand, the sequence and movement of the pericope, and on the other, the shifts or breaks in the development of the writer's thought."[45] In poetry one must also look for "refrains," as well as for other clusters of bicola and tricola termed "stanzas" or "strophes." Refrains are deemed rhetorically important by critics working outside the Bible.[46] Muilenburg was also of the opinion that Hebrew poetry contained "climactic or ballast lines."[47]

Muilenburg then did move beyond textual description by showing an interest in discerning the author's intent, development of thought, and meaning. But his agenda is still too limited for rhetorical critics with classical and modern interests. This is due more to the unique circumstances under which OT rhetorical criticism is forced to operate than to narrow scholarly interests on the part of Muilenburg. Rhetorical critics working on Lincoln's Second Inaugural, the Lincoln-Douglas Debates, Kennedy's speech at the Berlin Wall, or Martin Luther King's "Moses on the Mountain" speech have at their disposal vast amounts of information on speaker and audience and seldom, if ever, do they need wonder where their text begins and ends. Even those working with classical texts have an easier time delimiting speeches and coming up with speaker and audience data.

---

44. Ibid., 9.

45. Ibid., 10, 14–16.

46. Gene Montague, "Rhetoric in Literary Criticism," *CCC* 14 (1963), 173.

47. Muilenburg, "Form Criticism and Beyond," 9.

Whereas the beginning of OT "rhetorical criticism" is dated from Muilenburg's 1968 lecture to the Society of Biblical Literature, for Muilenburg's graduate students at the San Francisco Theological Seminary and the GTU the beginning came a year earlier. In a graduate seminar on Deuteronomy, offered in the fall of 1967, members of the seminar told Muilenburg that what they wanted from him was less "form criticism" and more "rhetoric and composition." Though the master teacher continued to serve up a healthy amount of both—and a healthy amount of much else, I might add—this seminar marked a turning point. Muilenburg did in fact accent rhetoric and composition in his teaching, and this emphasis continued in subsequent seminars taught up until his retirement in 1971. Largely as a result of these seminars and his SBL address of December, 1968, the GTU saw a flurry of dissertations on rhetorical criticism in the decade following—in both Old and New Testament. GTU faculty also came under Muilenburg's influence. Since then, rhetorical criticism following Muilenburg's lead, if not done precisely along Muilenburg lines, has become widely practiced in America and abroad.[48]

The Question of Method

It has been argued since Aristotle that rhetoric is an art, not a science.[49] What then is rhetorical criticism? Is it also an art? Hunt, as we mentioned earlier, believed speech to be a humane discipline, but his senior colleague at Cornell, James Winans, was of the opinion that the study of speech must be carried on along scientific lines. The program developed by Charles H. Woolbert of the University of Illinois and adopted in the midwestern universities built on the same premise.[50] It seems that

---

48. Clifton Black, "Rhetorical Criticism and Biblical Interpretation"; Phyllis Trible, *Rhetorical Criticism: Context, Method, and the Book of Jonah* (Minneapolis: Fortress Press, 1994); see more recently the studies of Pieter van der Lugt, *Rhetorical Criticism and the Poetry of the Book of Job* (OS 32; Leiden: E. J. Brill, 1995); P. A. Smith, *Rhetoric and Redaction in Trito-Isaiah* (VTSupp 62; Leiden: E. J. Brill, 1995); and Robert H. O'Connell, *The Rhetoric of the Book of Judges* (VTSupp 63; Leiden: E. J. Brill, 1996).

49. See W. R. Fisher, *A Tradition in Transition*, x; D. C. Stewart, "The Status of Composition and Rhetoric in American Colleges, 1880–1902," 738–39.

50. Corbett, "The Cornell School of Rhetoric," 292–94.

with "method" being more at home in the sciences, the question becomes, "Can criticism of and within a basically humane discipline be reduced to a method?"

Muilenburg called rhetorical criticism a method, yet for him it was a practiced art, not a science. He said, "in matters of this sort there is no substitute for literary sensitivity."[51] Although he might cite Near Eastern materials to compare with the biblical text when it was possible, when it came to identifying a climactic line, an inclusio, an important shift signaled by a particle, and so on, it was the sensitivity of the critic that controlled interpretation. If you asked him how he knew it was a climactic line, an inclusio, or an important shift by a particle, he would likely say, "Well, it just is!" The charge then sometimes made about there being too much subjectivity in Muilenburg's method is not entirely groundless. Muilenburg believed that subjectivity was required to do the job.

Clifton Black says that the Muilenburg program is not a *bona fide* method, as is the rhetorical criticism of George Kennedy, which "is truly a method, not merely an interpretative perspective."[52] Some rhetorical critics, however, fear that once rhetorical criticism becomes a method, the freedom of the critic is taken away and the whole enterprise returns to being prescriptive.[53]

A mediating position is that rhetoric is a "mixture of science and art,"[54] which would seem to allow for the possibility that rhetorical criticism too might be both science and art. This seems to be a happy compromise, particularly if an art admittedly ancient is subjected to an analysis admittedly modern. Whatever the final verdict on art versus science, the method question is one that must be addressed. When dealing with an ancient text—particularly a biblical text where interpretation rides on so many variables—one had better employ some method, with some controls; otherwise what is passed off as art may not be art at all but simply random and subjective reflections producing little or no yield. Sad to say, much current rhetorical criticism of the Bible is precisely this.

---

51. Muilenburg, "Form Criticism and Beyond," 9.
52. So Clifton Black, "Rhetorical Criticism and Biblical Interpretation," 256–57.
53. Klyn, "Toward a Pluralistic Rhetorical Criticism."
54. Arnold, "Rhetoric in America since 1900," 7.

University scholars doing rhetorical criticism of the broad variety have understood their work as being methodological in nature,[55] although some insist that method ought to be pluralistic.[56] It would seem that method is as appropriate to the study of rhetoric as to the study of any other humanistic discipline. The term is not wholly owned by the sciences. If Muilenburg's rhetorical criticism assumes for "method" an interpretation too loose to be meaningful, then some controls must be put into place that will either objectify insights credited to a critic's acute sensitivity or else show the same to be invalid, and if not invalid, at least unlikely.

Rhetorical Criticism and the Book of Jeremiah

We turn now to discuss an agenda for rhetorical criticism in the biblical book of Jeremiah. Some overlap here with matters of composition will be unavoidable, since at virtually every point the prophet's discourse has been preserved in combination with other discourse to serve the ongoing needs of a worshiping community.

The Text. Rhetorical criticism of the book of Jeremiah must begin with the text, that is, the biblical text. There really is no other place to begin. Extrabiblical sources telling us about the prophet and audiences he addressed in the late 7th and early 6th centuries B.C. are nonexistent. Also largely nonexistent are outside sources corroborating the book's narrative and other prose. All the speaker and audience information we possess is within the book of Jeremiah, and only there.

This brings us to clarify at the outset our use of the word *text*. In the Bible *text* has both a broad and a narrow meaning. *Text* in the broad sense means *the present biblical text in all its complexities.* Any portion of the Jeremiah book is text—4, 8, or 12 lines of poetry, with or without supplements; oracles, confessions, and liturgies, with or without interpolations, singly or in collections; small and large blocks of narrative prose; and books

---

55. Montague, "Rhetoric in Literary Criticism," 168.

56. C. J. Stewart, "Historical Survey: Rhetorical Criticism in Twentieth Century America," 22–23. Klyn ("Toward a Pluralistic Rhetorical Criticism," 146) earlier lobbied for pluralism, but not when it came to methodology. For him "rhetorical criticism . . . should only mean intelligent writing about rhetoric."

within the present book, for example, chapters 1–20; 21–23; 30–33; 50–51; 46–51. All this is text and may be subjected to rhetorical criticism.

Embedded in the biblical text are also "texts" that were at one time self-standing, namely oracles, confessions, prayers, liturgies, letters, proverbs, memoirs, narratives, colophons, and so on. On these rhetorical criticism may also be done, and with potentially greater yield. Once individual texts are delimited, one may begin asking questions about speaker—or speakers, if the discourse happens to be a dialogue of which there are many in Jeremiah; how the discourse begins and ends; the flow of the argument; who the audience might be; and so on. The context in some cases will be of help. But more often the rhetorical situation has to be recreated—with help from the imagination—on the basis of the text alone.

Delimitation of the Literary Unit. For Muilenburg the first order of business was delimiting the literary unit. This had priority also on the form-critical agenda, although criteria there were different, and in the case of certain literary genres—not the prophetic speeches, however—content alone would make clear where the unit began and ended. Delimitation of prophetic speeches is difficult, though not as difficult as one might imagine. The attempt, in any event, has to be made. Synchronic analysis that pays little or no attention to literary units will not pass for rhetorical criticism and ends up being a throw-back to precritical study of the Bible. University scholars, also, who have the broad agenda for doing rhetorical criticism betray a similar narrowness when they use as their text a King James or rabbinic Bible, neither of which distinguishes prose from poetry or has any of the other interpretive formatting derived from modern biblical research.

In Jeremiah the delimitation of literary and discourse units can in fact be done reasonably well with the use of both rhetorical and nonrhetorical criteria. There is a relative abundance of *setumah* (ס) and *petuḥah* (פ) section markers, which we now know from the Dead Sea Scrolls to be very old.[57] In chapters 1–20, where poetic texts are compiled end to end, these are particularly useful and more often than not corroborate rhetorical

---

57. The Dead Sea Scrolls do not contain the sigla; they simply have spacing in the text.

data in marking the end of one unit and beginning of another. Yet these are not always present. Also, ancient and medieval manuscripts are not entirely consistent in their use. Occasionally they have to be disregarded. But section markings should always be taken into account. In the main, they are reliable indicators of where the breaks should be.

Chapter divisions go back only to about the 8th or 9th centuries A.D., and verse numbers come later—with the advent of printed Bibles in the 15th and 16th centuries. Both have only limited value. Superscriptions are much older and generally prove to be reliable markers for delimitation. Messenger formulas—usually 'thus said Yahweh' (*kōh ᵓāmar yhwh*) or 'oracle of Yahweh' (*nĕᵓūm yhwh*)—are likewise helpful when present. In Jeremiah these formulas appear at the beginning or end of oracles, occasionally at both beginning and end, and only rarely in the middle. Once other textual assessments have been made, it is usually clear where the formula fits in a given oracle.

In Jeremiah interspersed prose and poetry give an added bonus in delimitation. Sometimes one can delimit on the basis of content or genre, but both are tricky, especially in the poetry, and corroborating criteria are a must. The form-critical search for genres, such as the "lawsuit" (*rîb*), "prophetic call," "judgment oracle on the individual," "judgment oracle on the nation," "summons to repentance," and so on, has been largely unsuccessful, the reason being that Jeremianic discourse is structured not according to form-critical models but according to canons of ancient Hebrew rhetoric.

The inclusio, once established, has proved to be of great value in delimitation, since by definition it ties in beginning and end.[58] Some scholars use *inclusio* to refer to almost any repetition, but the term should be reserved for repeated or balanced

---

58. Muilenburg, "Form Criticism and Beyond," 9–10; J. R. Lundbom, *Jeremiah: A Study in Ancient Hebrew Rhetoric* (SBLDS 18; Missoula, Mont.: Society of Biblical Literature and Scholars Press, 1975), 23–60 [[36–81]]. Moulton, *The Literary Study of the Bible*, 56–58, spoke of an "envelope figure." Barbara Herrnstein Smith, *Poetic Closure: A Study of How Poems End* (Chicago: University of Chicago Press, 1968), 53–54, does not use the term *inclusio* but recognizes the phenomenon all the same. Classical scholars use the term *ring composition*; see J. A. Notopoulos, "Continuity and Interconnection in Homeric Oral Composition," *TAPA* 82 (1951), 81–101; and Whitman, *Homer and the Heroic Tradition*, 252–54.

vocabulary or else a clear return of thought that brings about closure. In ancient as in modern discourse the inclusio returns the audience to the point of beginning. Chiastic structures— both keyword and speaker—also aid in delimitation. Occasionally a chiasmus will exist within a larger unit, in which case other data must help determine the beginning and end.

Structure. Once the literary or discourse unit is delimited, the rhetorical critic moves on to discern the arrangement of parts, that is, the unit's structure. Some refer to this as "formal analysis."[59] A structural feature of discourse, defined most simply, is any portion of the discourse that, if missing, substantially diminishes the whole. The controlling structures of the Jeremianic oracles, confessions, and other utterances are all rhetorical. Larger compositional structures in the book are both rhetorical and non-rhetorical.

In Jeremiah entire poems are structured by the inclusio and the chiasmus. These are usually formed by repeated or balancing words or, if the discourse has dialogue, by alternate speaking voices (6:8–12; 8:18–21; 17:13–16a). Sometimes poems have both (5:1–8; 8:13–17). It is difficult to overestimate the importance of repetition, which Muilenburg considered the very basis of ancient Hebrew rhetoric.[60] Jeremianic poetry is seen in other ways to be particularly well balanced, for example, the wordplay on 'see' (*yir⁾eh*) and 'fear' (*yirā⁾* Q) in the parallel stanzas of 17:5–8.

One finds in Jeremiah much argument, some of it stimulated by rhetorical questions. The threefold question in the form *hă . . . ⁾im . . . maddûaᶜ . . .* ('If . . . if . . . why then . . . ?') is a signature of the prophet (2:14, 31; 8:4–5, 19, 22; etc.), as also the question used to set up the "but my people" contrast (2:11, 32; 5:22a, 23; 18:14–15). Arguments make use of the classical *distributio* (28:8–9). In 26:14, the prophet defends himself by using wha t ancient rhetoricians called *surrender* (classical *permissio*). Jeremiah is familiar also with the argument *a minori ad maius* (Heb. *qal vechomer*; 3:1; 12:5; 25:29; 49:12), with protasis–apodosis (4:1–2;

---

59. Bernard Weinberg, "Formal Analysis in Poetry and Rhetoric," in *Papers in Rhetoric and Poetic* (ed. Donald C. Bryant; Iowa City: University of Iowa Press, 1965), 36.

60. Muilenburg, "A Study in Hebrew Rhetoric: Repetition and Style," *Congress Volume: Copenhagen, 1953* (VTSupp 1; Leiden: E. J. Brill, 1953), 97–111.

7:5–7; 16:11–13; 31:36, 37), and with the technique of arguing by way of circumlocution (inclusio: 3:1–5; chiasmus: 5:1–8).

Particles signal discourse shifts, as Muilenburg rightly pointed out, for example, *wĕ ʿattâ* ('and now') in 2:18, which not only divides a poem in two but separates a foil from the prophet's preferred subject. Shifts in speaker perform a structural function in the Jeremianic oracles (2:5–9; 5:1–8; 8:18–21), with dialogue occurring everywhere—between Yahweh and Jeremiah, between Yahweh and the people, between Jeremiah and the people, and between Jeremiah and himself. Even the enemy is heard from (6:4–5).

Refrains, which were important for Muilenburg as they are also for rhetorical critics working in modern poetry,[61] in Jeremiah conclude stanzas of oracles (2:14–19); take the form of doxologies in liturgical compositions (10:6–7, 10); and appear as stereotyped rhetorical questions later added at the end of oracles (5:9; 9:8 [Eng 9:9]) or else interpolated into them (5:29).

Juxtaposition is another structural device in composition, a way for theological statements to be made without so much as a word being said. In Jeremiah the juxtaposition of chapters 34 and 35, which are out of chronological sequence, sets up a contrast between disobedience and obedience.[62]

In discerning the structure of discourse, rhetorical criticism can isolate added material in the text and material that appears to have fallen out.[63] It can point up major breaks, minor breaks, and breaks that are not breaks at all.[64] Now and then it will illuminate differences between the MT and the LXX, helping to decide which text is better, if not the one that is more original (e.g., 10:1–10).

Style. Rhetorical criticism pays attention to matters of style in order to discern the texture of a text, as well as to measure

---

61. Muilenburg, "Form Criticism and Beyond," 11; Montague, "Rhetoric in Literary Criticism," 173.

62. Lundbom, "Scribal Contributions to Old Testament Theology," forthcoming in *Festschrift for Frederick C. Holmgren* (eds. Paul Koptak and Bradley Bergfalk; Chicago: Covenant Publications, 1997).

63. On possible loss in Jer 9:2–5[3–6], see Lundbom, *Jeremiah: A Study in Ancient Hebrew Rhetoric,* 86–88 [[114–16]]; in Jer 20:14–18, see ibid., 46–48 [[65–67]]; idem, "The Double Curse in Jeremiah 20:14–18," *JBL* 104 (1985), 589–600.

64. Lundbom, "Rhetorical Structures in Jeremiah 1," *ZAW* 103 (1991), 193–210.

such things as the level of abstraction, degree of ambiguity, and whether there is hidden meaning. Style has much to do with effect. Jeremiah's discourse is filled with wordplays, metaphors, similes, accumulation (*accumulatio*), and various other types of repetition. Here the interest goes beyond mere identification and cataloguing. The rhetorical critic seeks to find out how figures *function* in discourse,[65] with the great resources here being the classical rhetorical handbooks, such as Aristotle's *Rhetoric*, the *ad Herennium*, and Quintilian's *Institutes*.

Repetition may be for emphasis (*geminatio*) or embellishment (*exergasia*), but it has other functions. Anaphora simulates the sense (*onomatopoeia*) by driving home judgment (the fourfold "they shall eat up" simulating a consuming enemy in 5:17; the fivefold "sword" simulating the repeated stabbing of the victim in 50:35–38; the ninefold "I will break in pieces" simulating a pounding hammer in 51:20–23) or building up hope (the threefold "again" simulating renewed activity in Zion in 31:4–5). Asyndeton functions to create a sense of urgency (verbs in 4:5 and 5:1). *Accumulatio* functions as it does for the later classical orators to heap up praise or blame. The accumulation of six infinitives absolute in 7:9 heaps up blame.

Metaphors, similes, and other tropes add strength to discourse, functioning also to kindle the hearer's imagination. Jeremiah's metaphors describe Yahweh, false gods, the nation, Judah's kings, the enemy, and even Jeremiah himself. They also heighten the enormity of evil and the destruction this evil will bring upon the nation. One of the harsher tropes is the *abusio*, which is an implied metaphor. It behaves somewhat extravagantly, in that a word is taken from a common usage and put to a usage that is uncommon, perhaps unique. So, for example, in 4:4: "remove the foreskins of your *hearts*; 5:8: "each man *neighing* for his neighbor's wife; in 18:18: "come, let us smite him with the *tongue*; in 51:44: "the nations shall no longer *flow* to him."

Jeremiah's style includes an abundance of paronomasia, hyperbole, and verbal irony, showing also an unmistakable flair for the dramatic. On paronomasia, see 1:10; 18:7; 31:28; on hyperbole see 1:5 (where Yahweh is speaker); 2:20, 28; 6:10; 8:16;

---

65. Donald C. Bryant, "Uses of Rhetoric in Criticism," in *Papers in Rhetoric and Poetic* (ed. Donald C. Bryant; Iowa City: University of Iowa Press, 1965), 9.

and on verbal irony see 2:33; 4:22; 5:31. Fertility worship is mocked when Jeremiah deliberately reverses sexual preferences in 2:27, making the tree masculine and the stone feminine. Drama is seen in the use of apostrophe (2:12; 4:14; 22:29, 30; 47:6) and in the alternation of speakers.

Keywords. Rhetorical critics make much of "keywords," which are normally repeated words or word cognates in a given discourse.[66] But they can also be synonyms, antonyms, or fixed pairs that balance one another. According to Martin Buber, "the recurrence of keywords is a basic law of composition in the Psalms."[67] It is a basic law of composition in Jeremiah as well.

How does one identify keywords? Repeated words, for example, may have little significance or none at all. Muilenburg says keywords are words appearing in "strategic collocations" or in "crucial or climactic contexts." Repetitions at the beginning or end of successive cola, lines, or stanzas (anaphora; epiphora) qualify as keywords (see both in 8:22–9:1 [Eng 9:2]). So also do verb clusters, regardless of position (*šûb* in 8:4–5), as well as repetitions at the beginning and end of a discourse unit (inclusio) or repetitions forming an abb'a' pattern (chiasmus) in the same. In the commission passage (1:13–19), keywords structure the parts and connect parts to one another.[68]

What controls exist for identifying keyword inclusios or chiasmi, which returns us to the method question raised earlier in connection with the Muilenburg program of rhetorical criticism? The most obvious answer would be other data delimiting the same unit. But what if there are no corroborating data, or the corroborating data remain ambiguous? The proposed inclusio may simply rest upon the repetition of one or two words in 8 lines of poetry or poetry where 10 or 20 chapters lie in between. In such cases one internal control can be applied that

---

66. Thomson, "Notes on *Prometheus Vinctus*," 157; Muilenburg, "Form Criticism and Beyond," 11, 13, 16–17; Montague, "Rhetoric in Literary Criticism," 173–74; Richard L. Graves, "Symmetrical Form and the Rhetoric of the Sentence," in *Essays on Classical Rhetoric and Modern Discourse* (eds. Robert J. Connors, *et al.*; Carbondale, Ill.: Southern Illinois University Press, 1984), 174.

67. *Good and Evil* (New York: Charles Scribner's Sons, 1953), 52.

68. Lundbom, "Rhetorical Structures in Jeremiah 1," 205; idem, *The Early Career of the Prophet Jeremiah* (Lewiston, N.Y.: Mellen Biblical Press, 1993), 65.

seems to have validity. If a word or word combination repeats at what appears to be the beginning and end of a rhetorical unit *but occurs nowhere else in reasonable proximity to that beginning or end*, one may reasonably propose that the said repetition is an inclusio. Holladay, for example, has argued that the repetition of "sow" in 2:2 and 4:3 makes an inclusio between two oracles, 2:2b–3 and 4:3–4, noting that the verb does not appear again in the book until 12:13.[69]

As it turns out, Holladay has other data to support his argument. Rubrics introducing the two oracles contain other keywords, namely "Jerusalem" in both 2:2 and 4:3. This is significant, because in 2:1–4:4 the audience is otherwise (Northern) Israel (2:4; 3:12). Also 2:1–4:4, which is the unit delimited by Holladay's inclusio, is agreed on other grounds as being a "harlotry cycle" of oracles. This example, then, has an internal control of "isolated keywords in context" and an external control of corroborating non-rhetorical data. Rhetorical criticism that works in this fashion is a method; keywords are not randomly identified, nor are judgments based solely on "literary sensitivity."

One other example. Questions have been raised about my inclusio delimiting chapters 1–20,[70] which is based upon the repetition "you came forth from the womb" in 1:5 and "from the womb I came forth" in 20:18.[71] This verb-noun combination appears in these two places and nowhere else in chapters 1–20, in fact, nowhere else in the entire book of Jeremiah. The keywords are also inverted, which is a stylistic nicety often seen in this type of inclusio.

Corroborating non-rhetorical data were also cited in support of this inclusio. That 1:5 begins a literary unit needs no defense; it is the first poetry after the book's superscription. As for 20:18, a number of things point to its being a conclusion,

---

69. William L. Holladay, *Jeremiah I* (Hermeneia; Philadelphia: Fortress Press, 1986), 68.

70. Clifton Black, "Rhetorical Criticism and Biblical Interpretation," 254, and earlier James Crenshaw, "A Living Tradition: The Book of Jeremiah in Current Research," *Int* 37 (1983), 119. Crenshaw expresses a preference for the linking of chapters 1 and 24; see also Alexander Rofé, "The Arrangement of the Book of Jeremiah," *ZAW* 101 (1989), 390–98.

71. Lundbom, *Jeremiah: A Study in Ancient Hebrew Rhetoric*, 28 [[42]].

besides the universal judgment that the verse ends the confession in 20:14–18:

(a) after 20:18 is a change from poetry to prose;
(b) a *petuḥah* (פ) section marker appears after 20:18; and
(c) there is a chapter designation at 21.

That 20:18 marks an even greater termination point is indicated by the onset of dated prose in 21:1, the verse following. I pointed out that no dated prose from the reigns of either Jehoiakim or Zedekiah exists prior to 21:1; in fact, Jehoiakim and Zedekiah are not even mentioned in chapters 1–20, except in the superscription of 1:1–3.[72] Finally, a major break after 20:18 is indicated by the separate delimitation of chapters 21–23, which is a collection of utterances against kings and prophets. All this corroborates the keyword inclusio said to occur in 1:5 and 20:18. We are not talking here about proof; we are talking about method and controls that make for sound biblical interpretation.

Other keyword repetitions combine to form chiastic structures.[73] These occur in bicola and double bicola and in stanzas of oracles where they become the controlling structure (2:5–9; 5:1–8; 8:13–17; 51:34–45). Again, questions of method and controls are rightly asked about such structures. In Lamentations 1–2, where the phenomenon was first discovered by Condamin,[74] stanzas of an acrostic provided a control over the keyword distribution. In Jeremiah, stanzas delimited by speaker provide in some cases, though not all, a control for the keyword distribution. There is interpretation here, to be sure, but there is also the working out of a method and results that merit consideration. And it should also be pointed out that these chiastic structures, like the inclusio structures, are frequently supported at various points by non-rhetorical data as well.

Catchwords. Catchwords (hook words; *Stichwörter*; *mots crochets*) are keywords, basically, that connect originally independent discourse or literary units in the present biblical text. These

---

72. Ibid., 28–30.

73. Nils W. Lund, "The Presence of Chiasmus in the Old Testament," *AJSLL* 46 (1930), 104–26; idem, *Chiasmus in the New Testament*; Lundbom, *Jeremiah: A Study in Ancient Hebrew Rhetoric*, 61–112 [[82–146]]; and John W. Welch (ed.), *Chiasmus in Antiquity* (Hildesheim: Gerstenberg, 1981).

74. Albert Condamin, "Symmetrical Repetitions in *Lamentations* I and II," *JThS* 7 (1905), 137–40.

could be mnemonic devices used by the oral poet that have been carried over into the written text or else scribal devices used in early editing of the scrolls.[75] In chapters 1–20 almost all the individual poems, and some of the prose units, show a linking by catchwords.

It stands to reason that catchwords cannot be identified until after the discourse or literary units have been delimited. In Amos 1–2 stereotyped oracles provide a ready-made control for catchword identification.[76] In Jeremiah, catchwords can be identified in prose juxtaposed to poetry (e.g., "terror on every side" in 20:3 and 10), or when passages are delimited on other grounds. One notes in Jeremiah that some of the same words, for example, *hinnēh* ('look!') and *ᵓsp* ('gather'), turn up as catchwords in different parts of the book.

Audience.   Once discourse and literary units have been delimited and rhetorical criticism has done its full complement of work on the text, insights will be forthcoming on the speaker's interaction with his audience. In 3:1–5, for example, the audience is brought back at the oracle's end to the "Would you return to me" question posed at the beginning. In 5:1–8, Jeremiah abandons authority preaching by leaving it to the audience to decide at the end whether Yahweh can indeed pardon Jerusalem.[77] It is said that speakers commonly "work against a pattern of expectation, and that expectation is not in the work but in the audience."[78] Jeremiah plays with audience expectation in 50:35–38, where, after a fivefold repetition of *ḥereb* ('sword') he ends

---

75. Theophile J. Meek, "The Poetry of Jeremiah," *JQR* 14 (1923–24), 283; Sigmund Mowinckel, "Die Komposition des deuterojesajanischen Buches," *ZAW* 49 (1931), 242–60; Edwin M. Good, "The Composition of Hosea," *SEÅ* 31 (1966), 24; and Menahem Haran, "Book-Size and the Device of Catch-Lines in the Biblical Canon," *JJS* 36 (1985), 8–11. In the commentaries see W. Rudolph, *Jeremia* (HAT; 3d ed. Tübingen: J. C. B. Mohr [Paul Siebeck], 1968), 75; J. Bright, *Jeremiah* (AB 21; Garden City, N.Y.: Doubleday & Co., 1965), lxxv, 73, 134; and Claus Rietzschel, *Das Problem der Urrolle* (Gütersloh: Gütersloher Verlagshaus Gerd Mohn, 1966), 24, 128.

76. Shalom M. Paul, "Amos 1:3–2:3: A Concatenous Literary Pattern," *JBL* 90 (1971), 397–403.

77. Lundbom, "Jeremiah and the Break-Away from Authority Preaching," *SEÅ* 56 (1991), 7–28.

78. Montague, "Rhetoric in Literary Criticism," 169.

with the similar-sounding *ḥōreb* ('drought'). Amos, as has already been noted, did precisely the same sort of thing.[79]

I called attention earlier to Jeremiah's "rhetoric of descent."[80] Once discourse units are delimited, arguments are seen to go quite consistently from the ironic to the straightforward, the figurative to the literal, the general to the specific, and the abstract to the concrete. In the oracles and other utterances, Jeremiah moves in the direction of lowering the level of abstraction, which means the encounter with his audience is most immediate at the end. This observation and others are but a modest beginning in the kind of broad rhetorical criticism that doubtless holds more promise yet in future study of the book of Jeremiah.

---

79. David Noel Freedman, "Deliberate Deviation from an Established Pattern of Repetition in Hebrew Poetry as a Rhetorical Device," in *Proceedings of the Ninth World Congress of Jewish Studies (Jerusalem, August 4–12, 1985), Division A: The Period of the Bible* (Jerusalem: World Union of Jewish Studies, 1986), 45–52.

80. *Jeremiah: A Study in Ancient Hebrew Rhetoric*, 116–17 [[150–51]].

Chapter 1

Introduction

Call to Rhetorical Criticism

A renewed interest in rhetoric can be seen today in biblical as well as in non-biblical studies.[1] In the field of Old Testament, a keynote was sounded by James Muilenburg in his lecture "Form Criticism and Beyond," delivered to the Society of Biblical Literature at the University of California, Berkeley, in December 1968.[2] Muilenburg pleaded on that occasion for increased sensitivity to rhetorical features in the biblical text. The call was timely, even though it presented no major advance beyond the particular brand of literary criticism that has engaged him for the past 50 years.[3]

---

1. In non-biblical studies, see *inter alia, New Rhetorics*, ed. Martin Steinmann, Jr. (New York: Charles Scribner's Sons, 1967), especially the article by Wayne C. Booth, "The Revival of Rhetoric," 1–15; Thomas O. Sloan, "Restoration of Rhetoric to Literary Study," *ST* 16 (1967), 91–97. For the Cornell tradition see Everett L. Hunt's "Introduction" to *The Rhetorical Idiom*, ed. Donald C. Bryant (New York: Cornell University Press, 1958), "Herbert Wichelns and the Cornell Tradition of Rhetoric as a Humane Study," 1–4. Other works defining modern rhetoric and illustrating the method of rhetorical criticism include William J. Brandt, *The Rhetoric of Argumentation* (New York: Bobbs-Merrill Co., 1970); Edward P. J. Corbett, *Classical Rhetoric for the Modern Student*, 2nd ed. (New York: Oxford University Press, 1971); idem (ed.), *Rhetorical Analyses of Literary Works* (New York: Oxford University Press, 1969); Chaim Perelman and L. Olbrechts-Tyteca, *The New Rhetoric*, tr. John Wilkinson and Purcell Weaver (Notre Dame, Ind.: University of Notre Dame Press, 1969).

2. Published in *JBL* 88 (1969), 1–18.

3. Muilenburg was influenced early in his career by Richard G. Moulton's *The Literary Study of the Bible* (New York: D. C. Heath & Co., 1895), and his earliest work, *Specimens of Biblical Literature* (New York: Thomas Y.

Yet Muilenburg's concept of rhetoric is unmistakably modern. Written compositions are as much the object of study as oral speeches. And poetry also comes within its province.[4] But more important, rhetoric is not defined merely in terms of *style*, which was its chief meaning in the Renaissance,[5] and one that continued through the end of the 19th century.[6] Rhetoric is also made to include *structure*.[7] Muilenburg says,

> What I am interested in, above all, is in understanding the nature of Hebrew literary composition, in exhibiting the structural patterns that are employed for the fashioning of a literary unit, whether in poetry or in prose, and in discerning the many and various devices by which the predications are formulated and ordered into a unified whole. Such an enter-

---

Crowell Co., 1923) is quite similar to it. Early journal articles reflect the same "Bible as literature" interest: "Literary Form in the Fourth Gospel," *JBL* 51 (1932), 40–53; "The Literary Approach—the Old Testament as Hebrew Literature," *JNABI* 1 (1933), 14–22. Later works show deeper insight into matters of structure and style: "The Literary Character of Isaiah 34," *JBL* 59 (1940), 339–65; "Psalm 47," *JBL* 63 (1944), 235–56; "A Study in Hebrew Rhetoric: Repetition and Style," *VTSupp* 1 (Copenhagen, 1953), 97–111; *IB: Isaiah* 5, ed. G. A. Buttrick (Nashville: Abingdon-Cokesbury, 1956), 381–773; "The Form and Structure of the Covenantal Formulations," *VT* 9 (1959), 347–65; "The Linguistic and Rhetorical Usages of the Particle כי in the Old Testament," *HUCA* 32 (1961), 135–60; "A Liturgy on the Triumphs of Yahweh" in *Studia Biblica et Semitica* [Essays in Honor of Theodoro C. Vriezen] (Wageningen: H. V. Veenman en Zonen N. V., 1966), 233–51.

4. Professor Brandt of the University of California, Berkeley, has written a book entitled *The Rhetoric of Poetry* (unpublished).

5. Scholars of the Renaissance were fond of collecting figures of speech; cf. Richard E. Young and Alton L. Becker, "Toward a Modern Theory of Rhetoric: A Tagmemic Contribution" in *New Rhetorics*, 84. Young and Becker mention Henry Peacham's *Garden of Eloquence* (1577) which listed 184 schemes and tropes. A popular book of the same kind, only listing figures found in Scripture, was John Smith's *Mystery of Rhetoric Unveiled* (1657), facsimile reprint (Menston, England: Scholar Press, 1969).

6. Figures of speech in the Bible were catalogued by E. W. Bullinger, *Figures of Speech Used in the Bible*, 2nd ed. (Grand Rapids: Baker Book House, 1969 [1st ed., 1898]), and E. König, *Stilistik, Rhetorik, Poetik* (Leipzig: Dieterich'sche Verlagsbuchhandlung Theodor Weicher, 1900).

7. Two recent studies of structure in poetry are pioneering: Barbara Herrnstein Smith, *Poetic Closure* (Chicago: University of Chicago Press, 1970), and Leonard Nathan, "Conjectures on the Structural Principle of Vedic Poetry," subsequently published in *ComLit* 28 (1976), 122–34.

prise I should describe as rhetoric and the methodology as rhetorical criticism.[8]

Muilenburg is interested in "structural patterns" which make up a literary unit. One of these structural patterns is the "inclusio," which balances the end of a unit with its beginning.[9] Another means by which Muilenburg ferrets out structure is by observing *clusters* of bi-cola or tri-cola, which he defines loosely as "strophes."[10] These are a bit harder to determine, but we know they exist because of acrostics and refrains.[11] Many of the other features which Muilenburg points to could be termed stylistic, e.g., author's use of particles, figures of speech, repetition, etc., yet because these appear in "strategic collocations," or in "crucial or climactic contexts"[12] they serve a structural function. Actually, Muilenburg makes no attempt to distinguish structure from style (classical *dispositio* and *elocutio*), but then neither do other scholars working in the field such as Luis Alonso-Schökel[13] and William L. Holladay.[14] This should perhaps be done. But most important just now is that one realize how the modern definition of rhetoric has been expanded. It is in fact much more broadly defined, but discussion of this can wait until later.

According to Muilenburg the priorities in rhetorical criticism are (1) to define the limits of the literary unit,[15] and (2) to

---

8. "Form Criticism and Beyond," 8.

9. Ibid., 9–10; cf. *IB: Isaiah*, 385, 392. It is called "ring composition" by classicists; cf. J. A. Notopoulos, "Continuity and Interconnexion in Homeric Oral Composition," *TAPA* 82 (1951), 81–101; Moulton called the same an "envelope figure"; *The Literary Study of the Bible*, 56–58.

10. "Form Criticism and Beyond," 11ff.

11. Ibid., 11–12; cf. T. J. Meek, "The Structure of Hebrew Poetry," *JR* 9 (1929), 549; T. H. Robinson, "Basic Principles of Hebrew Poetic Form" in *Festschrift Alfred Bertholet*, ed. Walter Baumgartner *et al.* (Tübingen: J. C. B. Mohr [Paul Siebeck], 1950), 450; Charles F. Kraft, *The Strophic Structure of Hebrew Poetry* (Chicago: University of Chicago Press, 1938), 1–32.

12. "Form Criticism and Beyond," 14–16.

13. *Estudios de Poética Hebrea* (Barcelona: Juan Flors, 1963).

14. "Style, Irony and Authenticity in Jeremiah," *JBL* 81 (1962), 44–54; "The Recovery of Poetic Passages of Jeremiah," *JBL* 85 (1966), see especially "Theoretical Framework," 406–10; "Form and Word-play in David's Lament over Saul and Jonathan," *VT* 20 (1970), 153–89.

15. "Form Criticism and Beyond," 8–9.

determine the structure of the composition, or in Muilenburg's words, "discern the configuration of its component parts."[16] These are important methodological insights, and they have been echoed in a follow-up article by David Greenwood.[17]

Modern literary criticism of the Bible has brought us to this juncture. Despite all work previously done, we are still uncertain about delimiting literary units. This is basic, and explains in part why our knowledge of internal structures is less than complete. Advances have been made, especially since the 18th century, yet the precise understanding we seek is still for the most part based on subjective judgments.[18]

Nowhere is this more true than in the prophetic books. And yet it is to that corpus that we now turn to select the book providing for us the best point of departure: Jeremiah. Jeremiah is the largest prophetic book[19] and contains substantial amounts of poetry and prose. But more important, Jeremiah stands close in time to Deuteronomy,[20] the rhetorical book *par excellence* in the Old Testament. The stylistic affinities between these two books are well known,[21] and we might expect there to be structural affinities as well. But before we outline the course of our

---

16. Ibid., 10.

17. "Rhetorical Criticism and Formgeschichte: Some Methodological Considerations," *JBL* 89 (1970), 423–24.

18. Muilenburg is aware of this; cf. "Form Criticism and Beyond," 9.

19. In *BH*[3], Ezekiel is 83 pages of text, Jeremiah 107 pages. Isaiah is 93 pages, but since it is taken to be two separate collections (1–39; 40–66), the size of each is substantially smaller than Jeremiah.

20. De Wette argued in his *Dissertatio critica* (1805) that Deuteronomy was the lawbook found in Josiah's temple (2 Kings 22); cf. Eissfeldt, *The Old Testament: An Introduction*, tr. Peter Ackroyd (New York and Evanston: Harper & Row, 1965), 171f. De Wette further believed that Deuteronomy must have been written shortly before it was found, which is what gave the D source a firm date in the 7th century. The date has since been pushed back. *Urdeuteronomium* is now thought to derive from the time of Hezekiah (early 7th century). The Deuteronomic History, on the other hand, is dated in the time of Josiah (late 7th century); cf. D. N. Freedman, "Pentateuch" in *IDB* K–Q, 715–16; F. M. Cross, "The Structure of the Deuteronomic History" in *Perspectives in Jewish Learning* 3 (Chicago: College of Jewish Studies, 1968), 9–24.

21. S. R. Driver, *ICC: Deuteronomy*, 3rd ed. (Edinburgh: T. & T. Clark, 1965 [1st ed. 1895]), xciiff.; John Bright, "The Date of the Prose Sermons of Jeremiah," *JBL* 70 (1951), 15–29; cf. Bright, *AB: Jeremiah* (Garden City: Doubleday & Co., 1965), lxx–lxxiii.

work, it is necessary to give a brief survey of earlier attempts at literary criticism in the Old Testament. This we will do, paying particular attention to what has been done in Jeremiah.

Survey of Earlier Literary Criticism

In one way or another, all modern study of the prophetic books builds on the work of Robert Lowth. His *Lectures on the Sacred Poetry of the Hebrews* (1753)[22] argued two basic points: (1) that Hebrew poetry was dominated by a feature which he called "parallelism,"[23] and (2) that the prophetic books consisted primarily of poetry, not prose as was previously thought.[24] These theses were expanded and given specific application in Lowth's *Isaiah*, which appeared in 1778.[25] In Jeremiah, Lowth correctly recognized that the beginning and end of the book contained large poetical sections. He judged about half of the book to be poetry, and half prose.[26] Following Lowth's lead, Benjamin Blayney published a new translation with commentary of Jeremiah (1784)[27] which was modeled on Lowth's *Isaiah*. This work has been virtually forgotten, and unfortunately so since it is surprisingly discriminate in separating poetry from prose.[28]

During the same period, a new movement in source criticism was underway in Germany. By the 19th century it would be dominating not only biblical studies, but Homeric studies as well.[29] In Jeremiah, source criticism was from the first done in

---

22. Translated from the Latin by G. Gregory (Boston: Joseph T. Buckingham, 1815).

23. Lecture XIX.

24. Lecture XVIII.

25. *Isaiah, Preliminary Dissertation and Notes*, 10th ed. (London: T. T. & J. Tegg, 1833).

26. *Lectures on the Sacred Poetry of the Hebrews*, 291.

27. *Jeremiah and Lamentations*, 3rd ed. (London: Thomas Tegg & Son, 1836).

28. My impression is that it takes slightly more to be poetic than would presently be conceded, but nevertheless it is a respectable piece of work for its day.

29. See [Maurice Plaunauer (ed.)], *Fifty Years (and Twelve) of Classical Scholarship* (Oxford: Basil Blackwell, 1968), chap. I i, "Homer and the Analysts"; also Cedric Whitman, *Homer and the Heroic Tradition* (Cambridge: Harvard University Press, 1967), 4.

close conjunction with text criticism. It could hardly have been otherwise, since the Hebrew and Greek texts of Jeremiah are the most widely divergent in the Old Testament. The Greek (LXX) is one-eighth shorter than the Hebrew (MT), but more important, the Greek orders its material differently after 25:13.[30] These factors alone explain why even in recent times attention continues to be paid to the Jeremianic text.[31]

Eichhorn proposed in his *Einleitung* (1783) that the divergencies originated with Jeremiah himself (which parallels his views on Moses and Genesis). He believed that Jeremiah prepared successive editions. The first, with some augmentation, was sent to the exiles in Babylon. The second was prepared from a copy of the first in Egypt, after which it was sent to Palestine where it became the prototype of the MT.[32] Later in the early 19th century F. C. Movers proposed six separate books of Jeremiah which he argued were brought together into one compilation after the exile by the author of Kings. This is supported by the fact that Jeremiah 52 = 2 Kings 24:18–25:30, each being the concluding passage of the respective books. This view was the one adopted by De Wette.[33]

By the mid–19th century, when source criticism was well advanced, the same issues at stake in the Pentateuch were also at stake in the Prophets: authorship, composition and the dating of the sources. By 1850 the thesis for a "Second Isaiah" (Isaiah 40–66) had gained wide acceptance.[34] No "Second Jeremiah" emerged, but it was readily agreed that not everything in the

---

30. This is due mainly to the relocation of the Oracles to Foreign Nations; in the LXX they follow 25:13 while the MT places them in chapters 46–51.

31. A recently published thesis by J. Gerald Janzen entitled *Studies in the Text of Jeremiah* (Cambridge: Harvard University Press, 1973) is the most recent example and contains a useful introduction to earlier studies.

32. Ibid., 2; Frank Cross, however, had recently argued that the MT has a Babylonian provenance; see his article "The History of the Biblical Text in the Light of Discoveries in the Judaean Desert," *HThR* 57 (1964), 297.

33. Wilhelm De Wette, *A Critical and Historical Introduction to the Canonical Scriptures of the Old Testament* II, 3rd ed., tr. and enlarged by Theodore Parker (Boston: Little, Brown & Co., 1858), 416.

34. Ibid., 366; cf. S. DeVries, "Biblical Criticism, History of," *IDB* A–D, 415.

book of Jeremiah was to be attributed to the 7th–6th century prophet. Jer 10:1–16 was assigned to "pseudo-Isaiah,"[35] and sections from the Oracles to Foreign Nations (chaps. 46–51) were denied Jeremianic authorship.[36]

Graf's commentary (1862) also reflected the view that Jeremiah was a composite document.[37] Graf called attention to the fact that in the early chapters, Jeremiah speaks in the first person while he is referred to in chapters 20ff. in the third person. In the former we find the formulas ויהי דבר יהוה אלי לאמר or ויאמר יהוה אלי, while in the latter the corresponding formula is ויהי דבר יהוה אל־ירמיהו לאמר. Also in these latter chapters, both in the superscriptions as well as in the narrative portions, the designation ירמיהו הנביא is used, which Graf says, "in dem Munde des Jeremia selbst sonderbar wäre."[38]

By the end of the 19th century we see three sources emerging: (1) the Jeremiah source, consisting primarily of the early chapters; (2) a Baruch source, consisting of narrative which refers to Jeremiah in the third person, and (3) a Later-Compiler (*Bearbeiter*) source which supplements both Jeremiah and Baruch. This breakdown is seen most clearly in Giesebrecht's commentary.[39]

Yet the most important scholar of this period was Bernhard Duhm. A contemporary of Julius Wellhausen, who championed the cause of source criticism in the Pentateuch, Duhm wrote major commentaries on Isaiah (1892) and Jeremiah (1901).[40] Wellhausen limited himself to the Minor Prophets.[41] In Jeremiah Duhm refined the three-source theory by shifting the discussion to a new axis, viz., prose vs. poetry. The study of

---

35. De Wette, *A Critical and Historical Introduction . . .* , 403.

36. Ibid., 396ff.

37. *Der Prophet Jeremia* (Leipzig: T. O. Weigel, 1862).

38. Ibid., xxxix.

39. *HKAT: Das Buch Jeremia* (Göttingen: Vandenhoeck & Ruprecht, 1894), xv.

40. *HKAT: Das Buch Jesaia* (Göttingen: Vandenhoeck & Ruprecht, 1892); *Das Buch Jeremia* (Tübingen and Leipzig: Verlag von J. C. B. Mohr [Paul Siebeck], 1901).

41. *Die kleinen Propheten übersetzt und erklärt* (Berlin: Verlag von Georg Reimer, 1898); his views are carried over into the English *ICC* volumes on the Minor Prophets.

Hebrew poetry had been given new impetus in Germany as a result of the metrical theories of Julius Ley and Eduard Sievers.[42] Duhm was influenced by Ley,[43] and as is well known, applied Ley's theories to Jeremiah with astounding rigidity.[44] Nevertheless Duhm can be credited with isolating the core of the Jeremianic message in the poetry.

This in part reaffirmed the distinctions made by Lowth and Blayney more than a century ago, yet with the difference that neither Lowth nor Blayney was concerned as Duhm was with isolating Jeremiah's *ipsissima verba*. We must not overlook Kittel's 1906 edition of the MT, which for the first time printed poetry as poetry. Kittel himself did Jeremiah, and is largely responsible for the way the poetry is still read.

The last stage of source criticism in Jeremiah came with the early works of Sigmund Mowinckel and T. H. Robinson. Both later joined the new school of form criticism, but in Jeremiah their work proceeds along the old lines. Mowinckel's monograph *Zur Komposition des Buches Jeremia* (1914) is the most advanced discussion on the subject. In it Mowinckel refines the three-source theory further. Source A consists of poetry and is the *ipsissima verba* of Jeremiah. Source B consists of biographical prose written chiefly in the third person by an admirer. Source C is sermonic prose similar to what we find in Deuteronomy, and written in the first person.[45] Mowinckel was skeptical about

---

42. Julius Ley, *Grundzüge des Rhythmus des Vers- und Strophenbaues in der hebräischen Poesie* (Halle: Verlag der Buchhandlung des Waisenhauses, 1875); *Leitfaden der Metrik der hebräischen Poesie* (Halle: Verlag der Buchhandlung des Waisenhauses, 1887). Ed. Sievers, *Metrische Studien I* (Leipzig: B. G. Teubner, 1901).

43. He sided with Ley over Sievers choosing to count only accented syllables; see Duhm's article on "Poetical Literature" in *EncBib III*, col. 3802. This article of Duhm's is not well known because of a printing error attributing the article to a non-existent H. D.; see Key on p. xiv and cf. Israel Slotki, "Antiphony in Ancient Hebrew Poetry," *JQR* 26 (1936), 199 n. 3.

44. Duhm came to the conclusion that Jeremiah's words were written only in pentameter verse (3:2). After scanning Jer 2:2b as 3:2—a verse about which no one would quarrel—he remarked: "In diesem Versmass sind sämtliche prophetischen Dichtungen Jeremias geschrieben"; *Jeremia* 16. He then determined that Jeremiah's *ipsissima verba* amounted to 280 Massoretic verses, Baruch's memoirs 220 verses, while the chief contribution came from redactors, to whom the remaining 850 verses were assigned (xvi).

45. Sigmund Mowinckel, *Zur Komposition des Buches Jeremia* (Oslo: J. Dybwad, 1914), 20ff.

Baruch being the biographer (responsible for Source B), but he later gave that up.[46] Working independently of Mowinckel, Robinson came to similar conclusions.[47]

Source criticism has thus for the most part come and gone,[48] but not without leaving some lasting impressions. We are in the first place firmly committed to the idea that the book contains poetry and prose. Recent attempts by Holladay to identify presumed poetry within what has heretofore been taken as prose may alter the picture somewhat, but it does not bring into question the fact that both types of material are manifest.[49] This point must be made clear, for whether we realize it or not, our views of structure will be deeply influenced by what we take to be poetry and what we take to be prose. Where poetry and prose are interspersed, our judgments determine in many cases where we begin or end the literary unit. It is also clear that the core of the Jeremianic message is the poetry, and we will build on that assumption, even if we are not quite so concerned to recover the prophet's *ipsissima verba*.

Secondly, we are committed to the idea that Jeremiah is not the sole author of the book which bears his name. The view of total Jeremianic authorship is expressed in the Talmud.[50] A biographer was largely responsible for the book's composition (although Jeremiah cannot be excluded as collaborator), and Baruch is the likely candidate. Not only is it Baruch who prepares the first scroll dictated by Jeremiah (Jeremiah 36), but Mowinckel seems to be quite correct in proposing that Jeremiah's personal word to him (Jeremiah 45) was meant as an autobiographical postscript.[51] In the LXX, now generally regarded as the more original text,[52] this postscript concludes the book (less

---

46. Mowinckel, *Prophecy and Tradition* (Oslo: Jacob Dybwad, 1946), 61.

47. "Baruch's Roll," *ZAW* 42 (1924), 209–21.

48. As a movement that is; for current use of the methodology see works cited in n. 55.

49. William L. Holladay, "The Recovery of Poetic Passages of Jeremiah," 401–2.

50. Baba Bathra, 14b–15a.

51. *Prophecy and Tradition*, 61–62.

52. Janzen (*Studies in the Text of Jeremiah*, 135) concludes that the Greek text is superior, i.e., less developed. Muilenburg thinks that the Greek order (Oracles to Foreign Nations follow 25:1–13) is more original because Jeremiah's personal word to Baruch comes at the end of chapter 51; cf. "Baruch the Scribe" in *Proclamation and Presence* [Essays in Honour of G. Henton Davies] (Richmond: John Knox Press, 1970), 235.

chapter 52 of course). This in no way precludes there being
other biographers or editors who add and rearrange material
later on. But it does mean that the book in broad outline was
close to being in its present form by the beginning of the exile.

More could be said about source criticism. It has made substantial gains[53] even though some of its assumptions have had
to be modified.[54] Yet it has not been rendered unusable because
of newer methods which have come to replace it.[55] We need say
no more. Specific source-critical points can be discussed as they
arise along the way.

We turn now to form criticism (*Gattungskritik*),[56] which has
dominated biblical criticism since the turn of the century. Its
prime exponent was Hermann Gunkel, who did major studies
in both Genesis and the Psalms.[57] Gunkel was interested in the
pre-literary stage of Hebrew literature, which made form criticism particularly an inquiry into folk literature. Although some
would restrict its province to folk literature exclusively,[58]
Gunkel explicitly rejected the suggestion when it was made to

53. See T. H. Robinson's excellent article "Higher Criticism and the
Prophetic Literature," *ET* 50 (1938–39), 198–202.

54. In Jeremiah we no longer refer to Mowinckel's B and C material
as "sources." Mowinckel himself modified this earlier view in *Prophecy
and Tradition*, 62. Recent Jeremianic scholars are now questioning further
the distinction between B and C; see William L. Holladay, "Prototypes
and Copies: A New Approach to the Poetry-Prose Problem in the Book of
Jeremiah," *JBL* 79 (1960), 354. E. W. Nicholson in *Preaching to the Exiles*
(New York: Schocken Books, 1971) adopts a traditio-historial point of
view (see ahead pp. 25–27) and takes all the prose simply as "tradition."

55. G. W. Anderson makes the point very well: "It is perhaps not
superfluous to state the obvious fact that the scientific study of the Old
Testament must begin with the material which we now have in the form
in which we now have it"; "Some Aspects of the Uppsala School of Old
Testament Study," *HThR* 43 (1950), 248. Klaus Koch agrees; cf. *The Growth
of the Biblical Tradition*, tr. S. M. Cupitt (New York: Charles Scribner's Sons,
1969), 77–78.

56. It also goes by the names of *Gattungsforschung* and *Gattungs-
geschichte*; in New Testament studies, following Dibelius, it is *Formgeschichte*.

57. *Genesis*, 7th ed. (Göttingen: Vandenhoeck & Ruprecht, 1966); *Einleitung in die Psalmen*. Completed by J. Begrich, 2nd ed. (Göttingen: Vandenhoeck & Ruprecht, 1966).

58. Grobel, "Form Criticism" in *IDB* E–J, 320, implies this in his statement of definition.

him.[59] In this characteristic eclectic fashion, he believed that the method could be applied *mutatis mutandis* to the Prophets, and subsequent form-critics agreed.[60]

The primary concern of the form-critic was the identification of *Gattungen*, or to use the more common term, *genres*. Gunkel's article "Die Grundprobleme der israelitischen Literaturgeschichte"[61] was programmatic. Gunkel was also concerned to find the genre's *Sitz im Leben* (setting in life). Hymns he said were sung in the temple, lawsuits originated in the city gate, and prophetic oracles were uttered in the outer court of the temple.[62]

Gunkel said very little about Jeremiah. Actually from a form-critical standpoint, he developed his thoughts very little on any of the prophets.[63] Yet the methodology which became so fruitful for the study of folklore,[64] together with Gunkel's few comments about the prophets, have set in motion a movement in prophetical criticism that is at best a mixed blessing. But much work has been done, so it is necessary to examine the most basic form-critical assumptions as they apply to the Prophets.

Since Gunkel was interested in the earliest forms of prophetic literature, it was natural to begin in the poetry. Gunkel accepted the axiom that poetry was older than prose,[65] and,

---

59. "The Close of Micah: A Prophetical Liturgy" in *What Remains of the Old Testament and Other Essays*, tr. A. K. Dallas (New York: Macmillan Co., 1928), 116.

60. Hugo Gressmann, "Die literarische Analyse Deuterojesajas," *ZAW* 34 (1914), 254–97; Johannes Lindblom, "Die prophetische Orakelformel," *Die literarische Gattung der prophetischen Literatur* (Uppsala: A-B Lundequistska Bokhandeln, 1924)—for a summary see Claus Westermann, *Basic Forms of Prophetic Speech*, tr. Hugh Clayton White (Philadelphia: Westminster Press, 1967), 34–36; Walter Baumgartner, *Die Klagegedichte des Jeremia* (Giessen: Verlag von Alfred Töpelmann, 1917); English: *Jeremiah's Poems of Lament* (tr. David E. Orton; Sheffield: Sheffield Press, 1987).

61. *DLZ* 29 (1906), cols. 1797–1800; 1861–66; tr. later as "Fundamental Problems of Hebrew Literary History" in *What Remains of the Old Testament*, 57–68.

62. "Fundamental Problems of Hebrew Literary History," 61–62.

63. Yet he was not deficient in his psychological understanding; cf. "The Secret Experiences of the Prophets," *The Expositor*, 9th series, 1 (1924), 356–66; 427–35; 2 (1924), 23–32.

64. See James Muilenburg, "The Gains of Form Criticism in Old Testament Studies," *ET* 71 (1959–60), 229–33.

65. See *The Legends of Genesis* which is a translation of the Introduction to his *Genesis* commentary (New York: Schocken Books, 1966), 38.

following the source critics, he believed that this is where the core of the prophetic preaching would be found. Yet a problem arose in the investigation of the prophetic speeches which emerged in the investigation neither of Genesis nor of the Psalms, viz., how one delimits the literary unit. Gunkel used two criteria for delimitation: (1) stereotyped opening phrases, and (2) content. Genres begin in a certain way, e.g., the lament begins with "Woe," while the hymn begins with "Sing unto Yahweh."[66] Gunkel built here on the assumption of Norden that ancient man was more tied to convention than is modern man.[67] He nevertheless used *modern* examples to illustrate his point. The fairy tale begins with "Once upon a time," the letter with "Dear Sir," and the sermon with "Beloved in the Lord."[68] And scholars following Gunkel have made the modern evidence even more impressive.[69]

Content analysis provided other clues for genre classification. Gunkel's *Einleitung in die Psalmen*[70] classifies hymns in a way similar to what we find in our modern hymnbooks. Here content is quite clearly the main criterion for all Gunkel's genres and sub-genres. One cannot quarrel about basic categories (songs of praise, songs of thanksgiving, individual and communal laments), but neither can one confirm (or refute) the existence of all the sub-genres, if in fact they are sub-genres. In Genesis Gunkel was on better ground when he argued for legendary genres, for he had the extensive research of the Grimm

---

Gunkel's evolutionary views on the prophets manifest the same belief; see ahead p. 14.

66. "Fundamental Problems of Hebrew Literary History," 60.

67. Eduard Norden, in his *Antike Kuntsprosa* I (Stuttgart: B. G. Teubner, 1958) argued that Buffon's famous saying, "le style est l'homme même" could not be applied to men of antiquity: "Der Stil war im Altertum nicht der Mensch selbst, sondern ein Gewand, das er nach Belieben wechseln konnte," 11–12. Cf. Gunkel, "Fundamental Problem of Hebrew Literary History," 58–59.

68. Ibid., 60.

69. Koch, *The Growth of the Biblical Tradition*, 3ff.; Gene M. Tucker, *Form Criticism of the Old Testament* (Philadelphia: Fortress Press, 1971), 1ff.

70. This latest work was completed by Joachim Begrich (see note 57). Gunkel's earlier works included *Ausgewählte Psalmen überesetzt und erklärt*, 3rd ed. (Göttingen: Vandenhoeck & Ruprecht, 1911) and an article in *Old Testament Essays* entitled "The Poetry of the Psalms: Its Literary History and Its Application to the Dating of the Psalms," 118–42.

brothers and Axel Olrik to build on.[71] Furthermore, legends and fairy tales provide all kinds of clues from their content about beginning and end. It is thus easy to understand how Gunkel could say of a Genesis legend, "Everyone can see that the story ends here."[72] But everyone cannot see where the prophetic speech ends, and form-critics realize this. This is why more recent form-critics find their outlines in the prose and work back to the poetry,[73] instead of allowing the poetry to articulate itself.

Additional evidence showing the inability of form-critics to delimit the prophetic speeches comes from their arguments about length. Two arguments were used by Gunkel in the main, and both are erroneous.

The first was a psychological argument. Men of antiquity were unable to remember long units, therefore the units must be brief.[74] Gunkel used the analogy of a child (ancient man was "child-like") who only gradually develops to the point where he can absorb more.[75] Herder, a like-minded romantic from another era, interestingly enough argued just the reverse, viz., that ancients were fond of prolonged discourse.[76] This appears

---

71. The influence of the Grimm brothers is best seen in his *Das Märchen im Alten Testament* (Tübingen: J. C. B. Mohr [Paul Siebeck], 1921) where he traces the genre of the folktale throughout the Old Testament. Olrik published articles showing how oral saga follows regular laws of expression: "Episke Love i Folke-digtningen," *Danske Studier* 5 (1908), 69–89 [German: "Epische Gesetze der Volksdichtung," *ZDA* 51 (1909), 1–12; English: "Epic Laws of Folk Narrative," in Alan Dundes (ed.), *The Study of Folklore* (Englewood Cliffs, N.J.: Prentice-Hall, 1965), 129–41]. This latter article was used liberally by Gunkel in the 3rd edition of his *Genesis*; cf. xxxvi–liv.

72. *Legends of Genesis*, 43.

73. Koch, *The Growth of the Biblical Tradition*, 210; the same was done by Mowinckel; cf. *Prophecy and Tradition*, 45.

74. "Fundamental Problems of Hebrew Literary History," 62.

75. Gunkel says, "Just as we see the development of our children's mind in the gradually increasing amount that they can take in at a time, so we can trace one feature of the growth of civilization in the gradual increase of the literary units in Israel"; "Fundamental Problems of Hebrew Literary History," 63.

76. In explaining the reason for the long dialogues in Job, Herder says, "We are accustomed to prefer brevity in the dialogue, and a more obvious sequence of ideas, than we find here. The Orientals in their social intercourse heard each other quietly through, and were even fond of prolonged discourses, especially in verse"; *The Spirit of Hebrew Poetry* I, tr. James Marsh (Burlington: Edward Smith, 1833), 81.

to be the more valid psychological argument if one wishes to stay with Gunkel's analogy, for children are able to remember much longer units than adults, everything else being equal. Dependence upon the written word impairs memory, and anyone who has read stories to a child who cannot read will attest to the fact that the child can reproduce the story from memory much better than the adult who reads it to him night after night.

The second argument was an evolutionary one. Gunkel assumed that since the earliest prophets were ecstatics, their speeches must be brief. The earliest prophetic utterances were single words such as "Jezreel," "Not my People," etc., the names which prophets gave to their children.[77] "Dann haben es die P[rophet]en gelernt, längere Reden zu schaffen, die etwa ein Kapitel umfassen."[78] In Amos we get poems of four cola or more; Jer 2:14–19 is cited as one longer yet.[79] Ezekiel's speeches are the longest. Gunkel attributes this change to a development in culture. As writing became more and more common, the prophets turned into authors.[80] This latter point cannot be dismissed out of hand, for the prophets beginning with Amos and Hosea are clearly a different breed from those who preceded them. And they may also have written their speeches in a way that earlier prophets did not. But this will not support the thesis that speeches increase in length from Amos to Ezekiel. Gunkel was highly selective in the examples which he chose, and left far more unexplained than he explained. There is no observable distinction, for example, between the length of poems in Amos and Jeremiah. If anything, Amos 1–2 is probably one of the longest speeches in any of the prophetic books.[81]

We must conclude then that form-critics are on very subjective grounds when they argue for brief speeches. Further-

---

77. "Schriftstellerei und Formensprache der Propheten" in *Die Propheten* (Göttingen: Vandenhoeck & Ruprecht, 1917), 116.

78. "Propheten II B. Propheten Israels seit Amos," *RGG*[2] IV, col. 1548.

79. "Schriftstellerei und Formensprache der Propheten," 116–17.

80. Ibid., 112: "Inzwischen aber hatte sich die Zeit verändert; das allmählich zu höherer Kultur heranreifende Israel begann immer mehr zu schreiben. Und auch die Prophetie war, . . . eine andere geworden: ihr Gesichtskreis umfassender, ihre Einsichten tiefer, ihre Ziele weiter. So haben sich die Propheten der Schriftstellerei zugewandt."

81. Note how Mowinckel gives customary lip-service to the form-critical maxim of brief units when discussing this passage, but goes on to say that the passage makes more sense when treated as a unity; *Prophecy and Tradition*, 56–57.

more, we are still left with the obvious question of "How long is long?" or "How short is short?" In Jeremiah, Gunkel's delineations of 2:14–19[82] and 17:5–8[83] are perceptive enough, and I would say basically correct, but both of these poems are easily identifiable because of obvious poetic balance.

Another form-critical observation has been a mixed blessing. Gunkel realized that oral literature is characterized by loose connections. Legends are often brought together by a thematic principle, e.g., the central figure may provide the means of unification.[84] But by and large the various collections of legends, songs and proverbs are brought together without any discernible connection.[85] Form critics believed the same to be true of prophetic speeches, and from time to time we hear these being compared to "pearls on a string,"[86] a phrase apparently stemming from Herder.[87] This claim has been substantiated by the traditio-historical school and others who show how "catch-words" link poems together into chains of tradition. We will say more about this in a moment. But later form-critics, on the other hand, all too often use this point to argue that the present text has no discernible order.[88] John Bright has adopted this line in Jeremiah.[89] This has brought discredit upon form criticism since one of the original strengths of Gunkel's work was that it was holistic and treated the text with much greater respect than earlier works done by the source-critics.[90]

Recent form-critical work in the Prophets and in Jeremiah is plagued by these difficulties. The most ambitious study of prophetic speech forms is by Claus Westermann.[91] Westermann

---

82. "Schriftstellerei und Formensprache der Propheten," 117–18.

83. Gunkel thought that Psalm 1 was an imitation of this poem; *The Psalms: A Form-Critical Introduction* [Facet Books, Biblical Series, #19] (Philadelphia: Fortress Press, 1967), 27.

84. *Legends of Genesis*, 80.

85. "Fundamental Problems of Hebrew Literary History," 64.

86. Theophile J. Meek, "The Poetry of Jeremiah," *JQR* New Series 14 (1923–24), 283.

87. Herder spoke of "pearls from the depths of the ocean loosely arranged"; cf. *The Spirit of Hebrew Poetry* I, 81.

88. So Tucker, *Form Criticism of the Old Testament* 64.

89. "The impression he gains is one of extreme disarray"; *Jeremiah*, lvi.

90. See the comments of Israel Slotki as he contrasts treatments by Gunkel and Charles Briggs on Psalm 136; cf. "The Stichometry and Text of the Great Hallel," *JThS* 29 (1928), 255–56.

91. *Basic Forms of Prophetic Speech.*

sets forth what he believes to be the fundamental prophetic genre, viz., the "judgment speech." The judgment speech is directed at two main audiences: (1) the individual (JI), and (2) the nation (JN). Jeremiah contains both. Following Gunkel and Gressmann, Westermann accepted the idea that prophets were from oldest times foretellers of the future. Thus we could expect the true prophetic genre to be one which forecasts the future.[92] What resulted was two self-evident types: (1) predictions of salvation,[93] and (2) predictions of judgment. Westermann also used the Mari Letters as a basis of comparison.[94]

Thus far Westermann is on safe ground. There is no reason to object to the idea that prophets were foretellers of the future.[95] Neither is there any reason to quarrel over prophets making predictions of salvation and judgment. We can conclude both almost *a priori*. We need not even object to calling them separate genres. Perhaps they were.

But Westermann's work falls apart when he tries to set up structures for the prophetic speech. Two difficulties are apparent at once. In the first place, he is either unable or does not bother to defend the limits of his literary units. In his lone example of the JI from the Prophets (Amos 7:16–17), part of the known speech is excluded. That speech began in v. 14. In the poetry, which we agree is difficult to separate, Westermann could at least have availed himself of some outside help. But a comparison of his units with those in BH^3 and the modern versions, not to mention the commentaries, will show that the former seldom correspond with any of the latter.

A second major difficulty concerns the outline categories themselves. To say that a judgment speech has two main parts, the accusation and announcement of judgment, is to accent the obvious. Could it be otherwise? These and his other categories are so general that they become nondescript. Among the JNs,

---

92. Ibid., 26, where Westermann quotes Gunkel with approval; cf. Gunkel, "Fundamental Problems of Hebrew Literary History," 60.

93. Westermann did an earlier study of the salvation speech entitled "The Way of the Promise through the Old Testament" in *The Old Testament and Christian Faith*, ed. Bernhard W. Anderson (New York: Harper & Row, 1963), 200–224.

94. *Basic Forms of Prophetic Speech*, 115–28.

95. Earlier source critics de-emphasized this aspect of prophecy. Gunkel, on the other hand, takes Deut 18:22 seriously; cf. "The Secret Experiences of the Prophets," I, 433.

Jer 5:10–14 is made to fit by using the words of judgment, which should by his calculation come at the end, serve as "Introduction."[96] In Jer 7:16–18, 20 a command to Jeremiah not to intercede for the people is "Introduction." And other examples outside Jeremiah make it even more clear that the texts have been placed in a mould which just does not fit.[97]

When we look at the list of Jeremianic passages that supposedly fit the JI, of which Westermann finds ten,[98] only one of them, 36:29–30, corresponds tolerably to the outline given. Some lack "Accusations,"[99] while on two occasions the judgment is prophesied to *both* the nation and the individual.[100] In the case of 29:24–32, the order does not conform to the outline. Also there are many instances where one of the elements of the speech is not present.[101]

Taken together, these weaknesses greatly diminish the value of Westermann's work. Certainly his structural analysis cannot stand for the Jeremianic speech, if indeed it can stand for any of the prophetic speeches. So for our purposes, it provides virtually no help at all.

Other genres which the prophets supposedly borrowed[102] have also been studied since Gunkel. Westermann gives scant attention to them in his book,[103] while other scholars have

---

96. *Basic Forms of Prophetic Speech*, 175.

97. In Amos 4:1–2; Mic 3:1–2, 4; 9–12 it is a call to hear, while in Mic 2:1–4 the word "Woe" has been extrapolated to meet the need; other speeches are without an "Introduction"; cf. ibid., 174–75.

98. Ibid., 137.

99. In 22:24–27, what did Coniah do wrong? See also 22:30, 37:17.

100. 20:1–6; 28:12–16.

101. This problem is noticed by Tucker and causes him to reject such detailed structures; cf. *Form Criticism of the Old Testament*, 64, n. 94.

102. Gunkel believed that most of the genres used by the prophets did not originate with the prophets but were borrowed and appropriated to a new use. This they did because of a burning desire to win over the hearts of people who had a natural receptivity to such forms: "Für diese Geschichte aber ist die grundlegende Erkenntnis diese, dass die meisten der genannten Gattungen nicht ursprünglich p[rophet]isch sind, sondern dass die Prophetie fremde Gattungen in weitestem Umfange aufgenommen hat . . . Und auch der Grund, warum sie das geworden sind, ist deutlich: es ist der brennende Wunsch der P[rophet]en, Macht über das Gemüt ihres Volkes zu gewinnen, der sie dazu getrieben hat"; "Propheten II B. Propheten Israels seit Amos," col. 1550.

103. *Basic Forms of Prophetic Speech*, 199–204.

written up independent studies of them in the journals. In Jeremiah, most attention has been paid to a supposed "lawsuit" genre, which also goes by the name of *rib* (רִיב), the characteristic term of the genre meaning "contention."[104] Gunkel called it the *Gerichtsrede*, an example of which he found in Psalm 82.[105] Gunkel also laid out the outline of the genre,[106] and has since been followed by Herbert Huffmon.[107] Huffmon advanced the study by tying the רִיב in with George Mendenhall's classic study of Law and Covenant.[108] Mendenhall had compared the covenant of the Old Testament with Hittite treaties and shown striking similarities. Huffmon then interpreted the lawsuit in the context of the covenant, calling the רִיב a "covenant lawsuit." The prophets were seen as bringing a lawsuit by Yahweh against the people for breach of covenant. Huffmon also took over the main passages which Gunkel used to illustrate his *Gerichtsrede*, among them Jer 2:4ff. In addition he adds Deuteronomy 32, which is important for us since it is now clear that this poem had a decisive influence upon Jeremiah.[109]

Following Huffmon, Julien Harvey contributed to the discussion by modifying the Gunkel-Huffmon outline and comparing prominent biblical texts with a lawsuit from the Epic of Tukulti-Ninurta I, found among the Assyrian documents at Nineveh.[110] Both Jeremiah 2 and Deuteronomy 32 are central to his "Rîb à condamnation." Harvey also takes this form to have

---

104. For a study of this term, see James Limburg, "The Root רִיב and the Prophetic Lawsuit Speeches," *JBL* 88 (1969), 291–304.

105. *Einleitung in die Psalmen*, 329.

106. Ibid., 364–65.

107. "The Covenant Lawsuit in the Prophets," *JBL* 78 (1959), 285–89. Earlier, B. Gemser did a study entitled "The 'RÎB' or Controversy-Pattern in Hebrew Mentality" in *Wisdom in Israel and in the Ancient Near East* [VTSupp 3] (Leiden: E. J. Brill, 1955), 120–37.

108. *Law and Covenant in Israel and the Ancient Near East* (Pittsburgh: Presbyterian Board of Colportage, 1955).

109. See William L. Holladay, "Jeremiah and Moses: Further Observations," *JBL* 85 (1966), 17–27. For a separate analysis of Deuteronomy 32 as a lawsuit, see G. Ernest Wright, "The Lawsuit of God: A Form-Critical Study of Deuteronomy 32" in *Israel's Prophetic Heritage*, ed. Bernhard W. Anderson and Walter Harrelson (New York: Harper & Brothers, 1962), 26–67.

110. "Le 'RÎB-Pattern' Réquisitoire Prophétique sur la Rupture de l'Alliance," *Biblica* 43 (1962), 172–96.

originated in international law where it was used by a suzerain against his unfaithful vassal.

Finally Joseph Blenkinsopp has written an article on the "prophetic reproach"[111] which he takes to be similar to the lawsuit, and includes among his examples Jer 2:4–13. The significance of his work is that he refrains from making an outline, and recognizes further that in at least one case (though not in Jeremiah), it is the repetition in the poem that provides the poem with its structure.[112]

Again we do not quarrel with this general approach. The idea that Jeremiah would use a lawsuit form in one of his speeches is reasonable. We can readily imagine him denouncing the people for breach of contract. The only possible objection to the overall comparison might be that, of all the extra-biblical texts cited thus far, none refers to a divorce proceeding. This is important, for Jeremiah often views the covenant in marital terms. Jer 2:2–3, which is introductory, describes the early relationship of Yahweh and Israel as a time of honeymoon.[113]

The main criticism is again with structure. There is no agreement among these scholars on what constitutes the literary unit.[114] Also explanations of the internal structure of the Jeremianic lawsuit tend to leave one confused. Elements in the Jeremianic text are again "out of order." Gunkel noted long ago that the opening summons, instead of coming at the beginning of the suit where it belonged, came instead at v. 12.[115] Huffmon admits also that the suit begins with a summons to the accused, which he says should come later.[116] Then there is the same problem which we found with Westermann's work, viz., that the categories in neither the Gunkel-Huffmon outline nor the

---

111. "The Prophetic Reproach," *JBL* 90 (1971), 267–78.

112. In Amos 4:6–12 the phrase "yet you did not return to me" repeated five times impresses him as a structural feature; cf. ibid., 267–68.

113. Perhaps this is why Huffmon leaves out these verses.

114. In Jeremiah, Huffmon limits the pericope to 2:4–13; Harvey takes all of 2:2–37, and Gemser extends the lawsuit all the way to 4:4! With Deuteronomy 32, Huffmon takes the whole poem, for which he is to be commended, while Harvey omits vv. 26–43 leaving a good bit of the poem unexplained.

115. *Einleitung in die Psalmen*, 364; cf. Huffmon, "The Covenant Lawsuit in the Prophets," 288.

116. Ibid.

Harvey outline do an adequate job of explaining the Jeremianic
text.[117]

It is clear that the advocates of these "lawsuit" genres have
over-extended themselves in drawing their parallels. And the
most serious result is that they have thereby failed to illuminate
the way in which the text articulates itself. Exegetically this
method is almost of no value. Anyone who reads the text carefully is constantly at pains to see how such outlines are made to
fit the evidence. That Jeremiah is using legal language we will
not deny. Neither will we object to the thesis that his speech
contains allusions to legal proceedings from the court.[118] But it
remains unproven that Jeremiah is using a borrowed genre in

---

117. In Huffmon's analysis, besides the admission that components
are in a different order, it is not clear what difference exists between the
speech of the plaintiff (II) and the accusation to the defendant (II C 1).
Huffmon considers v. 5 as "accusation" (p. 288), and I would ask if this
doesn't continue on through to v. 8. The only verse where Yahweh speaks
in the first person about his mighty acts is v. 7. Also where is the indictment? And why does v. 13 reiterate the accusation of v. 9? It is clear that
Yahweh is accusing Israel of wrong—yes even breach of covenant—but a
comparison of the Jeremianic text with the Gunkel-Huffmon outline is by
no means clear. With Harvey the situation is much worse. Beginning in
the middle of his "Indictment" (III) and continuing through the "Declaration of Guilt" (V) there is no direct correspondence to the Jeremianic text.
The only part of Harvey's outline which rings true—and here it does so
in both Jer 2:5ff. and Deut 32:4ff.—is the first part of the Indictment,
where it is clear in both texts that Yahweh's gracious deeds are followed
by Israel's ingratitude. But this correspondence will not support Harvey's
entire scheme. To begin with, the inclusion of vv. 14–19 is doubtful since
this is generally taken to be a separate poem (so Gunkel; cf. p. 14 above).
If it is to be included, then Yahweh's goodness and Israel's ingratitude is
hardly the main thought. The point here is rather the futility of continued
political alliances with Egypt and Assyria (vv. 18–19) especially in light of
past failures (vv. 15–17). Within vv. 20–28, we have such a contrast in 21
alone, but nowhere else in the unit. In vv. 29–30 I do not see the contrast
at all. As for IV—The Uselessness of Ritual Expiation—there is nothing
in vv. 26–28 which stands out from the rest of the chapter. The mention of
idolatry appears in vv. 5, 8, 11, 13, 19, 20 and 23 in one form or another—
indeed it is the theme of the entire chapter. The same is true with V—The
Declaration of Guilt: it is mentioned in vv. 7, 9, 13, 19, 22, 23, etc. There is
thus no reason to isolate vv. 31–37 as a specific reference to judgment and
destruction.

118. Muilenburg, "Form Criticism and Beyond," 5, says that 2:1–4:4
contains *several* examples of the lawsuit, although he agrees that the biblical text does not give a complete reproduction of this genre as it was
carried on in the courtyard. He calls them "imitations of a Gattung." But

chapter 2, and we are certain that the structure of Jeremiah 2 is not controlled by any of the outlines set forth in the lawsuit proposals. It is to Blenkinsopp's credit that he refrains from making an outline, and the same may be said of Holladay, who proposes a lawsuit initiated by Jeremiah against Yahweh in Jer 12:1ff.[119]

With other genre studies the same situation obtains. Thomas Raitt has argued for a "summons to repentance" genre,[120] and Norman Habel has isolated what he believes to be a genre of the prophetic "call."[121] Both take into account texts from Jeremiah. Raitt has no agreed-upon units in mind when inserting texts into his scheme, nor does he keep the texts in their present order. This latter problem does not disturb Raitt, any more than it disturbs other form-critics, for it is assumed that the present order is one of disarray.[122] In Habel's study, the outline fails in part when applied to Jeremiah's call, and fails significantly when put to the call of Isaiah.[123] This is damaging to the whole

---

is even this necessary? Only after we provide a better analysis of structure can this question be answered.

119. "Jeremiah's Lawsuit with God," *Int.* 17 (1963), 280–87.

120. "The Prophetic Summons to Repentance," *ZAW* 83 (1971), 30–48.

121. "The Form and Significance of the Call Narratives," *ZAW* 77 (1965), 297–323.

122. Raitt says, "In the transition from an oral to a written representation—to say nothing of the continual tendency to re-work early speech elements to fit the needs of a later situation—any hypothetical speech-form is subject to the possibility of modifications and adaptations"; "The Prophetic Summons to Repentance," 37. It is one thing to say this when we have a known prototype and some known deviations, but in the absence of both, such reasoning goes in a circle.

123. In the call of Jeremiah, the "sign" is actually not present; vv. 9–10 can hardly be forced into this category. In the call of Isaiah, besides the modification which Habel admits for the beginning, the Introductory Word (II) does not fit the text. The words of the seraphim are to each other, not to Isaiah. Secondly, the "Woe is me" phrase (v. 5) comes much closer to an objection than "How long, O Yahweh" (v. 11). In any case, Isaiah does not offer an objection like Moses and Jeremiah; he accepts the call readily: "Here am I, send me" (v. 8). Also, the final Sign (VI) is missing in Isaiah's call as it is in the call of Jeremiah. We note too a problem of nondescript categories like those of Westermann, e.g., the Introductory Word can cover almost anything. If we are asked to take the call as a separate genre, we must insist that outlines be rejected which do not fit the text. Muilenburg issues a warning in this regard to those who would overly conventionalize the prophetic calls; cf. "The 'Office' of the Prophet in Ancient Israel" in *The Bible in Modern Scholarship*, ed. J. Philip Hyatt (Nashville & New York: Abingdon Press, 1965), 89.

argument, since the calls of Jeremiah and Isaiah are two of the most important in the prophetic corpus.

Actually the most form-critical help for delimiting literary units came as a result of the thesis of Ludwig Köhler who argued that prophetic speech was essentially "messenger speech."[124] The prophet now becomes a messenger who receives his message in the council of Yahweh and then delivers it to the people. Yahweh is the sender; the people are the sendee. The prophet remains an intermediary whose only function is to deliver the message as directed. This model then replaces the ecstatic model, which was accepted earlier on the basis of Hölscher's work.[125] The model of the messenger is seen elsewhere in the ancient Near East, notably at Mari, where a prophetic-type figure functions as a divine messenger of the god Dagan.[126] A comparison, moreover, of the formula "Thus says Yahweh . . ." (כה־אמר יהוה) with such formulas as "Thus says the king . . ." (כה־אמר המלך) or "Thus says Ben Hadad . . ." (כה־אמר בן־הדד), both of which are used in messenger contexts,[127] suggests that the prophetic formula was appropriated by the prophets for a new use. The "call" passages of Isaiah and Jeremiah further suggest that the commission to be Yahweh's messenger was part of the prophetic self-understanding. Köhler pointed this out in Isaiah 6. In Jeremiah, the call from Yahweh is made in order that Yahweh may *send* Jeremiah (אשלחך), after which he puts words into Jeremiah's mouth (1:7, 9).[128] Thus recent scholarship has adopted the mes-

---

124. "Formen und Stoffe," *Deuterojesaja (Jesaja 40–55) Stilkritisch Untersucht* [BZAW 37] (Giessen: Verlag von Alfred Töpelmann, 1923), 102–42.

125. Gustav Hölscher, *Die Propheten* (Leipzig: J. C. Hinrichs'sche Buchhandlung, 1914). Hölscher takes Jeremiah too as an ecstatic, frequently appearing in the temple court where he is under the discipline of the priests (Jer 20:2; 29:26). Like other prophets of his day he could appear mad and disturbed (29:26ff.), and in ecstasy could hear sounds and see images (3:21; 4:13, 15; etc.). Jeremiah also does not always have ready access to the word of Yahweh; sometimes he must wait many days for the spirit to grip him; cf. 294.

126. See Martin Noth, "History and the Word of God in the Old Testament," *BJRL* 32 (1950), 197ff.; also Herbert Huffmon, "Prophecy in the Mari Letters," *BA* 31 (1968), 101–24.

127. 1 Kgs 20:3, 5; 2 Kgs 9:18.

128. Jeremiah later distinguished himself from the false prophets by claiming to have stood in Yahweh's council where he was then given Yahweh's message. Others were quick enough to run and deliver, but they had not been sent (Jer 23:18, 21–22).

senger model,[129] although it is readily acknowledged that not all prophetic speeches are messenger speeches.[130] Meek isolates Jer 2:2–3 on these grounds since the speech is framed by כה אמר יהוה at the beginning, and נאם־יהוה at the end, the latter being another formula similar to כה אמר יהוה.[131]

These formulas are then a help in delimiting the literary unit. Yet they are not always reliable. It is conceded that some have been inserted by editors for later adaptations of the material,[132] in which case the original beginning or end of the speech is obscured. In actual practice the form-critics disregard these formulas almost as much as they follow them, which means we should probably regard them in about the same way as we regard chapter headings. They are useful ancient markers, but they need corroborating data before they can be judged to signal authentic breaks, or be in fact original messenger formulas. Also, we can get help from these formulas only when they are present, and a good bit of the Jeremianic text is without them.

Summing up then the contribution of form criticism, we can agree that it has asked some important questions even if it has not always been able to provide the correct answers. The question of genre is not unimportant. It was fundamental for Gunkel in Genesis, and it is equally fundamental in Jeremiah—especially when we come to the prose material. There what the source critics called "biography," some latter-day form-critics want to call "legend," which is clearly an error.[133] Gunkel's comments about this material indicate that he did not consider it to be legend,[134] and Muilenburg has recently affirmed the same.[135]

---

129. Westermann, *Basic Forms of Prophetic Speech*, 98ff.; James F. Ross, "The Prophet as Yahweh's Messenger" in *Israel's Prophetic Heritage*, 98–107.

130. Westermann, *Basic Forms of Prophetic Speech*, 111.

131. "The Poetry of Jeremiah," 281–82.

132. T. H. Robinson, *Prophecy and the Prophets in Ancient Israel*, 2nd ed. (London: Gerald Duckworth & Co., 1953), 52–53.

133. So Klaus Koch, *The Growth of the Biblical Tradition*, 201ff., and Martin Kessler, "Form-Critical Suggestions on Jer 36," *CBQ* 28 (1966), 390.

134. "The Secret Experiences of the Prophets," I, 434: "It is clear that many of these narratives [i.e., the narratives of Elijah and Elisha] are popular tales, for it is significant that the biography of Jeremiah, included in his book, *which is extraordinarily faithful* [italics mine], contains no such magical deeds concerning him."

135. "Baruch the Scribe," 233. Muilenburg here cites Kessler for support, but as we have just shown (n. 133), Kessler stated that the material was legend.

The prose of Jeremiah ought not be compared with either the Genesis legends or the legends of Elijah and Elisha; it is far more like the Court History in 2 Samuel 7–20; 1 Kings 1–2.[136]

As for the prophetic speeches, we are still lacking models for a proper genre analysis.[137] The most promising model to be used of late, viz., the letter,[138] is only of help when comparing opening and closing formulas. We get no insight into the *body* of the speech. Here we must judge form criticism to have failed, for it has been unable to throw light on the structure of the prophetic speech.[139]

The form-critical emphasis on the prophet as *speaker* is important. It is also worthwhile to recover when possible the *Sitz im Leben* of the prophetic speech, or to use a more appropriate term now in use, the *audience*. The speech needs to be understood in the context of the audience for which it was originally intended. And we must also find out more about how the speech—together with other comment—was used to address audiences removed in time from the original delivery.

---

136. Just to read Koch's description of the material is to wonder why he uses the term. He refers to this prose as "the first prophetic biography composed in Israel" and agrees it is completely reliable; cf. *The Growth of the Biblical Tradition*, 204. He also agrees that the "legends" were not collected by a circle of the prophet's disciples—which was the case with the Elijah-Elisha legends—and passed on then by oral transmission (p. 203). How then can he call such "legend" and say on p. 201 that it is similar to the Elijah-Elisha narratives?

137. Mowinckel pointed out quite rightly that the prophetic literature has no real counterpart in the literature of the *ANE*; see his article, "Literature," *IDB* K–Q, 142.

138. Westermann, *Basic Forms of Prophetic Speech*, 115ff.

139. Of course the form-critics could always say that by Jeremiah's time the forms were breaking up. Gunkel believed that forms have their own history: they are born, they flourish for a time, then they decay and die, after which come the imitations; cf. "Fundamental Problems of Hebrew Literary History," 65–66. Von Rad in fact says this quite specifically about Jeremiah: "In Jeremiah all the forms of expression to be found in classical prophecy are obviously breaking up"; cf. Gerhard von Rad, *Old Testament Theology* II, tr. D. M. G. Stalker (Edinburgh & London: Oliver and Boyd, 1967), 193. Yet it should be noted that Gunkel's desire to write a history of Israelite literature died with him and is now forgotten; see Koch, *The Growth of the Biblical Tradition*, 103. Furthermore, the so-called "forms of classical prophecy" have yet to be shown.

It remains only to comment briefly on the contribution of the traditio-historical school of Old Testament studies. This was another school of biblical criticism which flourished for a time at Uppsala, and like the school of form criticism, developed its own particular theories about oral tradition.[140] H. S. Nyberg began it all with some revolutionary comments at the beginning of a commentary on Hosea.[141] He argued in short that much of the Old Testament was transmitted in oral form until the exile, which was the crisis that forced it into writing. This amounted to a sweeping attack on source criticism, and with regard to the Prophets, it challenged the entire search for the prophet's *ipsissima verba*. All we have in the text are "tradition-complexes" which became fixed at the time when they were written down.

The upshot of this thesis was a lively debate which continued for a time on oral vs. written tradition. Today, however, it is generally agreed not only that writing was practiced quite early in Israel,[142] but also that *both* oral and written tradition existed side by side prior to the exile.[143]

With respect to the Prophets, the traditio-historical critics believed that a circle of disciples preserved the master's words for a time in oral form, after which they were eventually written down. Hosea has continued to have particular appeal for this methodology,[144] but Jeremiah is not neglected either despite the

---

140. There are three good surveys of this school: G. W. Anderson, "Some Aspects of the Uppsala School of Old Testament Study"; C. R. North, "The Place of Oral Tradition in the Growth of the Old Testament," *ET* 61 (1949–50), 292–96; and Walter E. Rast, *Tradition History and the Old Testament* (Philadelphia: Fortress Press, 1972).

141. *Studien zum Hoseabuche* (Uppsala: Lundequistska Bokhandeln, 1935).

142. Geo Widengren, *Literary and Psychological Aspects of the Hebrew Prophets* (Uppsala: Lundequistska Bokhandeln, 1948), 68ff.; 122. See also Solomon Gandz, "Oral Tradition in the Bible" in *Jewish Studies in Memory of George A. Kohut* (New York: Alexander Kohut Memorial Foundation, 1935), 251ff., and James Muilenburg, "Baruch the Scribe," 215ff.

143. J. Weingreen, "Oral Torah and Written Records" in *Holy Book and Holy Tradition*, ed. F. F. Bruce and E. G. Rupp (Grand Rapids: Eerdmans Press, 1968), 67. The suggestion by Moses Buttenwieser in *The Prophets of Israel* (New York: Macmillan Co., 1914), 133, that Jeremiah was unable to write, is not at all implied by Jeremiah 36.

144. See Edwin Good's "The Composition of Hosea," *SEÅ* 31 (1966), 21–63.

explicit statement in Jeremiah 36 that Baruch wrote Jeremiah's speeches down. This is a crucial chapter, and Birkeland, Mowinckel and Engnell begin there too.[145] They point out the fact that Jeremiah retained oracles for a long period (23 years according to 25:3) before committing them to writing (36:2–4). This alone says something about the preservation of literature in non-written form. The other point used to support their thesis is not so persuasive. Birkeland says that the final words of chapter 36, "and many similar words were added to them" cannot be ascribed to Baruch,[146] therefore someone else must be the biographer. But this however does not follow. And as we pointed out earlier, Mowinckel later gave up a similar skepticism which he once had on the same point.[147] But in the traditio-historical view, Baruch is just one member of a circle of disciples who preserved the Jeremianic traditions into the exile, at which time they were finally written down.

Thus in Jeremiah these scholars begin not with the Jeremianic speeches, but with what they believe to be large blocks of tradition still observable in the final composition. Methodologically they work just the reverse of the form-critics: they begin with the latest stage of development and work back. Four "tradition-complexes" are posited in Jeremiah:[148] (1) 1–24; (2) 25, 46–51; (3) 26–35/36; (4) 36/37–45. The complexes are isolated for rather obvious reasons. The break at 25:13 between the MT and the LXX is considered significant, and thus aids in marking off two blocks of tradition. Since 25:1–13 originally introduced the Oracles to Foreign Nations (as it still does in the LXX), it is grouped together with those oracles, which in the MT are found in 46–51. This forms the second group. By elimination, 1–24 becomes group one. The other two groups are arrived at by taking what is left and dividing at chapter 36, which is

---

145. Harris Birkeland, *Zum Hebräischen Traditionswesen* (Oslo: Jacob Dybwad, 1939), 43ff.; Mowinckel, *Prophecy and Tradition*, 61. For a summary of Engnell's late study on Jeremiah and the method he employed, see T. R. Hobbs, "Some Remarks on the Composition and Structure of the Book of Jeremiah," *CBQ* 34 (1972), 263ff.

146. Ibid., 43.

147. See pp. 8–9.

148. The views of Engnell and Claus Rietzschel (see note following) are conveniently summarized by Hobbs, "Some Remarks on the Composition and Structure of the Book of Jeremiah," 267ff.

pivotal. Only agreement does not exist on whether 36 ends the earlier complex, or begins the complex that follows. Engnell takes the first view, and Claus Rietzschel, a German scholar working along similar lines, takes the latter.[149] Kessler and Hobbs side with Engnell.[150]

The way these scholars continue their research into earlier stages of composition is worthy of comment. Like the form-critics, scholars of this school emphasize that earlier complexes were formed by rather loose connections. This is due to oral tradition, only the traditio-historical scholars are quick to point out that such arrangements are not haphazard or illogical.[151] Early units are grouped into chains by "catchwords" (Rietzschel: "thematischen Gesichtspunkten oder Stichwortverknüpfungen").[152] This is basically a sound observation, except that it is unfortunate that the major attempts to find such links in Jeremiah have been made in the prose. We reject the assumption that the prose is legend, and we are not prepared to grant the material any substantial period of oral transmission. Thus the prose does not contain catchwords.[153] The poetry is the proper place to look for catchwords. But since the units there are not firmly established, this would be a precarious venture. One can hardly show what is linked together without first knowing the limits of units being linked. Thus we can only conclude that such a study has promise, but cannot be done unless other controls are available.

This concludes our survey. It should be clear by now that a structural analysis of Jeremiah is much needed. We need to know the very things which Muilenburg listed as deserving top priority: the limits of the literary units, and the structure of

---

149. See *Das Problem der Urrolle* (Gütersloh: Gütersloher Verlagshaus Gerd Mohn, 1966), 17.

150. Kessler, "Form-Critical Suggestions on Jer 36," 389; Hobbs, "Some Remarks on the Composition and Structure of the Book of Jeremiah," 267–68.

151. The comment of Edwin Good ("The Composition of Hosea," 21) is to the point: "We have too often been satisfied merely to apply our own canons of logic to the Old Testament, and we are still groping after an understanding of the Old Testament's own logic."

152. *Das Problem der Urrolle*, 24.

153. As proposed by Martin Kessler in his unpublished dissertation, "A Prophetic Biography: A Form-Critical Study of Jer 26–29, 32–45" (Ph.D. thesis, Brandeis, 1965).

those units, whether in the prophetic speech or in the larger book of Jeremiah.

Outline of the Present Study

In order to speak to this problem, we are prepared to argue that two known rhetorical figures, the inclusio and the chiasmus, are important controlling structures in Jeremiah. They control not only the prophetic speeches, but also larger complexes which make up the *book* of Jeremiah.

We mentioned earlier that Muilenburg delimited units by the inclusio. Leon Liebreich also found the inclusio in both First and Second Isaiah.[154] In Deuteronomy a use of the inclusio has been recognized by Norbert Lohfink, although he has yet to realize the full extent to which this figure is employed in the composition of that book.[155] More recently Dahood has found it

---

154. Leon Liebreich, "The Compilation of the Book of Isaiah," *JQR* 46 (1956), 259–77; 47 (1956), 114–38.

155. Professor Lohfink kindly sent me a copy of his *Lectures in Deuteronomy*, tr. S. McEvenue S.J. (Rome: Pontifical Biblical Institute, 1968), in which he notes inclusios in Deut 14:1–21 and 14:22–15:23; cf. 24, 26. But there are others. Chapter 12 is framed by the words תשמרון לעשות (12:1) and תשמרו לעשות (13:1). The RSV and NEB correctly take the latter as the concluding verse of chapter 12 (against both MT and the LXX!). Also the liturgical-type injunction found duplicated in 6:6–9 and 11:18–20 (with the center sections inverted!) may likewise be an inclusio for 6–11. Two other inclusios are overlooked by Lohfink due to his view that Deuteronomy in its final form was modeled on an archive (*Lectures*, 7–9). According to this view four documents are placed side by side, each being introduced by a superscription. The four superscriptions would be 1:1; 4:44; 28:69 and 33:1. But 4:44 and 28:69 are *not* superscriptions. They are *subscriptions*—or in the case of 4:44 part of a subscription—which link up to 1:1–5 to make inclusios. It is true that the LXX takes MT 28:69 as 29:1, but Driver is quite correct in taking the verse as a subscription. He says it looks back to 5–26, 28 and not ahead to 29ff.; cf. S. R. Driver, *Deuteronomy*, 319. To show further that this verse makes an inclusio with 1:1– 5 we need only notice the following key words: אלה הדברים (1:1) and אלה דברי (28:69); also בארץ מואב in both 1:5 and 28:69. This suggests then that Deuteronomy was not modeled on an archive but had instead a rhetorical form even at this late stage. We also believe that 4:44–49 is yet another inclusio with 1:1–5. Here we lack the support of Driver and others (although Driver does admit that 4:44–49 is "superfluous" after 1:1–5; *Deuteronomy*, 79) but a close look at both pericopes will show that they are indeed intended as a frame for 1–4. 1:1–5 ends with את־התורה הזאת (this

in the Psalms,[156] and David Noel Freedman has shown it to be present in the poetry of Job and Hosea.[157] In Jeremiah some valuable insights can be gained from Condamin's commentary,[158] although Condamin's strophic notions detract from the overall value of this particular work. Not all inclusios are the same. Most consist of repeated vocabulary or phraseology at the beginning and end of a unit. But in the case of Hos 8:9–13, Freedman correctly points out that the final line is not mere repetition of the line which opens the poem;[159] the two lines are complementary, being broken parts of a standard bi-colon which the poet uses for purposes of inclusio. The inclusio must therefore not be defined too narrowly. It is necessary only that the end show continuity with the beginning, and that this continuity be taken as a deliberate attempt by the author to effect closure.

Chapter 2 of our study will show how the inclusio is used in Jeremiah. Examples will be grouped at three levels. One level will be the larger book of Jeremiah. Here we will show structures imposed on earlier material in the collection process, whether originating from a period of oral tradition or deriving from the hand of a writing scribe. The other two levels deal with the Jeremianic speech, both as a whole and in part. The inclusio is the surest way to delimit the speech, since, by definition, it ties the end together with the beginning. We will also show the

---

law) while 4:44–49 begins with וזאת התורה (And this is the law). The terms are nicely inverted too. Also there is mention of the "Arabah" at the beginning of 1:1–5 and at the end of 4:44–49. And both pericopes have "beyond the Jordan" at beginning and end. It is clear I think that 4:44–49 looks *back* to the events of chapters 2–3 just as 28:69 looks back to the covenant contained in 1–28. Both pericopes (1:1–5 and 4:44–49) reiterate the sojourn from Horeb to Moab, the high point being the victories over Sihon and Og. These victories are described more fully in chapters 2–3. Thus we conclude that both 4:44–49 and 28:69 were meant to form inclusios with 1:1–5 giving Deuteronomy 1–28 an overall rhetorical form.

156. Mitchell Dahood, *AB: Psalms I–III* (Garden City: Doubleday & Co., I, 1966; II, 1968; III, 1970). See I, 5 and indices for specific passages.

157. "The Structure of Job 3," *Biblica* 49 (1968), 503–8. The inclusio of Hos 8:9–13 is shown in the Prolegomenon to G. B. Gray's *The Forms of Hebrew Poetry* (New York: KTAV Publishing House, 1972), xxxvi–xxxvii.

158. Albert Condamin, *Le Livre de Jérémie*, 3rd ed. (Paris: Librairie Lecoffre, 1936).

159. *The Forms of Hebrew Poetry*, xxxvi.

inclusio functioning in units smaller than the speech. It will thus be seen to control certain parts even when it does not control the whole. This suggests to us that such units are stanzas within the poem.

The other rhetorical figure assuming a prominent role in Jeremiah is the *chiasmus*, or as is sometimes called, the *chiasm*.[160] In rhetorical handbooks, the chiasmus is an inverted syntactic structure which occurs in parallel or linked phrases.[161] It is well known from both classical and biblical sources.[162] In Hebrew poetry it was first cited as an inverted form of Lowth's parallelism, and was soon found to control much larger units also, both in poetry and in prose.[163] It is thus an ABB'A' structure, or in more developed form, ABCB'A', ABCC'B'A', etc. In larger units, it is also the name given to ABA' structures. The classic study of chiasmus in large panels was done by Nils W. Lund, who dem-

---

160. Also called "introverted parallelism" by John Jebb in his *Sacred Literature* (London: T. Cadell & W. Davies, 1820), 53ff., and John Forbes in *The Symmetrical Structure of Scripture* (Edinburgh: T & T Clark, 1854), 35ff. Roman Catholic scholars call the larger panels "concentric structures"; so Dennis J. McCarthy, "Moses' Dealings with Pharaoh: Ex 7,8—10,27," *CBQ* 27 (1965), 338. Lohfink refers to the same as "chiastische" or "konzentrische" in *Das Hauptgebot* (Rome: Pontifical Biblical Institute, 1963), 67, 181, *et passim*. In his *Lectures in Deuteronomy* the translated term is "concentric inclusion"; cf. 11, *et passim*. Aaron Mirsky considers the chiasmus as an expanded form of "anadiplosis," which he says is used often in the Mishnah, and even defined elsewhere in the Talmud (Vide Nazir, ii); see "The Origin of the *Anadiplosis* in Hebrew Literature" [Hebrew with English summary], *Tarbiz* 28 (1958–59), 171–80; cf. iv.

161. See Sheridan Baker, *The Complete Stylist* (New York: Thomas Y. Crowell Co., 1966), 4, 326; Edward P. J. Corbett, *Classical Rhetoric for the Modern Student*, 478. Brandt uses the Latin term, "commutatio"; cf. *The Rhetoric of Argumentation*, 162–63.

162. Lund argued that the LXX translators showed awareness of a chiastic structure in Amos 2:14–16 by choosing words which were euphonic; cf. "The Presence of Chiasmus in the New Testament," *JR* 10 (1930), 92. It has also been argued that chiastic structures appear in some Qumran documents; cf. Barbara Thiering, "The Poetic Forms of the Hodayot," *JSS* 8 (1963), 189–209; Jacob Licht, "An Analysis of the Treatise of the Two Spirits in DSD" in *Scripta Hierosolymitana* IV, ed. C. Rabin and Y. Yadin (Jerusalem: Magnes Press, 1965), 88–100; E. Parish Sanders, "Chiasmus and the Translation of *I Q Hodayot* VII, 26–27," *RQ* 23 (1968), 427–31.

163. By Jebb and Forbes; see above, n. 160.

onstrated that this was clearly a structure to be reckoned with in the biblical text.[164] Although Lund did most of his work in the New Testament, he argued that chiasmus was originally a Semitic form, and called it on more than one occasion "the gift of the East to the West."[165] Lund also maintained that the structure served a liturgical function in the Jewish community.[166]

Since the time of Lund numerous studies of chiastic structures have been done. The figure in one form or another has been found throughout the Old Testament,[167] including the Prophets.[168] Some impressive chiasmi have been shown by Lohfink to exist in Deuteronomy.[169] Thus while form-critics have either ignored or spoken disparagingly about such studies,[170] it is still recognized by scholars sensitive to literary structure that the quest for chiastic structures is far from being completed.[171] In Jeremiah some impressive chiasmi have been discovered by

---

164. *Chiasmus in the New Testament* (Chapel Hill: University of North Carolina Press, 1942).

165. *Outline Studies in the Book of Revelation* [Covenant Graded Lessons] (Chicago: Covenant Book Concern, 1935), 4; *Chiasmus in the New Testament*, viii.

166. *Chiasmus in the New Testament*, 93.

167. See *inter alia*, Dennis J. McCarthy, "Moses' Dealings with Pharaoh: Ex 7,8—10,27"; Stephen Bertman, "Symmetrical Design in the Book of Ruth," *JBL* 84 (1965), 165–68; Bezalel Porten, "The Structure and Theme of the Solomon Narrative (I Kings 3–11)," *HUCA* 37 (1967), 93–128; Norman K. Gottwald, "Samuel, Book of," *EJ* 14, 796–97.

168. In Isaiah, see Luis Alonso-Schökel, *Estudios de Poética Hebrea*, 319–36; Fredrick Holmgren, "Chiastic Structure in Isaiah LI 1–11," *VT* 19 (1969), 196–201; elsewhere in the Prophets: William L. Holladay, "Chiasmus, the Key to Hosea XII 3–6," *VT* 16 (1966), 53–64; R. Pesch, "Zur konzentrischen Struktur von Jona 1," *Biblica* 47 (1966), 577–81; John T. Willis, "The Structure of Micah 3–5 and the Function of Micah 5:9–14 in the Book," *ZAW* 81 (1969), 191–214.

169. See *Das Hauptgebot*. In *Lectures in Deuteronomy*, 15, Lohfink shows a chiasmus of *speaker* in Deut 1:20–31. This is an important discovery as we will see after having looked at many of the same type of structures in Jeremiah.

170. The remarks of Hans Dieter Betz in *JBL* 89 (1970), 126 are overreactionary to an author's views of inspiration, and thus basically uncritical. Less scholarly still are the remarks of John Elliott, *CBQ* 34 (1972), 371.

171. Gordis says of chiasmus: "it is the key to many difficult passages in Biblical literature, the value of which have not yet been fully explored"; cf. "On Methodology in Biblical Exegesis," *JQR* 61 (1970), 115.

Holladay,[172] and he has recently called for a full-scale study to be done in that book.[173] This thesis is an answer to that call.

Chapter 3 will be on chiasmus, and like the chapter on inclusio, examples will be grouped at three levels. The first level in this case will be the sub-poem level. Since chiasmus is first known as a syntactic structure, we will show how it is used in that manner. Then we will show how it functions in larger units within the poem. These we also think to be stanzas. Since our examples are few, additional research can perhaps test this to see if such a conclusion is valid. The second level will be the poem (or speech) level. There is no *a priori* reason why the chiasmus should delimit the speech like the inclusio, but for reasons which will be given along the way, we believe that to be the case in the Jeremianic speeches. The speech chiasmi will also give us valuable insight into stanza formation, providing us with clues to the "clusters" that make up the overall structure. The third level will be the larger book of Jeremiah. Here our examples will be varied. In all but one case, viz., the Letter to the Exiles (chap. 29), the chiasmus will be a structure imposed on material in the collection process. And even with the Letter to the Exiles, a superstructure has been imposed on the original letter to give it an expanded form.

This thesis then will take its lead from scholars who pursued similar lines of inquiry in the past. These scholars have met with varying degrees of success, but the evidence which has motivated them—be it little or much—is nevertheless incontrovertible. Jeremiah has been largely neglected, yet we aim to show that it is indeed a rich mine for such study. Our work will be based upon a close examination of the text, without which no rhetorical theory can stand. We will cover the entire book, presenting a systematic array of data from all levels.

In two respects we hope to go beyond previous work. First of all, our desire is to be eclectic insofar as other methodologies can contribute to overall understanding. Earlier studies of structure have gone along too much on their own. Even Lund, who hoped in his New Testament research to open dialogue with the form-critics,[174] stopped short of penetrating debate

---

172. "Style, Irony and Authenticity in Jeremiah," 45, 51–52.
173. "The Recovery of Poetic Passages of Jeremiah," 434.
174. *Chiasmus in the New Testament*, 25.

with them about the text. Corroborating data provide a control for one's research. Yet by being eclectic we do not mean to imply that all methodologies can be melted together and used synthetically. Rhetorical criticism is a distinct method, and makes possible a distinct way of looking at the text. As we aim to show, it can provide fresh insight into the text. But, the time is ripe for dialogue among the various disciplines, and this piece of research is devoted to that end.

The other point at which this thesis will go beyond previous work is by looking for the *function* of the rhetorical figures. We must do more than be descriptive, which has been the tendency from Lowth on. Analyses of balancing patterns could go on *ad infinitum* without our knowing anything of their rhetorical value.

To begin to see what we mean by "function," let us compare the different ways of viewing parallelism. Lowth described a relationship which existed between parallel lines. They were synonymous, antithetical, or synthetic, the latter being a balance of rhythm only. Following Lowth, refinements of the "parallelism doctrine" have amounted to more precise statements on word balance, whether or not the parallelism is complete or incomplete, has compensation or lacks compensation, etc.,[175] but these still remain essentially descriptive.

Another way of looking at the same phenomenon is seen in the work of Christian Schoettgen, who discussed this very thing in a section of his two-volume work *Horae Hebraica et Talmudica*.[176] What Lowth described as parallelism, Schoettgen took to be an example of the rhetorical figure "exergasia," which is described in the rhetorical handbooks as a figure that "polishes" or "refines" by repetition.[177] Schoettgen equated it with the Latin "expolitio," which is similarly defined in the *ad Herennium* (4.42). Schoettgen then set forth ten canons of "exergasia sacra" to show the different ways this is accomplished. In these canons

---

175. The most complete restatement is by G. B. Gray in *The Forms of Hebrew Poetry*.

176. 2 Vols., I (Leipzig & Dresden: Christoph. Hekelli B. Sons, Booksellers, 1733); II (Leipzig & Dresden: Fridericum Hekel Booksellers, 1742). In the first volume is a treatise entitled "Exergasia Sacra" (Dissertatio VI), 1249–63, in which he discusses his insights into Hebrew poetry.

177. John Smith, *Mystery of Rhetoric Unveiled* (1657), 221–22; Sheridan Baker, *The Complete Stylist* (1966), 327.

he becomes analytical as Lowth was to be, but going further in anticipating those who issued correctives to Lowth later on. A translation of these canons together with biographical information and comment appears in the Appendix.

We shall then be more than descriptive with the inclusio and the chiasmus. We want to know how the figures *function* in rhetorical discourse, whether it be in the original speeches of Jeremiah, or in the later re-presentation of those speeches along with other material to a worshipping congregation. In the Jeremianic speeches we will be interested in another dimension of the New Rhetoric: argumentation.[178] Do these figures function for Jeremiah in his argument, and if so, how? In structures that tie together large and originally separate units, we want to do more than point out the sense of order and artistry which the structures display. Lund suggested that the chiasmus had a liturgical function, and we will build on this idea with both the inclusio and the chiasmus in Jeremiah. In any case, the material must be viewed against its audience, and we will try whenever possible to distinguish between an original audience and a later audience removed from the former in time. The concluding chapter will bring together all the research in order that some statement can be made about (1) the rhetoric of Jeremiah, and (2) the rhetoric of the book of Jeremiah.

In our discussion of poetic material, we will use the terminology set forth by Albright and Holladay.[179] The basic unit in Hebrew is the *word*, which includes its prefixes and suffixes, and in some cases such particles which are attached by a maqqeph, e.g., כל־, ־את, etc. The basic thought unit is the *colon*, which consists in almost all cases of two or more words, but rarely more than five. Beyond the colon is the *line*, made up of two or three cola. A line of two cola may also be called a *bi-colon*, and a line of three cola a *tri-colon*. Beyond this is the *stanza*, which is a group of two or more lines. In Jeremiah the stanzas are usually four lines, rarely more. We will not retain the use of the term

---

178. See especially, Perelman and Olbrechts-Tyteca, *The New Rhetoric*, and Brandt, *The Rhetoric of Argumentation*.

179. William L. Holladay, "The Recovery of Poetic Passages of Jeremiah," 403–4; cf. W. F. Albright, "The Old Testament and Canaanite Language and Literature," *CBQ* 7 (1945), 19–22; *Yahweh and the Gods of Canaan* (Garden City: Doubleday & Co., 1968), 1–52.

"strophe," even though for many it means essentially what our "stanza" means.[180] Too often it implies an antistrophe common to Greek usage, and it further suggests units which are always equal in length. Here is an element of Condamin's work in Jeremiah with which we do not want to be associated.[181] The stanzas in Jeremiah are sometimes of equal length, but frequently they are not.

With regard to Hebrew meter, we will assume as little as possible since its canons are still as obscure as they were in the time of Lowth.[182] Where it is advantageous to measure cola quantitatively, we will count the number of syllables in a manner currently being done by Freedman and others.[183]

We now proceed to our study, which is to exhibit and discuss two rhetorical structures in Jeremiah: the inclusio and the chiasmus. Stated in terms of a thesis, we will argue the following: *that rhetorical structures are controlling structures of the prophetic speeches in Jeremiah, and that any other structures, gained as they may be from various genres known to the poet Jeremiah, are clearly secondary in influence—if they have influence at all—and in no case do they supply the basic model for the speech.* A corollary to this will also be argued: *that rhetorical structures are controlling structures for collections of speeches and collections of other material about Jeremiah which go together to make up the composite work now known to us as the book of Jeremiah.*

---

180. Muilenburg retains "strophe" because of its wide usage, but also agrees that it has these unfortunate connotations; "Form Criticism and Beyond," 12.

181. One exception is Condamin's work on Lamentations 1–2 where his concentric structure had the advantage of being found within an acrostic. The acrostic provides a valuable control for stanza division, and thus Condamin's insight is substantiated; cf. "Symmetrical Repetitions in *Lamentations* Chapters I and II," *JThS* 7 (1905), 137–40.

182. Lowth's position was that Hebrew poetry was indeed metrical, but since the true pronunciation was lost when Hebrew ceased to be a living language, we are now unable to recover the original meter; *Lectures on the Sacred Poetry of the Hebrews*, 44.

183. David Noel Freedman, "Archaic Forms in Early Hebrew Poetry," *ZAW* 72 (1960), 101–7; more recently see the Prolegomenon to Gray's *The Forms of Hebrew Poetry*, vii–xlvi; "The Structure of Psalm 137" in *Near Eastern Studies in Honor of William Foxwell Albright*, ed. Hans Goedicke (Baltimore: Johns Hopkins Press, 1971), 187–205; "Acrostics and Metrics in Hebrew Poetry," *HThR* 65 (1972), 367–92. See also Mitchell Dahood, "A New Metrical Pattern in Biblical Poetry," *CBQ* 29 (1967), 574–79.

Chapter 2

Inclusio

The largest number of inclusios to be found thus far in datable passages of the Old Testament occurs in Isaiah. Muilenburg noted the inclusio in the poems of II Isaiah, and Liebreich has argued for many more in Isaiah, both I and II. One of Liebreich's more impressive examples ties the whole book together: chapter 66 is made to balance chapter 1.[1] Adding then to these the inclusios already mentioned from Deuteronomy,[2] we see that the figure is well established in Deuteronomic literature. This is most important for any study of the rhetoric of Jeremiah since Jeremiah too is part of that same Deuteronomic tradition.

At the present time we are able to do little more than show where the inclusio is concentrated in the Old Testament. While we might prefer a sketch of its development, any attempt at such would surely be premature. Albright sketched the evolution of stylistic features in Hebrew poetry,[3] but even there, despite the fact that much is already known, we are still less than certain about the results. Perhaps at some future date we can write a history of Hebrew rhetoric. But for now we will be content to plant our feet firmly in what is generally agreed to be *the* rhetorical literature of the Old Testament, and then to work out from there.

Deuteronomy is by far the most important comparative document for Jeremiah, thus a few words are in order about Deuteronomy's provenance, authorship and composition. Deuteronomy has long been recognized to consist primarily of rhetorical prose. Von Rad has said that Deuteronomy is not mere

---

1. Liebreich, "The Compilation of the Book of Isaiah," 276–77.
2. See n. 155 on pp. 28–29.
3. W. F. Albright, *Yahweh and the Gods of Canaan*, 1ff.

law, but parenesis on the law.[4] And because it is "preached law" it must be seen *vis à vis* a gathered congregation. Von Rad also believed that Deuteronomy was written by the Levites, i.e., the Levitical priests,[5] and had as its *Sitz im Leben* the covenant renewal festival at Shechem.[6] But recently these views, especially the latter, have been called into question. Many scholars now believe that Deuteronomy was written not by Levitical priests but by scribes.[7] Lohfink reflects this shift of opinion, nevertheless his position is more moderate. He sees much truth in von Rad's theory and is perfectly willing to relate the text of Deuteronomy to earlier liturgy.[8] But he does not believe that von Rad's theory explains the *final stage* of the book's composition. In this final stage, Deuteronomy is a scribal document modeled on an archive. Lohfink says,

> In archives are collected various written documents, placed one beside the other, each with its title to indicate the contents. This is very prosaic and common, but it seems to be the type of writing which the book of Deuteronomy follows. In its final form Dt presents itself as an archive, a collection of what Moses uttered during the last days of his life.[9]

Lohfink does not advance this as an original theory but rather as one expounded long ago by P. Kleinert (1872). Lohfink supports this theory by arguing that four major headings in 1:1, 4:44, 28:69 and 33:1 isolate four separate collections making up the archive. But in our view 4:44 and 28:69 are not headings at all but conclusions. Each in its own distinct way forms an inclusio with 1:1–5.[10] This appears to be the crucial point of disagreement with Lohfink since he is not otherwise predisposed to discount rhetorical structures in Deuteronomy. He readily concedes that such structures exist and in fact has done more than most to call attention to where they exist. Moreover, he correctly perceives that such structures are auditory signals for people

---

4. *Studies in Deuteronomy* (London: SCM Press, 1963).

5. "Deuteronomy," *IDB* A–D, 836.

6. *Studies in Deuteronomy*, 14.

7. See Moshe Weinfeld, "Deuteronomy—the Present State of Inquiry," *JBL* 86 (1967), 249–62.

8. *Lectures in Deuteronomy*, 6.

9. Ibid., 7.

10. See n. 155 on pp. 28–29.

who must listen to documents read to them aloud. The ancients did not read Deuteronomy silently as we do today.[11] Nevertheless Lohfink considers *the final stage of composition* to be a scribal work, and given his interpretation of 4:44 and 28:69, we assume this means a *non-rhetorical* work.

In our view 1–28[12] is a rhetorical unit. The inclusio functions here to signal to a gathered audience that the end has come. The function of the other subscription in 4:44–49 is to frame the Introduction of 1–4. It restores focus before the main presentation of legal material in chaps. 5ff. Thus we believe that Deuteronomy 1–28 in its entirety was read to a gathered group of people, possibly at Shechem, but more probably at the temple in Jerusalem. If 1–28 dates from the time of Hezekiah, which is most probable,[13] then the material was tailored for temple use at that time The compilers used the inclusio because it was used earlier to tie together sermons within the collection. Also the people could be expected to respond again to a rhetorical structure that was now well known. This will all be very important when we come to explaining the function of the Jeremianic structures. Jeremiah uses structures already in existence and so also does his scribe Baruch. Deuteronomy was a model for both of them—for Jeremiah the sermons became models for his speeches, and for Baruch the composition of this book became a model for the book that he was to compile: the book of Jeremiah.

Finally, concerning the Levite/scribe debate, we suggest that the question is not properly put. According to 2 Chr 34:13 some Levites were scribes (ומהללים סופרים) which means that we may in fact be talking about one and the same group of persons.

Inclusio in the Larger Book of Jeremiah

We begin with the larger entity: the *book* of Jeremiah. All the inclusio structures in this section we judge to be editorial,

---

11. *Lectures in Deuteronomy*, 5.

12. Von Rad took the "original Deuteronomy" to end at chapter 26 after the formula of commitment to the covenant (vv. 16–19); cf. "Deuteronomy," *IDB* 831. Driver includes chapter 28; cf. *Deuteronomy*, ii. Our inclusio tying 1–28 together supports Driver. Chaps. 29–34 form a supplement.

13. So Freedman, "Pentateuch," *IDB* K–Q, 715.

whether they are to be attributed to Jeremiah, Baruch or some other unknown. They are structures beyond the prophetic speech *per se.*

1–51

Our first inclusio is found at the limits of the present book—or at least almost at the limits. Jeremiah has a chapter 52 but this duplicates 2 Kgs 24:18–25:30 and served as a historical epilogue in the exilic or post-exilic period (Jer 52:31 gives us a *terminus a quo* of ca. 561 B.C.). The book of Jeremiah proper ends at 51:64. There we find what is generally regarded as a scribal summary statement.[14] It is indeed that and more. Taken together with the opening words of the book, the two form an inclusio:

1:1 *The words of Jeremiah,*   דברי ירמיהו בן־חלקיהו
   the son of Hilkiah, ...

51:64 Thus far *the words of Jeremiah* עד־הנה דברי ירמיהו

Like Deut 1:1–5 and 28:69 this ties an entire composition together. Everything within these limits is taken to be דברי ירמיהו, which includes Jeremiah's own words as well as words *about* Jeremiah. We note too a chiasmus: דברי ירמיהו begins 1:1 and concludes 51:64.

This could be the work of any Deuteronomic scribe, and we would leave it at that were it not possible in this case to attach to the inclusio the name of an individual. Immediately preceding the subscription is a personal note from Jeremiah to Seraiah (51:59–64a). This man is the brother of Baruch,[15] Jeremiah's close friend and scribe. Seraiah is designated "quartermaster" (שר מנוחה) in v. 59, but he is also no doubt a Deuteronomic scribe the same as Baruch (scribes came in families later on in the time of the Massoretes). Jeremiah then is said to have given Seraiah custody of a scroll that went to Babylon. This personal word—which we believe Seraiah adds—functions the same way as the personal word given by Jeremiah to Baruch (which in the MT

---

14. *BDB* under הֵנָּה, 244.

15. *BDB* 633. The name "Neriah" does not occur in the OT outside Jeremiah, and since Baruch is also "son of Neriah, son of Mahseiah" (32:12) we can assume he and Seraiah were brothers.

comes in 45 but in the LXX comes *in exactly this position!*). Both are autobiographical postscripts. We are thus led to wonder if it is not Seraiah who also adds the subscription in 51:64b.

The matter can be pursued further by comparing the Hebrew and Greek texts more closely. We recall that the Greek places the Oracles to Foreign Nations after 25:13. In the Hebrew they come in 46–51. Now if we take Baruch to be the custodian of the text which was the *Vorlage* to the LXX, and Seraiah to be the custodian of the text which became the MT, we can then isolate the two text traditions originating in Babylon and Egypt. Baruch went to Egypt while Seraiah went to Babylon.[16] We assume that the LXX has an Egyptian provenance, and a Babylonian provenance for the MT is also likely. Frank Cross has recently argued that the MT is Babylonian,[17] and we believe he is right.

The different positions of the Oracles to Foreign Nations can be explained as follows. Seraiah took the oracles from 25:13ff., which is where Baruch placed them originally, and put them at the end of the book. He then took Jeremiah's personal word to him and placed it at the new end as an autobiographical postscript (in the LXX its position is of no special importance).[18] Then he added the subscription עד־הנה דברי ירמיהו at the very end to make an inclusio with 1:1. And here is the most important point of all: *this subscription is lacking in the LXX*, which is precisely what we would expect if Seraiah's text is the expanded MT.[19] We should observe also that although Seraiah relocates the Oracles to Foreign Nations, the rest of Baruch's book is left intact: Baruch's own postscript still comes at what was formerly the end of the book (chapter 45).

What can we say about the function of this inclusio? It clearly delimits the final book of Jeremiah, but are we to assume

---

16. He is recorded, however, as going in the 4th year of Zedekiah (51:59), which means that the rest of the biographical prose (37–44) must have followed him at a later time. Since there was frequent travel between Jerusalem and Babylon (cf. chapter 29), this would not be an impossibility.

17. Cross has come to this conclusion as a result of his study of text recensions; cf. n. 32 on p. 6. For a recent challenge to Cross, however, see George Howard, "Frank Cross and Recensional Criticism," *VT* 21 (1971), 440–50.

18. There it comes in 28:59–64.

19. So Janzen on the MT; see *Studies in the Text of Jeremiah*, 135.

that an entire 51 chapters were read to a sitting congregation as with Deuteronomy 1–28? This would be a long reading, but perhaps it is not altogether out of the question given the situation in exile. If this be the case, then Seraiah too prepared his book for worship. For him the inclusio would function just as it had in Deut 28:69: to signal that the end had finally come.

49:34–39

This is our one specimen from the Oracles to Foreign Nations. The inclusio comes only in the Greek, where the superscription of the MT is divided in two and placed half at the beginning and half at the end. The oracle is against Elam, and the MT introduces it with the following:

49:34 The word of Yahweh that came to Jeremiah the prophet concerning Elam, in the beginning of the reign of Zedekiah king of Judah:

אשר היה דבר־יהוה
אל־ירמיהו הנביא
אל־עילם
בראשית מלכות
צדקיה מלך־יהודה
לאמר

The oracle in the LXX is found in 25:14–20 and appears there as follows:

25:14 What Jeremiah said concerning the nation of Elam:

Ἃ ἐπροφήτευσεν Ιερεμιας ἐπί τά ἔθνη τά Αιλαμ

25:20 In the beginning of the reign of Zedekiah the king, this word came concerning Elam

ἐν ἀρχῇ βασιλεύοντος Σεδεκιου τοῦ βασιλέως ἐγένετο ὁ λόγος οὗτος περί Αιλαμ

It appears that the LXX reflects a text tradition in which some scribe took the usual superscription and divided it up between beginning and end. It is possible that the process could have worked in the reverse except for the fact that all poems in this collection are introduced with superscriptions, and none with the exception of the Moab poems have subscriptions. Also, the subscription to the Moab poems (48:47) is of the same type as 51:64 and does not read like the subscription we have here.

The Elam oracle occupies a strategic location in the LXX, being there the first of the Oracles to Foreign Nations. But we can do little more than speculate as to why it has the inclusio. Perhaps it circulated independently for a time.

1–20

Here we find an inclusio of major importance.[20] It is formed by linking the first fragment of poetry in chapter 1 with the last lines of the poem in chapter 20. And according to established custom the key words are inverted in the closing section.

1:5	Before I formed you in the belly I knew you	בטרם אצורך בבטן ידעתיך
	and before *you came forth from the womb*, I consecrated you	ובטרם תצא מרחם הקדשתיך
20:18	Why *from the womb did I come forth*	למה זה מרחם יצאתי
	to see trouble and sorrow	לראות עמל ויגון
	and have my days end in shame?	ויכלו בבשת ימי

The opening line is from Jeremiah's call. He says that his call took place before emerging from his mother's womb. The latter poem reflects a moment of great despair. Jeremiah asks why his birth was ever allowed to take place. With the exception of a brief reference in 15:10, these are the only instances in which Jeremiah refers to the event of his birth.

The poem of 20:14–18 is well known, especially for its tone of despair. The last colon of 20:18 reads ויכלו בבשת ימי, where the verb כלה should be translated "end" rather than "spend" (so RSV). The AV translates "consume," which is literal enough. The point is that Jeremiah fears his days will be ended, i.e., he will die. At such a time it is natural to recall one's birth, for that was when life began. It was natural at least for Jeremiah, because as we shall see before this study is concluded, he more than most was particularly conscious of beginnings and ends.

---

20. While commentators generally take 1–25:13 as the first major collection, Rudolph (*Jeremia*, xix) recognizes that 21–24 comes from a later period than 1–20. Rietzschel takes 1–20 as an *Überlieferungsblock* within 1–25:15 (*Das Problem der Urrolle*, 17, 128). He also thinks that Jeremiah's personal word to Baruch (chap. 45) stood originally after 20:18.

Another point has also been made about his poem: it ends without any hope. This is unusual since in other confessions (e.g., 11:18–23; 12:1–6; 15:15–21; etc.) where Jeremiah boldly confronts Yahweh we have an answer from Yahweh. It is true that Jeremiah does not here address Yahweh—he curses "the day" and "the man who brought his father the news"—nevertheless the passage is still generally agreed to be a confession in which Jeremiah pours out his heart to Yahweh. Von Rad says, "the God whom the prophet addresses no longer answers him."[21] Our inclusio, however, makes possible another interpretation, viz., that the conclusion of the poem was perhaps meant to be read together with the opening words of the call. Jeremiah says, "Why did I come forth from the womb?" Answer: "Because Yahweh called me before I came forth from the womb." Whatever despair the original poem of 20:14–18 may have had, in the larger composition *it contains an answer* which is one of hope and affirmation. 1:5 also serves to give the large composition its authority. In disguised form, Jeremiah is affirming his call to be a prophet. He is saying that he was born because Yahweh called him forth to be born. And the listener with an ear for this kind of rhetoric would be able to make the connection. It is quite likely too that such a unit was deliberately prepared for temple worship, in which case the call could be reread as a final conclusion. We know that later custom dictated the rereading of the penultimate verse in Isaiah in order to provide a "happy ending."[22] A similar return, only this time to the beginning, could have been employed here so as not to conclude the composition on a dismal note.

We have suggested that 1–20 is an early major composition. Corroborating evidence can also be brought forth to show that a major break comes after 20. We note that chapter 21 contains the first *dated* biographical prose in the book. None of the prose in 1–20 is dated, while in 21ff., almost all the prose is pegged either in the reign of Jehoiakim or in the reign of Zedekiah. (Actually, neither of these kings is even mentioned before 21, except in the superscription of 1:3.) We will also demonstrate

---

21. *Old Testament Theology* II, 204.
22. This was required by the Massoretes; see Liebreich, "The Compilation of the Book of Isaiah," 277.

shortly how 21 serves as the beginning of the first of two appendices that follow 1–20.

A firm delimitation of this major unit invites a reopening of the question of the *Urrolle*. Scholars are generally agreed that the *Urrolle* is contained within 1–25,[23] but so far no objective data has been made available which would enable us to determine more precisely its limits. Now we can put forth 1–20 as the *Urrolle* since 1–20 is a clearly defined composition within 1–25. Also, what we have proposed in the way of structure fits well with the situation described in chapter 36. Baruch brings a scroll to the temple and reads it to the people who are assembled there. Jeremiah is not allowed to go but the structure of the scroll material makes clear his authorship as well as his authority to the careful listener. Some may perhaps think that 1–20 is too large to have been read three times within a short period. Maybe so, but it is not at least out of the question. Also it is always possible that material was inserted *into* 1–20 at a later time making the present composition larger. Our only argument is that what is now 1–20 manifests the marks of a distinct composition made in the Deuteronomic manner. It is therefore a more likely unit than, say 1–6, for the *Urrolle*.[24]

8:13–9:21 [Eng. 9:22]

This has not been put forth as a unit before, but our inclusio is supported by the fact that 8:12 ends a previous unit[25] and 9:22–25 [Eng. 23–26] is prose expansion. The inclusio is made up of the verb אסף, "to gather," used together with אין.

8:13 *Gathering* I will end them[26] says Yahweh   אָסֹף אֲסִיפֵם נְאֻם־יְהוָה
        no grapes there are on the vine   אֵין עֲנָבִים בַּגֶּפֶן

---

23. Muilenburg, "Baruch the Scribe," 231; Bright, *Jeremiah*, lvii–lviii, 162–63; S. R. Driver, *The Book of the Prophet Jeremiah* (London: Hodder and Stoughton, 1908), xlvii.

24. Rietzschel, *Das Problem der Urrolle*, 136; cf. Rudolph, *Jeremia*, xix; Philip Hyatt, "The Deuteronomic Edition of Jeremiah" in *Vanderbilt Studies in the Humanities* I (Nashville: Vanderbilt University Press, 1951), 93.

25. Not only does 8:12 conclude with אמר יהוה, but 8:10–12 less the first line is duplicated in 6:13–15. This suggests that 8:10–12 was originally independent.

26. No need to revocalize with Bright (*Jeremiah*, 61); Jeremiah is engaging in word-play with two verbs that sound alike, אסף, meaning "to gather," and סוף, meaning "to make an end of " (H stem).

and *no* figs there are on the fig tree ואין תאנים בתאנה

even the leaves are withered והעלה נבל

9:21 The dead bodies of men shall fall ונפלה נבלת האדם

like dung on the open field כדמן על־פני השדה

like sheaves after the reaper וכעמיר מאהרי הקצר

and *no one* shall *gather* them ואין מאסף

We can see how 8:13 calls attention to both key words which will occur later in the words of closure. The verb is given attention by the word-play אסף אסיפם, and אין is equally prominent, appearing twice at the beginning of successive cola (anaphora). Condamin has noticed the repetition of אסף,[27] but he goes astray in forcing the text into a different order.

Since there is no real semantic link between the two verses, it appears that the inclusio functions only to tie together poems originally separate into a larger collection. Perhaps it is also here a mnemonic device used by Jeremiah. We can imagine that he needed some such devices to hold speeches together in his head for those 23 years before they were put into writing (Jeremiah 36). If the unit was not part of the dictated material which went into the *Urrolle*, then it could have been material added later. Poems within this unit are also nicely structured as we shall see later on when we come to the chapter on chiasmus.

21:1–23:8

This collection forms one of two appendices which follow 1–20. It contains words which Jeremiah delivered specifically to Judah's kings. The other collection is made up of words specifically directed to the prophets (23:9–40). As Westermann has pointed out, the criterion for collection in both of these cases is "audience."[28] In the latter collection the introductory לנבאים identifies the audience. The "king collection" has no such introduction, although Adam Welch suggested some years ago that a title לבית מלך יהודה may originally have exited at 21:11. This he took to be the beginning of the collection,[29] which he thought

---

27. *Le Livre de Jérémie*, 82–83. Bright takes "gather" as a catchword linking 9:21 with 10:17.

28. *Basic Forms of Prophetic Speech*, 95–96.

29. "A Problem in Jeremiah," *ET* 26 (1914–15), 429; Bright agrees; cf. *Jeremiah*, 144.

was comprised primarily of the poetry. Welch likewise ended the collection at 22:30 which is where the poetry ends.

There is definitely a poetic core in the king collection and we will discuss its structure in the next chapter. Here we are only concerned with the outer frame, i.e., 21:1–10 and 23:1–8. The problematic unit is 21:1–10, which appears to be nothing more than an ordinary prose account about one of Jeremiah's encounters with Zedekiah. It need not be part of the king collection at all since it is essentially no different from chapters 34 or 37. Perhaps this is why Bright groups it with those chapters.[30] Yet we will now argue that 21:1–10 is definitely meant to be a part of the king collection. A final editor meant to balance this account with the messianic prophecy in 23:1–8. Thus another inclusio.

We notice first of all that prior to the messianic verses Judah's kings are listed in chronological order. Josiah is referred to by implication in 22:10 (he is the one who is dead); then comes Shallum (Jehoahaz) (vv. 11–12); Jehoiakim (22:18–19); and finally Jeconiah (22:24–30). We now expect a word about Zedekiah, but there is none. Instead comes the messianic prophecy. Yet it is in this messianic prophecy that we find the key to our outer structure. It comes in the name of the future king, which is to be יהוה צדקנו, "Yahweh is our righteousness" (23:6). As commentators have already noted, this is an obvious play on "Zedekiah," צדקיהו, which can be translated "Yahweh is righteous," "righteous of Yahweh," or something similar.[31] Comparing the two names we note a small difference, but it is important. The component parts are switched around. In the name Zedekiah the Yahwistic appellative יהו comes in normal fashion at the end. But in the name of the new Davidic king יהוה comes first. The reversal must be deliberate.[32] Jeremiah wants to point out the *discontinuity* between the present king and the future king. The future king will be what Zedekiah ought to be but is not, viz., a sign of Yahweh's righteousness. Or the new king will be a complete "turn-around" from the present king.

---

30. Bright, *Jeremiah*, 213ff.

31. Condamin, *Le Livre de Jérémie*, 177, following Cornill and Giesebrecht. More recently see Holladay, "The Covenant with the Patriarchs Overturned: Jeremiah's Intention in 'Terror on Every Side' (Jer 20:1–6)," *JBL* 91 (1972), 314.

32. Holladay argues (ibid.) that Jeremiah is playing the same kind of word game with the name Pashhur.

Let us now return to the structure of the section. Having seen what Jeremiah did with Zedekiah's name in the first place, it should amuse us even more to see how *the very same point is silently made* by the creator of our structure. The word to Zedekiah about his fate, instead of being placed at the end (after 22:30) where we anticipated it, is placed at the beginning. And at the end comes the messianic prophecy providing the compiler with the contrast he wanted to make. The compiler then in his final composition makes the same contrast which Jeremiah made earlier in 23:6. The inclusio becomes a vehicle for theology. It affirms something not too dissimilar from what was affirmed by the Deuteronomic Historian when he set up David as the model of the good king and Jeroboam as the model of the bad king (cf. 2 Kgs 14:3, 24; 15:9, 18, 24, 28; 17:21–23; 18:3, etc.). Zedekiah is now the antitype of the messiah, and we can imagine that such a contrast could forcefully be made to a worshipping congregation over and over and over again.

30–31

Chapters 30–33 form a separate collection containing primarily words of hope, thus the name "Book of Comfort" or "Book of Consolation." A superscription tells us that Jeremiah was commanded by Yahweh to write these words in a book (30:2). The limits of this book—in its various stages of growth—can now be seen because a compiler (or compilers) made use of the inclusio.

Within the collection is a poetic core extending from 30:5 to 31:22. This core to begin with is held together by an inclusio: the end of the last poem balances the beginning of the first.

30:5–6	We have heard a cry of panic	קול הרדה שמענו
	of terror and no peace	פחד ואין שלום
	Ask now and see	שאלו־נא וראו
	can a *male* bear a child?	אם־ילד זכר
	Why then do I see every *soldier*	מדוע ראיתי כל־גבר
	with his hands on his loins	ידיו על־חלציו כיולדה
	like a woman in labor?	
31:22b	For Yahweh has created a new	כי־ברא יהוה חדשה
	thing on the earth:	בארץ
	the *female* protects the *soldier*	נקבה תסובב גבר

This final bi-colon was considered an appendage by Duhm, but Holladay has recently argued that it belongs with the poem which it concludes.[33] The bi-colon is also a *crux interpretum.* Many solutions have been proposed but none is completely satisfactory.[34] I take the line as an ironic statement expressing shock and surprise at the weakness of Israel's soldiers in defeat. Jeremiah is saying, "My, a new thing on earth! the woman must protect the soldier." It should of course be the other way around, but Jeremiah can only articulate another of the incongruous sights before his eyes. Full play is given to the sexual distinction. The common term for "woman," אשה, is not used; instead Jeremiah employs the generic נקבה, "female."

In the counterpart passage the same is true. There Jeremiah mocks the soldiers asking, "Can a male (זכר) bear a child?" Taken together these verses form an inclusio for the core. They say the same thing only in different ways. In 30:6 the soldiers are said to be behaving like weak women in labor; in 31:22b they are depicted as being so weak that they need women for protection.

The inclusio also sets the controlling mood for the core, which is not hope but despair. This has not been properly recognized. The tendency is usually to read the core in light of the rest of the material which is all hope. But the core is a "mixed bag." Some of the poems are judgment pure and simple. The opening poem in 30:5–7 is a clear example. Holladay shows how the final colon of that poem, "Yet he shall be saved out of it" was not originally meant this way at all. It was an ironic question to which the answer was a firm "No!"[35] Other judgment poems are 30:12–15, 30:23–24 and 31:15. We must therefore recognize that the core contains *both* poems of judgment and poems of hope.[36]

---

33. "Jer xxxi 22b Reconsidered: 'The Woman Encompasses the Man'," *VT* 16 (1966), 236–39.

34. See the Holladay article (ibid.) for a survey of other explanations. Holladay himself takes the line to be a word to the personified daughter of Israel which bids her to return from exile.

35. "Style, Irony and Authenticity in Jeremiah," 53–54.

36. I have outlined the structure of the core in an earlier study entitled "Patterns of Poetic Balance in the Book of Jeremiah" (Unpublished B.D. Thesis, North Park Theological Seminary, 1967), 66–67.

It has also been pointed out that at least some of the hope poems in this collection derive from the *earliest* part of Jeremiah's ministry when he awaited the return of the exiles from Assyria.[37] Maybe all are early, i.e., pre-exilic, in which case we would have an earlier collection than is usually assumed.[38] My reading of 31:22b would support such an interpretation since I think this line cannot be a sober statement about the "new age" even if it does belong with a poem which looks ahead to the return from exile. It is a word of desperation reflecting the present state of affairs. And in forming an inclusio with 30:5–6 it creates an entire mood of the same. To be sure the core certainly falls short of the confidence expressed in 31:23ff.

We spoke earlier of the desire to end a collection on a happy note, for that appears to have been the function of the inclusio which tied together 1–20. Now we are suggesting just the reverse, viz., that the inclusio which ties together the poetic core within the Book of Comfort creates an overall tone of despair. Is this possible? Our answer must be in the affirmative not only because we know that the canons of Hebrew composition made this allowable (Ecclesiastes, the Book of the Twelve and Isaiah all end on a note of judgment), but also because there is *a priori* no reason why an inclusio must function the same way every time it is used. If the core was put together when the outlook was not good it could be made to reflect such a time, and the compiler is then one who "tells it like it is." We may then have a basis for dating the core. The final years of Jehoiakim would fit perfectly culminating in the attack on Jerusalem in 597 B.C. and the exile of Jehoiachin with many of the leading citizens (cf. 2 Kgs 24:10–17). These were the years when Jeremiah and Baruch were in hiding (Jer 36:19) and any circulation of this core at such a time would certainly serve to weaken the people's resistance. It would not give them hope. Only later when the people are broken and Jeremiah gives additional words of hope does this core get expanded into the Book of Comfort it becomes. Yet the marks of the earlier composition remain.

---

37. See Theodore M. Ludwig, "The Shape of Hope: Jeremiah's Book of Consolation," *CTM* 39 (1968), 526–41. Ludwig follows the lead of Volz although not accepting an early date for all the hope poems in 30–31.

38. Bright wants to date the collection in the middle of the exilic period or thereabouts, which I think is too late.

We will now look at the structure of a portion of that expansion. The remaining verses of chapter 31 are nicely framed and held together by an inclusio. Since there appear to be two stages of development we will discuss one at a time.

In the first stage material in vv. 23 to 34 was added. The stereotyped phrases making the frames and the inclusio will show the structure in outline:

23	Thus says Yahweh of Hosts God of Israel: *Again they shall speak* these words . . .	כה־אמר יהוה צבאות אלהי ישראל <u>עוד</u> <u>יאמרו</u> את־הדבר הזה
27	*Behold, the days are coming,* says Yahweh, when I will sow . . .	<u>הנה ימים באים</u> <u>נאם־יהוה</u> וזרעתי
29	In those days, *they shall not again speak*: . . .	בימים ההם <u>לא־יאמרו</u> <u>עוד</u>
31	*Behold, the days are coming,* says Yahweh, when I will make . . . a new covenant . . .	<u>הנה ימים באים</u> <u>נאם־יהוה</u> וכרתי . . . ברית חדשה
34a	And *they shall not again teach* each man his neighbor, . . .	<u>ולא ילמדו עוד</u> איש את־רעהו
34b	And their sin *I will not remember again*	ולחטאתם לא <u>אזכר־עוד</u>

The two sections in the center are framed by opening and closing formulas. At the extremes (vv. 23, 34b) we have single closing formulas which make the inclusio. One of the key words in the closing formulas is עוד which I have translated in all cases as "again" to accentuate the intended repetition. עוד occurs with three different verbs, which, in all but the first instance (v. 23) is coupled with the negative לא. The key words emphasize the theme of the unit, which is the discontinuity between the future and the present. The future will be a new time when old proverbs are abandoned and even a new covenant is made.

In the second stage of development the poetic fragment in vv. 35–37 is added along with another framed prophecy much like those added in stage one:

38 *Behold the days are coming,*[39]   הנה ימים (באים)[39]
     says Yahweh, when the city   נאם־יהוה ונבנתה
     shall be rebuilt . . .   העיר

39 *And it shall go out again*   ויצא עוד קוה המדה
     the measuring line . . .

Verse 40 concludes the material added in stage two and contains
a single stereotyped phrase like those found in vv. 23, 29, 34a
and 34b. It makes an inclusio with yet one more opening formula found in 30:3:

30:3 For *behold, the days are coming*   כי הנה ימים באים
      says Yahweh, when I will restore   נאם־יהוה ושבתי
      the fortunes of my people . . .   את־שבות עמי

31:40 And *it shall not be overthrown*   ולא־יהרס עוד
       again forever   לעולם

Since there is the mention of a "book" immediately prior to the
beginning formula in 30:3 (v. 2), we conclude that this book is
delimited by the above inclusio. Thus while we have earlier
compositions preceding it, the first Book of Comfort contains
only the material in chapters 30–31. What appears in chapters
32–33 is added from yet a later time.

     A concordance check on עוד in chapters 30–33 only adds to
what we have already come to realize about its importance. In
31:4–5, which is poetry, it is used as an anaphora for three successive cola making it a key word in the poem. In chapters 32–
33 it occurs five times: 32:15; 33:10, 12, 13, 24, and in one of
these, viz., 33:13, it may signal another conclusion. We note that
in the LXX this verse concludes the chapter (MT 33:14–26 is
omitted). Chapter 33 is admittedly a difficult chapter to unravel
so we cannot say more than this at the present time.

     In summary the core is an early compilation of poetry found
in 30:5–31:22. It contains judgment and hope but the inclusio
gives the whole a tone of irony and despair. Nevertheless the
hope which it contained gave rise to two subsequent additions,
which, when completed became the Book of Comfort referred

---

39. Add באים with Qere; omission due to haplography.

to in 30:2. This book consisted of chapters 30–31, but was later expanded to include chapters 32–33. And if 33:14–26 is taken to be yet another addition we have five stages of composition instead of four.

Inclusio in the Poems of Jeremiah

We come now to the poetic speeches of Jeremiah. The main problem as we have said before is their delimitation. It will now be argued that 12 poems in Jeremiah employ the inclusio device. In a variety of ways, Jeremiah forces his audience to return at the end to the beginning. In so doing he uses a rhetorical technique already well established, and one to which his audience can respond if they are so inclined.

We will now look at each poem separately. The structure of the whole will be laid out including a breakdown into stanzas. In the chiastic poems to be looked at later our criteria for establishing the rhetorical structure will also aid us in stanza division. But here the stanza division is based not upon the controlling inclusio but upon other criteria, some rhetorical, e.g., balancing terms, repetition, both in some cases making smaller inclusios or chiasmi, and some non-rhetorical, e.g., a messenger formula, change of speaker, content, etc. These will be discussed but only in a cursory way since our main concern is with the controlling inclusio.

3:1–5

The limits of this poem are easily established. The chapter divisions mark the upper limit and most commentators take this as the beginning.[40] The lower limit is marked by the introduction of prose comment beginning in v. 6, although debate still goes on whether this is the end or whether the poetry in vv. 12–14 or vv. 19ff. continues the poem.[41] This latter poetry does have

---

40. The MT prefixes לאמר which Bright fills out with the complete formula, "The word of Yahweh came to me saying . . ."; cf. *Jeremiah*, 19. One Ms., the LXX and Syriac omit; Rudolph suggests we delete.

41. Hyatt, in his *Jeremiah* commentary (*IB* 5, 829), ends the unit at 3:20. Muilenburg ("Hebrew Rhetoric: Repetition and Style," 105) and Bright (*Jeremiah*, 25) follow Volz and take all of 3:1–4:4 as a single unit. Giesebrecht (*Jeremia*, 13), however, takes 1–5 as a self-contained unit.

affinities with 1–5 which means, I think, that we may have a larger editorial unit. But for now we will argue only that 1–5 was originally a separate poem, and indeed it was a poem of uncompromising judgment.

הֵן ישלח איש את־אשתו והלכה מאתו   1
והיתה לאיש־אחר הישוב אליה עוד
הלוא חנוף תחנף הארץ ההיא
ואת זנית רעים רבים ושוב אלי נאם־יהוה

שְׁאִי־עיניך על־שפים וראי איפה לא שגלת   2
על־דרכים ישבת להם כערבי במדבר
ותחניפי ארץ בזנותיך וברעתך

וימנעו רבבים ומלקוש לוא היה   3

ומצח אשה זונה היה לך מאנת הכלם

הלוא מעתה קראתי לי אבי אלוף נערי אתה   4

הינטר לעולם אם־ישמר לנצח   5
הִנֵּה דברתי ותעשי הרעות ותוכל

1   *Behold*, a man divorces his wife
       and she goes from him
     And becomes the wife of another
       Will he return to her?
     Would it not be greatly polluted
       that land?
     But you have played the harlot with many lovers
       and would you return to me? Oracle of Yahweh

2   Lift up yours eyes to the bare hills and see
       where have you not been ravished?
     Along the roads you sat for them
       like an Arab in the wilderness
     You have polluted the land with your harlotry
       and with your evil deeds

3   Therefore the showers have been withheld
       and the spring rain has not come

     Yet you have a harlot's brow
       you refuse to be ashamed

4   Have you not just now called to me "My father,
       you are the friend of my youth,

5   Will he be angry forever,
        will he be indignant to the end?"
    Behold, you have spoken but done
        all the evil that you could.

The poem contains many nice balances. Stanza 1 balances
lines 2 and 4 with forms of the verb שׁוב, and stanza 3 has assonantal balance with וּמֶצֶה and לָנֶצַח. There is also a play on sound
in the last lines of stanzas 1 and 2: רַבִּים and רְבָבִים. Finally, both
stanzas 1 and 3 have double rhetorical questions in the center.
The inclusio is formed by "behold" which begins the poem and
is then repeated again at the end. Different forms of the inter-
jection are used, but it is nevertheless the same word. Modern
translators overlook the repetition completely translating הן in
v. 1 with "If " (so RSV, JB, NEB).[42] And Bright follows Volz in
emending הִנֵּה in v. 5 to הֵנָּה which does away with the final "behold."[43] Both should be left intact. Neither reading is problematic, and rhetorically the repetition is significant.

Jeremiah is here making a case for judgment and he begins
by citing the only law in the Old Testament dealing with divorce: Deut 24:1–4. This law states that a man cannot reunite
with a divorced wife if she has contracted another marriage.[44]
Jeremiah then uses this law to make an analogy—actually he
does more than that since the argument contains in addition an
inference *a minori ad maius*, or to use talmudic terminology, a *kal
vechomer* (cf. 12:5).[45] The man cannot return to his former wife
because she has known (or been known) by *one* other man; in
Jeremiah's argument Israel has had *many* lovers (רעים רבים).[46]

_____

42. Granted the "if " is understood, but there is nothing wrong with
reading simply "Behold." "Behold" can carry the conditional element even
in English.

43. Bright, *Jeremiah*, 19; cf. Volz, *Der Prophet Jeremia* [KAT] (Leipzig:
A. Deichertsche Verlagsbuchhandlung, 1928), 35.

44. For an important discussion of this text, see Reuven Yaron, "The
Restoration of Marriage," *JJS* 17 (1966), 1–11.

45. Brandt (*The Rhetoric of Argumentation*, 130) calls the same a *con-
trarium*.

46. Yaron ("The Restoration of Marriage," 8) argues that the law of
Deut 24:1–4 is designed to *preserve* the second marriage. If this is the
case, then Jeremiah is taking it out of its legal context and using it to
make a different point. It seems unlikely that Jeremiah would want
Israel's second, third and fourth marriages to be preserved, unless of
course he is being highly ironic.

Thus Jeremiah's audience would have to answer "No" to the question ending verse 1. Israel certainly cannot return now to Yahweh after being so polluted by foreign affairs.[47] What follows in stanza 2 is more indictment. Stanza 3 ends the poem by pointing up an incongruity between what the people say and what their actions betray, and the final "behold" brings the hearer back to the beginning. It reminds him of the "No" answer he just gave. The inclusio thus forces the application which Jeremiah intends, viz., that Israel—on the basis of old friendship—cannot now plead forgiveness after violating so completely her vow to be faithful to Yahweh in marriage. That the line "and would you return to me?" was later read as a call for restoration is easy enough to understand,[48] but we do not believe it to be consonant with Jeremiah's original intent.

This analysis has given us additional insight into Jeremiah's rhetoric. We said earlier that this was a poem of uncompromising judgment, yet it is to be noted that the judgment is never explicitly given. The rhetorical question ending v. 1 may evoke a judgment, and the conclusion may also "beg" judgment as it returns the hearer to v. 1; but in each case the hearer must furnish the answer of judgment himself. Jeremiah does not give it. He gives the hearer plenty of indictment, but no judgment. Thus while we recovered a much harsher tone in the poem, at the same time we showed Jeremiah to be more subtle, less judgmental and rhetorically more astute. He engages his audience at a point of common agreement—citing a law which all know well—and then makes a quick application by analogy. A final rhetorical question together with a repetition making an inclusio forces the hearer to *himself* bring the matter to completion. The real twist of course does not come until the end. After

---

47. See James D. Martin, "The Forensic Background to Jeremiah III 1," *VT* 19 (1969), 82–92. Yaron's translation "yet return again to me" (ibid., 3) does not take the Hebrew as having interrogative force. This interpretation goes back, as Yaron points out, to the Talmud where this text was used to show how Yahweh's mercy is not subject to law. But see the modern Jewish commentary by Rabbi Harry Freedman, *Jeremiah* [Soncino Books of the Bible] (London: Soncino Press, 1961), 18, which translates the Hebrew as a question. For a more complete discussion of the omission of the interrogative ה, see H. G. Mitchell, "The Omission of the Interrogative Particle" in *Old Testament and Semitic Studies in Memory of William Rainey Harper* I (Chicago: University of Chicago Press, 1908), 115–29.

48. See note above.

hearing many examples of wayward behavior which embellish the indictment, the hearer is forced to see the impossibility of expecting acquittal for wrongdoing. This kind of rhetoric will not be grasped by everyone. Only those who are perceptive will pick up the judgment Jeremiah intends. Others must wait for someone to explain it to them.

5:10–13

The versions and the commentaries do not give much help in delimiting this unit. Rudolph, Volz, Condamin and Bright all extend through v. 14. And Rudolph and Volz begin back at 5:1. Condamin takes 10–14 as a strophe of a much larger unit. The RSV breaks before v. 10 and after v. 13, but also after v. 11. Bright too says that 10–14 is composed of separate fragments.[49] Our only support for isolating 10–13 comes from the Massoretes who marked the ends of verses 9 and 13 as closed (ס) sections.[50] We take these verses then to comprise a poem of 2 stanzas, each having 3 lines. The main division points up a change of speaker. Yahweh speaks in the first stanza (v. 11 ends with נאם־יהוה), and Jeremiah in the second. There also appears to be crescendo in the stanzas for each has a long final line.[51]

10   עלו בשרותיה ושחתו וכלה אל־<u>תעשו</u>
        הסירו נטישותיה כי לוא ליהוה המה

11   כי בגוד בגדו בי בית ישראל ובית יהודה נאם־יהוה

12   כחשו ביהוה ויאמרו לא־הוא
        ולא־תבוא עלינו רעה והרב ורעב לוא נראה

13   והנביאים יהיו לרוח והדבר אין בהם כה <u>יעשה</u> להם

    10   Go up through her vinerows and destroy
            and *make* a full end[52]

---

49. Bright, *Jeremiah*, 42.

50. Professor Freedman reminds me that the Dead Sea Scrolls show the open and closed sections to be very old, dating from at least pre-Christian times.

51. Although made in a slightly different context, David Daube's comments about long final lines are a warning to those who would require all the lines of a poem to be of the same length; cf. David Daube, "Three Questions of Form in Matthew V," *JThS* 45 (1944), 21–22.

52. This colon has long been a crux because of the אַל־. Older commentators deleted it, as they also deleted the לֹא־ in 4:27 (so Volz and Rudolph).

> Strip away her branches
>> for they are not Yahweh's
> 11 For they've been utterly faithless to me
>> the house of Israel and the house of Judah
>>> oracle of Yahweh
>
> 12 They've spoken falsely of Yahweh
>> and said "Surely not he;
> Evil will not come upon us
>> and sword and famine we will not see"
> 13 The prophets will become wind
>> the word is not in them
>>> thus *he will make* them[53]

The inclusio is formed by the verb עשה, meaning "make." There is no reason to follow the Alexandrinus and Arabic which omit the last colon (so Rudolph and Bright). It does not "fit poorly";[54] rather it gives a poem the closure which Jeremiah intended.

Like 3:1–5, this poem has also had the judgment softened. Whether the אַל in v. 10 is to be read as an ancient asseverative, or is a negative added later to harmonize the poem with 30:11 (cf. 4:27; 5:18)—in either case the colon did not originally read "but make not a full end."[55] The whole poem is strong judgment and can hardly admit such immediate qualification.

How then does the structure give insight into the interaction between Jeremiah and his audience? Jeremiah averts any immediate wrath by beginning with generalities. The object of Yahweh's attack is stated metaphorically, and the audience is not yet offended because the "branches" are not identified. But at the end Jeremiah becomes specific. The culprits turn out to be the prophets (v. 13), and we are even given their words before

---

We know now from Ugaritic, however, that אַל (like לֹא) can have asseverative meaning, i.e., it can mean "surely." That seems to be the meaning here. On the asseverative אַל, see C. H. Gordon, *Ugaritic Textbook* (Rome: Pontifical Biblical Institute, 1965), 357; also M. Dahood, "Hebrew-Ugaritic Lexicography I," *Biblica* 44 (1963), 293–94.

53. My translation of this colon does not reflect the fact that the Hebrew verb is N stem and should be translated passively: "thus it will be done to them." I wanted, however, to force the link between עשה here and in v. 10, which the poet intends.

54. Bright, *Jeremiah*, 37.

55. See n. 52 above.

they themselves are specified. The inclusio helps make the desired connection: יעשה in the final colon echoes תעשו at the beginning. And what might otherwise be an ambiguous conclusion is now very clear. The antecedent of כה, "thus" is כלה, "full end." Yahweh will make a full end of the prophets. Now we know that *they* are the dead branches in Yahweh's vineyard.

This type of argument has subtlety. Jeremiah does not come right out and damn the prophets; he uses his structure in such a way that the audience can end up doing it. And Jeremiah is also able to keep his audience with him because the total message does not come across until the end, or perhaps we should say, after the end.

5:26–31

Chapter 5 ends with v. 31 and most commentators (except Volz) break there. The beginning has been less clear. Only Volz breaks before v. 26, but neither he nor anyone else makes the divisions we propose. Verse 29 is the same stereotyped refrain found in 5:9 and 9:8. Condamin places it after v. 31. We take it as an insertion, and therefore omit it. What remains then is a nicely balanced 3:3:3 poem with inclusio.

כי־נמצאו <u>בעמי</u> רשעים ישור כשך   26
יקושים הציבו משחית אנשים ילכדו

ככלוב מלא עוף <u>כן</u> בתיהם מלאים מרמה   27

על־כן גדלו ויעשירו *שמנו עשתו   28*
גם עברו דברי־רע דין לא־דנו
דין יתום ויצליחו ומשפט אביונים לא שפטו

שמה ושערורה נהיתה בארץ   30
הנביאים נבאו־בשקר והכהנים ירדו על־ידיהם   31
<u>ועמי</u> אהבו <u>כן</u> ומה־תעשו לאחריתה

  26   For scoundrels are found among *my people*
       they lurk like fowlers[56]
     Bait-layers setting their traps
       it is men they catch
  27   Like a basket full of birds
      so their houses are filled with deceit

---

56. Text obscure; see commentaries.

> Therefore they've become great and rich
> 28   they are fat and sleek
> Yes, they overlook bad deeds
>   not judging with justice
> The cause of the orphan to win it;
>   they defend not the rights of the needy
>
> 30   An appalling and horrible thing
>   has happened in the land
> 31   The prophets prophesy falsely
>   and the priests rule at their direction[57]
> But *my people* love it *so*
>   therefore what will you do when the end comes?

Despite some textual difficulties, we generally know what the poem is about. The prophets and priests are being flayed for acting in self-interest. They disregard the admonition of Deuteronomy to help the orphan and the needy (cf. Deut 10:18; 14:29; 16:11, 14; etc.). Jeremiah again is slow to identify them specifically. The poem begins by referring to רשעים (scoundrels). But we soon know from the description in stanza 2 who these are. Now one might think that the poem is exclusively about prophets and priests, but it is not. The inclusio gives a peculiar twist in that it shifts the focus *off* the *prophets and priests* and *on* to the *people*. These people—who had been prey to the scoundrels—*they* "love" it this way. The verse is also ironic. Jeremiah says that the people do not really mind injustice prevailing. So understood, the part about prophets and priests is merely *foil*; the *preferred subject* is the people themselves, making the last two cola the *cap* of the poem.[58] If the "people" happen to be the audience, we can see how they might cheer Jeremiah along most of the way. But the cap makes them accomplices with the prophets and priests, meaning that they too must share the blame. What we have is an "unholy alliance" between clergy and people against society's helpless. Thus the concluding question "And what will you do when the end comes?" addresses *both* clergy and people.

---

57. For a different reading, see W. L. Holladay, " 'The Priests Scrape Out on Their Hands,' Jeremiah V 31," *VT* 15 (1965), 111–13.

58. The use of "cap" and "foil" to analyze poetic structure is developed by Professor Brandt in his unpublished "The Rhetoric of Poetry" (Chapter V, "The Structures of Lyric Poetry").

9:9b–10 [Eng. 9:10b–11]

This is a brief 4-line poem. Verse 11 begins prose comment establishing the power limit. The upper limit is not so clear. Condamin and Bright begin with 9a (verse 8 is again the stereotyped
refrain seen earlier in 5:29, and in this context signals the conclusion of the poem preceding). Volz completely rearranges the
text and therefore is of no help. Our inclusio argues for 9a being
outside the poem and thus an introductory line. In the next
chapter we will explain why it is there.

כי נצתו מבלי־איש עבר ולא שמער קול מקנה   9b
מעוף השמים ועד־בהמה נדדו הלכו

ונתתי את־ירושלם לגלים מעון תנים   10
ואת־ערי יהודה אתן שממה מבלי יושב

9b For they are laid waste *without man* passing through
        and the lowing of cattle is not heard
    Both birds of the air and beasts
        have fled and are gone

10 I will make Jerusalem a ruin-heap
        a lair for jackals
    And the cities of Judah I will make a total waste
        without inhabitant

The poem is also divided in half by speaker. Jeremiah speaks
in the first stanza, and Yahweh in the second. The one in fact
echoes the other. Jeremiah says he sees a land "without inhab-
itant," and Yahweh says that is what he sees too. The function
of this inclusio appears to be simple reinforcement. Yahweh
echoes Jeremiah's thought like in 1:12 ("You have seen well").
The inclusio builds here on similar—not identical—expressions, yet we prefer MT מבלי in v. 10 to מאין, the latter occurring
in 24 Mss.

10:6–7

As we mentioned earlier, 10:1–16 is not usually attributed to
Jeremiah. Nevertheless we have in vv. 6–7 an unusually intri-
cate poem that deserves to be seen. These verses can be isolated
form-critically. They comprise one of two doxologies that follow

separate poems mocking false gods. These poems come in vv. 2–5 and vv. 8–9. The other doxology praising Yahweh is in v. 10. The entire unit of 10:2–10 alternates, then, between a mocking poem to false gods (2–5); a doxology praising Yahweh (6–7); a mocking poem to false gods (8–9); and a doxology praising Yahweh (10). In its present form it appears to be a liturgy recited antiphonally. We now look to the doxology of 6–7. It is 3 lines with each line a tri-colon.

6   <u>מאין כמוך</u>   יהוה גדול אתה   וגדול שמך בגבורה

7   מי לא יראך   מלך הגוים   כי לך יאתה

כי בכל־חכמי הגוים   ובכל־מלכותם   <u>מאין כמוך</u>

6   *There is none like you*
     Yahweh you are great
         and great is your name in power
7   Who would not fear you
     King of the Nations
         for that is your due
For among all the wise men of the nations
     and among all their kingdoms
         there is none like you

The subject of the doxology is in the exact center: King of the Nations. And the inclusio repeats words which are the poem's theme, i.e., the incomparability of Yahweh.[59] If then 10:2–10 is a liturgy, our doxology with its inclusio gives the whole even greater suitability for use in temple worship.

14:7–9

This next poem can also be isolated form-critically. It is a liturgy of penitence to be recited by the people in the temple.[60] It follows a judgment oracle (2–6) and was probably used together with it. Condamin has again noticed the key words making up the inclusio.

7   אם־עונינו ענו בנו   <u>יהוה</u> עשה למען <u>שמך</u>

כי־רבו משובתינו   לך חטאנו

---

59. These verses are lacking in the shorter LXX text.
60. So Volz, *Der Prophet Jeremia*, 162; Bright, *Jeremiah*, 102.

מקוה ישראל מושיעו בעת צרה 8

למה תהיה כגר בארץ וכארח נטה ללון

למה תהיה כאיש נדהם כגבור לא־יוכל להושיע 9

ואתה בקרבנו יהוה ושמך עלינו נקרא אל־תנחנו

7   Though our iniquities testify against us
    act *Yahweh* for *your name's* sake
For our backslidings are many
    against you we have sinned

8   O Hope of Israel
    its savior in time of trouble
Why are you like a stranger in the land
    like a traveler who stops only for a night?

9   Why are you like a man surprised
    like a soldier who cannot save?
Yet you *Yahweh* are in the midst of us
    we are called by *your name*
      do not leave us.

Taken by itself the second colon of stanza 1 sounds a bit altruistic: "act Yahweh for your name's sake." The inclusio however focuses on the poet's main intent, i.e., to persuade Yahweh that only *by saving Israel* he will save his own name. Yahweh's name is inextricably tied up with the fate of his people, and their defeat will harm his as well.

20:4, 6

This is a poem which Holladay recently uncovered in the prose of 20:1–6.[61] He calls attention to its inclusio, even as Condamin did much earlier. I take the poem as 6 bi-colic lines, the last being very short because of the poem's diminution.

הנני נתנך למגור לך ולכל־אהביך 4

ונפלו בחרב איביהם ועיניך ראות

ואתה פשחור וכל ישבי ביתך 6

תלכו בשבי ובבל תבוא

ושם תמות ושם תקבר

אתה וכל־אהביך

---

61. "The Covenant with the Patriarchs Overturned . . . ," 307ff.

4   Behold, I make you a terror[62]
       yourself and all your 'dear ones'
     And they shall fall by the sword of their enemies
       while your eyes are looking on
6   And you Pashhur
       and all the inhabitants of your house
     You shall go into captivity
       to Babylon you shall enter
     And there you shall die
       and there you shall be buried
     You
       and all your 'dear ones'

Holladay eliminated vv. 4b–5 and the final phrase of v. 6 as expansion. Perhaps this expansion merely attempts to explain the term אהביך, which is ironic.[63] There seem to be two groups of "dear ones." The first are those mentioned in v. 4 who will die violently before Pashhur's eyes. The second group in v. 6 go into exile and will die there. They are members of Pashhur's house. At any rate, Pashhur and his colleagues will all suffer an ignominious fate, and the inclusio functions to reinforce the comprehensive quality of Yahweh's judgment.

20:7–10

Condamin correctly sees the limits of this poem and also its inclusio. But we do not agree with him that it is an antistrophe to vv. 4–6.[64] It goes instead with vv. 11–13 following, which some commentators include with 7–10 to make one poem.[65] In our view, 11–13 is a companion poem to 7–10, and the two were probably meant to be read together at some later stage. Let us now look at the inclusio in 7–10.

7   פתיתני יהוה ואפת חזקתני ותוכל
     הייתי לשחוק כל־היום כלה לעג לי

---

62. Holladay leaves מגור untranslated because of a threefold meaning which he believes Jeremiah intends for it.

63. Jeremiah uses the verb אהב and its cognate nouns with ironic meaning in 2:33; 5:31; 22:20, 22; and 30:14.

64. Condamin, *Le Livre de Jérémie*, 164.

65. So Bright.

כי־מדי אדבר אזעק המס ושד אקרא 8
כי־היה דבר־יהוה לי   לחרפה ולקלס כל־היום

ואמרתי לא־אזכרנו ולא־אדבר עוד בשמו 9
והיה בלבי כאש בערת עצר בעצמתי
ונלאיתי כלכל   ולא אוכל

כי שמעתי דבת רבים מגור מסביב 10
הגידו ונגידנו   כל אנוש שלומי שמרי צלעי
אולי יפתה ונוכלה לו   ונקחה נקמתנו ממנו

7   *You deceived me*, Yahweh, and *I was deceived*
     you seized and *overcame* me
     I have become a joke all the day
     everyone mocks me
8   For whenever I speak, I cry out
     'Violence and destruction' I shout
     For the word of Yahweh has become for me
     a reproach and derision all the day

9   If I say 'I'll not remember him
     and not speak anymore in his name'
     In my heart there is like a burning fire
     shut up in my bones
     And I weary of holding it in
     and I cannot

10   For I hear many whispering
     'Terror On Every Side,[66]
     Denounce him, let us denounce him'
     say all my friends of shalom who wait for my fall
     'Perhaps *he will be deceived* and *we can overcome* him
     and take our revenge on him'

This is one of the Jeremianic confessions. It is a brutally
frank word to Yahweh accusing him of deception and also of being overpowering. The inclusio gives added theological insight.
Yahweh is here charged with the very thing that comes to Jeremiah from his opponents. Jeremiah calls these opponents אנוש
שלומי, "my friends of shalom" (v. 10), suggesting some concern
on his part about their genuineness. Only if he suspects that

---

66. Bright ingeniously recognizes that "Terror On Every Side" is here
a nickname which Jeremiah has been given; cf. *Jeremiah*, 132–33.

they perhaps be right and he perhaps be wrong can Jeremiah
turn to accuse Yahweh. Were he sure of his rightness, he would
instead write them off and be confident. His confidence does
come in vv. 11–13, but this we take to be later since Yahweh has
by then delivered him from the grip of these men (v. 13). Taken
by itself, however, the poem of 7–10 preserves the ambiguity so
often existing in real life situations. Certainty must come sometime later.

20:14–18

This final poem in the 1–20 collection is the most moving in
Jeremiah, and perhaps one of the most moving in all of ancient
literature. Its unity is contested by no one since the poem is easily delimited by content. In this poem Jeremiah curses his birth.
We saw earlier how this poem was made to balance the call in
chapter 1. Now we can see its own structure, which also has an
inclusio made up of "day" and "days." These key terms are
noted by Condamin. For reasons which will be given later, we
believe that the poem divides up into stanzas of 2 lines each.[67]
With also the position of אשר beginning each second colon, we
propose that the poem in its original form was 5 stanzas
(2:2:2:2:2) which means that two of the cola have fallen out.[68]
This would further explain the abrupt beginning of v. 17.[69]

14 ארור היום אשר ילדתי בו
    יום אשר־ילדתני אמי אל־יהי ברוך

15 ארור האיש אשר בשר את־אבי לאמר
    ילד־לך בן זכר שמח שמחהר

16 והיה האיש ההוא כערים אשר־הפך יהוה ולא נחם
    ושמע זעקה בבקר ותרועה בעת צהרים

---

67. See Chapter 3, pp. 90–91.

68. On the subject of textual omissions, Albright has said the following: There is "increasing evidence from the Qumran Scrolls that our
Hebrew originals, once edited in antiquity, suffered far more from omissions by copyists than from additions"; cf. W. F. Albright, "Some Remarks
on the Song of Moses in Deuteronomy XXXII," *VT* 9 (1959), 341.

69. One cannot help but wonder if the lost colon beginning v. 17 was
not omitted intentionally since it no doubt named the one who could
have killed Jeremiah while he was still in the womb. This may have been
too offensive, especially if Yahweh was in any way implied.

17 [.........]   אשר לא־מותתני מרחם
ותהי־לי אמי קברי   ורחמה הרת עולם

18 למה זה מרחם יצאתי   [אשר ....]
לראות עמל ויגון   ויכלו בבשת <u>ימי</u>

14   Cursed be *the day*
     on which I was born
  The day when my mother bore me
     let it not be blessed

15   Cursed be the man
     who brought the news to my father
  'A son is born to you'
     making him very glad

16   Let that man be like the cities
     which Yahweh overthrew without pity
  Let him hear a cry in the morning
     and an alarm at noon

17   ....
     who did not kill me in the womb
  So my mother would have been my grave
     and her womb forever great

18   Why did I come forth from the womb
     ....
  To see toil and sorrow
     and end in shame *my days*?

Jeremiah begins the poem by recalling the *day* of his birth.
He ends it with a reference to the most recent of *days*, which apparently were very trying. The poem is probably to be dated
from the time around 605–604 B.C. when Jehoiakim was threat-
ening his life, and if so, we can well understand Jeremiah's fear
and despair. The inclusio puts in tension his beginning and
what Jeremiah feared would be his end. And at such a time his
thoughts return to the beginning: "Why did I come forth from
the womb . . ." (v. 18). Verse 15 suggests that for Jeremiah's father at least, his birth was a joyous event. Indications elsewhere
in the poetry suggest that for Jeremiah too the early years of his
life were filled with happiness.[70] But now in light of present

---

70. See 15:16 and also my translation of 8:18 discussed in Chapter 3,
pp. 112–13.

despair, what originally was a happy event becomes tragic, and Jeremiah curses the event strongly. History has a way of changing one's perspective, and that appears to have been the case here with Jeremiah.

We discussed earlier how the inclusio tying this poem together with the call *did just the opposite*. It made over time what was originally a desperate cry into a larger statement of hope. The compiled form then gives us the "long view" of Jeremiah, which is the more balanced view. He is not just the prophet of doom; he both breaks down and builds up (cf. 1:10).

22:6–7

This is a short poem of 4 lines framed by prose comment on either side (so Volz, Condamin and Bright). It is one of three main poems in the "King Collection" (21:1–23:8), all of which play upon the luxury of Jerusalem's royal complex. The other two are 22:13–17 and 22:20–23. So plush were these buildings with their cedar interiors that Jeremiah addresses them metaphorically as "Lebanon."[71] This poem forms its inclusio by using words of common association: "Lebanon" and "cedars." They may even be a fixed pair (cf. 22:23), although their use in the Old Testament is usually in the construct chain ארזי הלבנון (Ps 29:5; 104:16; etc.).

6 גלעד אתה לי ראש הלבנון
אם־לא אשיתך מדבר ערים לא נושבה
7 וקדשתי עליך משחתים איש וכליו
וכרתו מבחר ארזיך והפילו על־האש

6   You are as Gilead to me
        as the summit of *Lebanon*
    Yet I will surely make you a desert
        uninhabited quarters[72]
7   I will sanctify destroyers against you
        each with his weapons
    And they shall cut down your choicest *cedars*
        and cast them into the fire

---

71. For later metaphorical uses of "Lebanon" in the Targums, see Geza Vermes, "The Symbolical Interpretation of *Lebanon* in the Targums: The Origin and Development of an Exegetical Tradition," *JThS* 9 (1958), 1–12.

72. עיר can mean "temple quarter"; see L. R. Fisher, "The Temple Quarter," *JSS* 8 (1963), 34–41.

Jeremiah could have placed the line about the "cedars" immediately following the line about "Lebanon," but instead he delays it until the end. And if the key terms are a fixed pair, he is also playing with the hearer's expectations: the second of the pair is bound to be anticipated soon after the first is given.

22:20–23

This is the third poem on "Lebanon," and its limits are agreed upon by all commentators.[73] It contains other metaphorical terms, e.g., "shepherds," which is a favorite Jeremianic term for kings (cf. 2:8; 23:1–4; etc.). The inclusio here is formed by the repetition of "Lebanon" with an added "cedars" at the end.[74] And each stanza has its own inclusio as we will see in the next section.

עלי הלבנון וצעקי ובבשן תני קולך 20
וצעקי מעברים כי נשברו כל־מאהביך
דברתי אליך בשלותיך אמרת לא אשמע 21
זה דרכך מנעוריך כי לא־שמעת בקולי

כל־רעיך תרעה־רוח ומאהביך בשבי ילכו 22
כי אז תבשי ונכלמת מכל רעתך
ישבתי בלבנון מקננתי בארזים 23
מה־נחנת בבא־לך חבלים חיל כילדה

20 Go up to *Lebanon* and cry out
  and in Bashan lift up your voice
  Cry out from Abarim
  for all your lovers are destroyed
21 I spoke to you in your prosperity
  but you said, 'I will not listen'
  This has been your way from your youth
  that you have not obeyed my voice

22 The wind shall shepherd all your shepherds
  and your lovers shall go into captivity
  Then you will be ashamed and confounded
  because of all your wickedness
23 O inhabitants of *Lebanon*
  nested among the *cedars*

---

73. So Volz, Condamin, Hyatt, Bright, etc.
74. Condamin sees the "Lebanon" balance; *Le Livre de Jérémie*, 172.

> How you will groan when your pangs come upon you
> pain as of a woman in travail

The poem begins with Jeremiah ironically telling the king to go ahead with his pagan worship on "Holy Hill." This is the classical figure called *epitrope*. Now if the hearer does not detect the irony with which Jeremiah begins, he might catch the word-play in כל־רעיך תרעה־רוה beginning stanza 2. There is more irony in the next colon where Jeremiah uses "lovers" as he did in v. 20.[75] In the final lines of the poem Jeremiah is still using metaphors to indicate how royalty will suffer in the coming day of judgment. These figures—especially the metaphors—all create *distance* between Jeremiah and his audience. Perhaps such a stance was the only safe one to take. It is dangerous to come right out and tell the king and his court that they will be defeated, although Jeremiah was evidently able to speak this candidly with Zedekiah (see chaps. 21, 34 and 37).

51:11–14

In spite of some prosaic-sounding lines (11bcd), we nevertheless take this to be a 3-stanza poem of four lines each. The lower limit is established by the doxology in vv. 15–19 (= 10:12–16) and commentators generally take v. 11 as the beginning.[76] Condamin has again caught the key word מלא, which means "to fill" or "to supply."

11 הברו החצים מלאו השלטים
העיר יהוה את־רוח מלכי מדי
כי־על־בבל מזמתו להשחיתה
כי־נקמת יהוה היא נקמת היכלו

12 אל־חומת בבל שאו־נס החזיקו המשמר
הקימו שמרים הכינו הארבים
כי גם־זמם יהוה גם־עשה
את אשר־דבר אל־ישבי בבל

13 שכנתי על־מים רבים רבת אוצרת
בא קצך אמת בצעך

---

75. See also 2:33; 20:4, 6 (although in discussing 20:4, 6 we used Holladay's translation of "dear ones") and 30:14.
76. So Condamin and Bright.

14 נשבע יהוה צבאות בנפשו
כי אם־מַלֵּאתִיךְ אדם כילק וענו עליך הידד

11   Sharpen the arrows
        supply the shields
     Yahweh has stirred up
        the spirit of the kings of the Medes
     For his purpose against Babylon
        is to destroy it
     For that is the vengeance of Yahweh
        the vengeance for his temple

12   Signal attack against Babylon's walls
        make the watch strong
     Set up watchmen
        prepare the ambushes
     For even Yahweh has planned
        even he has done
     That which he said
        concerning the inhabitants of Babylon

13   You who dwell by many waters
        rich in treasures
     Your end has come
        the thread of your life is cut
14   Yahweh of Hosts has sworn
        by his own very self
     Surely *I will supply you* with men like locusts
        and they will raise the victory shout over you

Any translation of the two uses of מלא will be inadequate
because of the shift in meaning. The verb normally means "to
fill," which fits well into v. 14, but not into v. 11. Our use of "supply" follows Condamin who translates with "remplir." This tension only serves to point up again how Jeremiah plays with
word meanings, and since the less common usage occurs at the
beginning, the audience will be alerted to notice the term when
it appears again at the end. The inclusio helps to focus on a
battlefield filled with armor and men and thereby functions to
emphasize what is meant to be the main point, viz., that Babylon will soon be faced with an enemy whose strength is nothing
less than overpowering.

*   *   *   *   *

This concludes our section on the use of the inclusio in the Jeremianic speeches. Yet we have not exhausted the number of speeches that end by a return to the beginning. Chiastic speeches to be shown in the next chapter do this and more. But we have made a beginning. And we have also for the first time discovered strategies of argumentation used by Jeremiah against his audience.

Since the inclusio was employed in the earlier rhetoric of Deuteronomy and is now found quite frequently in the rhetoric of Jeremiah, we may perhaps be permitted some speculation about Jeremiah's dependence on Deuteronomy. It would appear that Jeremiah appropriated the structures of Deuteronomy for his own use. Why? A slightly revised answer of Herman Gunkel's would be suitable enough. When asked why the prophets borrowed certain genres, Gunkel answered that they did so in order to win over the hearts of a people who were already receptive to those genres.[77] We think rather that Jeremiah used the rhetorical structures of Deuteronomy because *they* were already familiar to the people, and were no doubt structures to which the people could conceivably respond.

Inclusio within the Jeremianic Poems

We have seen that the inclusio delimits whole poems. Now, as we look within various poems, we see the inclusio again where it appears to delimit certain parts. These we offer as stanzas within poems. As we mentioned earlier, stanzas are already conceded in Hebrew poetry, and we think that the inclusio can now be listed as another criterion for their delimitation. It is of course possible that some of the units to be discussed here are in reality whole poems; we cannot be sure, but our present judgment is that they are not. Most important is that Jeremiah structured smaller segments of his poems in the same way that he structured whole poems. That is the point we wish to make clear.

---

77. See n. 102 on p. 17.

4:22

This unit is usually taken to be a part of 4:19–22 (so Condamin and Bright). Volz, however, separates it out as being independent. We take it as a 3-line stanza of 4:19–22 with לא ידעו at the end of lines 1 and 3 making the inclusio.

22 כי אויל עמי   אותי <u>לא ידעו</u>
בנים סכלים המה   ולא נבונים המה
הכמים המה להרע   ולהיטיב <u>לא ידעו</u>

> 22   For my people are foolish
>   me *they do not know*
>   Stupid children are they
>   no understanding have they
>   Wise are they to do evil
>   but to do good, *they do not know*

To lack a knowledge of Yahweh is to lack a knowledge of how to do good. The people lack both. This entire unit is finely constructed: the center cola balance one another by both ending in המה. The final bi-colon is a chiasmus, and the positive "Wise are they . . ." sets up the negative "they do not know," which enables the tie-up with the beginning.

4:29

This is a 3-line stanza in the poem of 4:29–31.[78] The rest of the poem divides up into two additional stanzas of 3 lines each making the whole a 3:3:3 structure.[79] The inclusio here is made by the repetition of כל־העיר. It appears at the end of the first line and at the beginning of the third. We see no reason to emend (with Rudolph) the first of these to כל־הארץ (Greek: πᾶσα χῶρα). Bright says כל־העיר in line 1 is an intrusion from line 3, but we disagree.[80] We also find it unnecessary to expand the center of

---

78. So Bright.
79. When the poem is taken as a 3:3:3 structure, some other nice balancing terms emerge, e.g., נפשך (v. 30) and נפשי (v. 31). Also, although we did not identify this as an inclusio poem, it may very well be one with מקול beginning the first stanza (v. 29) and כי קול beginning the third stanza (v. 31).
80. Bright, *Jeremiah*, 31.

the unit as the Greek does. The Hebrew has here a nice syntactic chiasmus giving the stanza added structure.

29 מקול פרש ורמה קשת ברחת כל־העיר
באו בעבים ובכפים עלו
כל־העיר עזובה ואין־יושב בהן איש

29 At the noise of horseman and archer
every city takes to flight
They enter into the thickets
and into rocks they climb
Every city is deserted
and no man dwells in them

When Jeremiah first speaks of "every city," he is using "city" as a metonymy for "people of the city." But in the second instance "every city" means every *place* where people so live together. Thus after *every city* evacuates, *every city* is deserted.

5:21

5:21, though a brief 2 lines, contains a nice inclusio using שמע (hear):

21 שמעו־נא זאת עם סכל ואין לב
עינים להם ולא יראו אזנים להם ולא ישמעו

21 *Hear* this please
foolish people without sense
Who have eyes but do not see
who have ears but do not *hear*

It is ironic. Jeremiah asks a people to hear who cannot hear. Perhaps by placing the key term at the extremes he will make an impression on the *ear*, in which case their deafness can be penetrated. A comparison of this verse with Isa 6:9–10 and Ps 135:16–17 shows that the thought was not original to Jeremiah, but the structure which he gave it was.

8:4–5

This is the first of four stanzas in the poem of 8:4–9, and three make use of the inclusio in one way or another. The key term in this stanza is שוב (to return). Not only does this verb make the inclusio, but together with its cognate nouns it occurs in the stanza no fewer than five times. In Holladay's major study of שוב[81] this text is crucial for determining the root's basic meaning.[82]

4   היפלו ולא יקומו אם־ישוב ולא ישוב

5   מדוע שובבה העם הזה ירושלם משבה נצחת
     החזיקו בתרמת מאנו לשוב

4   When men fall, do they not rise again?
     If one turns away, does he not *return*?
5   Why then has this people turned away
     Jerusalem, the 'turncoat pre-eminent'?
     They hold fast to deceit
     They refuse *to return*

My translation differs from most in that it follows the MT in line 2 which includes "Jerusalem." One Ms. and the LXX omit, and so also does the RSV. Commentators are similarly divided.[83] This line, however, is a syntactic chiasmus: Why then / turned away / this people // Jerusalem / the 'turncoat / pre-eminent'. The second colon in the line is ironic: Jerusalem (= the people of Jerusalem) is "exhibit A" of apostasy. She is outstanding in her field.

The inclusio in this brief stanza reveals a rhetorical strategy seen earlier in the full poem of 3:1–5. Jeremiah begins with a rhetorical question, to which his audience can be expected to give an obvious answer. He then goes on to use a link term to point up an incongruity. The obvious answer to the question in colon 2 is, "Of course such a person will return" (although in 3:1 it was just the opposite!). Then at the end comes the twist: but this people *refuses* to return. Here lies the incongruity Jeremiah wants his audience to see. We have here from Jeremiah no "authority preaching." He appeals only to the listener's sense of order, and after an analogy pointing up the incongruity, the listener is left with the decision to accept or reject.

---

81. *The Root ŠÛBH in the Old Testament* (Leiden: E. J. Brill, 1958).
82. Ibid., 1.
83. Bright (*Jeremiah*, 60) omits; Volz (*Der Prophet Jeremia*, 107) retains.

8:7

This is the third stanza of the same poem and plays on the verb
ידע. That same verb formed the inclusio in 4:22. Here Jeremiah
uses it to contrast people with birds, and in a way very typically
Jeremianic, it is unfavorable to the people.

7 גם חסידה בשמים <u>ידעה</u> מועדיה
וחר וסוס ועגור שמרו את־עת באנה
ועמי לא <u>ידעו</u> את משפט יהוה

7   Even the stork in the heavens
        knows her times
     And the turtledove, swallow and crane[84]
        keep the time of their coming
     But my people do not *know*
        the ordinance of Yahweh

Again Jeremiah uses an argument from the natural order. The
repetition of "know" helps underscore the contrast and also to
point up the incongruity which Jeremiah has come to see. How
different a view of man within the created order from what is
found in Gen 1:26ff. and Ps 8:6!

8:8–9

The final stanza of this poem is 4 lines, and the inclusio here is
made up of balancing terms in *both* cola of the opening and closing lines.

8 איכה תאמרו <u>חכמים</u> אנחנו <u>ותורת יהוה</u> אתנו
אכן הנה לשקר עשה עט שקר ספרים
9 הבישו חכמים חתו וילכדו
הנה <u>בדבר־יהוה</u> מאסו <u>וחכמת</u>־מה להם

8   How can you say, 'We are *wise*
        and the *law of Yahweh* is with us?'
     But, behold, the false pen of the scribes
        has made it into a lie
9   The wise men shall be shamed
        they shall be dismayed and taken

---

84. Bird names are not known for certain; see the commentaries.

> Behold they have rejected the *word of Yahweh*
> so what *wisdom* is in them?

Here Jeremiah quotes his opponents in order to engage them, or perhaps he may be putting words in their mouth. Then by showing that their claim is mere pretension, he uses synonyms and cognate terms to turn and accuse them. But the question at the end still leaves the answer with the audience.

<u>10:20–21</u>

This cluster of 4 lines is usually taken to be part of a 6-line poem beginning at v. 19.[85] Yet they may be independent. We are faced at the outset with textual difficulty primarily because of some metaphors. Verse 20 begins by mentioning a "destroyed tent," which is followed by "destroyed children" no longer able to set up a tent (is it Yahweh's tent?). Without discussing other alternatives the following solution is proposed. First we must omit אהלי שדד, "my tent is destroyed" as a gloss (so Rudolph).[86] What emerges then is an inclusio that helps clear up the sense.

20 <u>וכל־מיתרי</u> נתקו בני יצאני ואינם
אין־נטה עוד אהלי ומקים יריעותי
21 כי נבערו הרעים ואת־יהוה לא דרשו
על־כן לא השכילו <u>וכל־מרעיתם</u> נפוצה

20 *All my cords* are broken
        my children have left me and are not
    There is no one to spread again my tent
        and to set up my curtains
21 For the shepherds are stupid
        and of Yahweh they do not inquire
    Therefore they have not prospered
        and *all their flock* is scattered

The problematic term is מיתר, which is an uncommon word meaning "cord" or "string."[87] It usually refers to a "tent cord"

---

85. Closed sections (setumahs) mark off 19–21 as a unit. Bright calls these verses a soliloquy in which Jeremiah speaks for the nation; cf. *Jeremiah*, 73.

86. In the apparatus to *BH*[3] he suggests that it is probably added from 4:20.

87. So *BDB* 452; *KBH* 193.

(Exod 39:40; Isa 54:2; etc.) which no doubt explains the attempted gloss: the tent cords are broken // the tent is destroyed. But if one reads "All my cords are broken" with the colon *following*, then "cords" end up in parallelism with "children." This would require a metaphorical use of "cords"—albeit a rare one (but again who knows since the term is uncommon to begin with). Yet if the inclusio is made up of equivalent terms, i.e., if both metaphors refer to *people*, then this interpretation is substantiated. The "cords" become the same as the "flock," which is also equivalent to the "children." Jeremiah is of course responsible for the confusion, but he seems to want to say something like "My cords are no longer able to set up my tent. Why? Because they are broken, i.e., they are gone away."

Such a pattern of though is true to form. Jeremiah begins with an obscure term—in this case a metaphor—and one that does not reveal his preferred subject. The "broken cords" only enlist the audience's sympathy. The preferred subject is "shepherds" (i.e., the kings). *They* have become alienated from Yahweh, and as a result the flock/children/cords are scattered. The end of the unit in this way brings us right back to the beginning.

22:20–21

We looked earlier at this stanza when we discussed the whole poem.[88] Now we can see how an inclusio isolates vv. 20–21 into a stanza of four lines, making the poem a 4:4 structure. Stanza 2 also has an inclusio and will be our next example. Here the structure is created by "your voice/my voice," which comes at the end of lines 1 and 4.

20 עלי הלבנון וצעקי ובבשן תני קולך
וצעקי מעברים כי נשברו כל־מאהביך
21 דברתי אליך בשלותיך אמרת לא אשמע
זה דרכך מנעוריך כי לא־שמעת בקולי

20 Go up to Lebanon and cry out
 and in Bashan lift up *your voice*
 Cry out from Abarim
 for all your lovers are destroyed

---

88. See pp. 68–69.

21 I spoke to you in your prosperity
     but you said, 'I will not listen'
     This has been your way from your youth
     that you have not obeyed *my voice*

The repetition making this inclusio brings out the lack of communication between Yahweh and the personified daughter of
Jerusalem. The whole is of course ironic. Jeremiah tells her to go
ahead and *continue* crying to her deity (so also Elijah on Mt. Car-
mel; cf. 1 Kgs 18:27), while at the same time reminding her of
her *continual* refusal to listen to the voice of Yahweh.

22:22–23

Inclusios which tie together stanzas of poems seem to be appearing in clusters. We found three such stanzas in 8:4–9, and
now two are present in 22:20–23. These four lines contain an inclusio which is assonantal. We give the Hebrew only.

22 כל־רעיך תרעה־רוח ומאהביך בשבי יֵלֵכוּ
     כי אז תבשי ונכלמת מכל רעתך
23 ישבתי בלבנון מקננתי בארזים
     מה־נחנת בבא־לך חבלים חיל כַּיֹּלֵדָה

The play on sound is made by two words containing יל followed
by a sere vowel. In addition we have כ following the combination in the first term, whereas it precedes the combination in the
final term. Assonantal balance is common in Jeremiah as Holladay has already shown us.[89] Thus far in this study we have put
the emphasis on *key words*, which in turn create semantic links.
But the possibilities of *sound* for making associations should not
be minimized. Here by sound alone Jeremiah associates "tra-
vail" with "going into captivity," the former very clearly de-
scribing what the latter will be like.

30:12–14

This is the larger of two stanzas which make up a poem in
30:12–15. That poem, taken as a whole, is a companion piece to

---

89. A good example is the word-play on ראה and ירא in balancing
stanzas of Jer 17:5–8; cf. Holladay, "Style, Irony and Authenticity in Jeremiah," 52.

30:16–18.[90] The inclusio here is formed by the repetition of מכה (wound), which is a central term of the poem. This word in fact also links the poem to its companion piece (v. 17: וממכותיך ארפאך).

12 אנוש לשברך נחלה מַכתך
13 אין־דן דינך למזור רפאות תעלה אין לך
14 כל־מאהביך שכחוך אותך לא ידרשו
כי מַכת אויב הכיתיך מוסר אכזרי

12 Your hurt is incurable
   your wound is grievous
13 No salve for your sore[91]
   no healing for you
14 All your lovers have forgotten you
   they care nothing for you
   An enemy's wound I dealt you
   a cruel chastisement

The movement is again from the general to the specific. Only in the final line does Jeremiah make it clear that the wound is from Yahweh. And if the "wound" stated at the beginning is not readily perceived to be at the same time a wound from the enemy, then the hearer must wait until the end for this revelation also.

31:35–36

This stanza is another cluster of 4 lines in a 4:2 poem. 31:35–37 was inserted into the Book of Comfort in what we determined earlier to be the third stage of its growth. Such shapes of unequal but proportional stanzas are now commonly seen in Jeremiah—the 4:2 and 2:4 structures being most prevalent in the Book of Comfort.

35 נתן שמש לאור יומַם חקת ירח וכוכבים לאור לילה
רגע הים ויהמו גליו יהוה צבאות שמו

---

90. So Bright, *Jeremiah*, 286, although he breaks at v. 17 as do other commentators. I would however see 16–18 as another 4:2 structure just like 12–15. This structure predominates in these poems: 30:5–7 is 4:2, while its companion piece in 30:10–11 is 2:4. I also take 30:19–20 as 4:2. Outside the Book of Comfort, we noted earlier that 10:19–21 was 2:4 (see p. 76).

91. This is Bright's translation; for a discussion of the textual difficulties, see Bright, *Jeremiah*, 271.

אִם־יִמֻּשׁוּ הַחֻקִּים הָאֵלֶּה מִלְּפָנַי נְאֻם־יְהוָה 36
גַּם זֶרַע יִשְׂרָאֵל יִשְׁבְּתוּ מִהְיוֹת גּוֹי לְפָנַי כָּל־הַיָּמִים

35 Who gives the sun for light by *day*
    and the ordered moon and stars to illumine the night?
  Who lashes the sea to make its waves roar?
    Yahweh of Hosts is his name
36 If this fixed order should vanish
    from before me—oracle of Yahweh
  Then Israel's descendants will cease
    from being a nation before me, *all the days*

The balance of "day/days" is exactly what we had in 20:14–18.[92] There Jeremiah cursed the *day* of his birth at the beginning, and concluded with a lament about ending his *days* in shame. It would appear that Jeremiah not only uses the same structures more than once, but even some of the same word-pairs over again.

The "if/then" form at the end leaves the final answer again with the audience. If the fixed order departs, then Israel's descendants will cease from being a nation. We can hear the audience respond to this with a loud "No!" The people are now broken and Jeremiah must raise them up, so he uses the same strategy of former times when he gave them a message of judgment. Before the people needed to supply an answer that would break them; now they need to articulate words that will sustain them in the days ahead.

46:20–21

Our final example is a cluster of 4 lines which comes from a speech given by Jeremiah against Egypt. I take the speech to include all of 46:18–23, and since this cluster comprises the middle 4 lines, the poem appears to be a 4:4:4 structure.[93] The verb בוא makes the inclusio.

---

92. See pp. 65–66.
93. Commentators are not agreed on the limits of this poem. If we take it as a 4:4:4 structure, then some rather impressive balancing features emerge. Each final line begins with כי and each stanza has a simile at the beginning.

20 עגלה יפה־פיה מצרים קרץ מצפון בָא בָא[94]
21 גם־שכריה בקרבה כעגלי מרבק
כי גם־המה הפנו נסו יחדיו לא עמדו
כי יום אידם בָא עליהם עת פקדתם

20 A beautiful heifer is Egypt
       but a fly from the north has *come* upon her[94]
21 The mercenaries too in her midst
       are like fatted calves
   They too have turned and fled together
       they did not stand
   For the day of their disaster has *come* upon them
       the time of their punishment

Jeremiah begins again with metaphors, only when speaking
against Egypt it is apparently safe to identify her from the start.
Yet we still move from the figurative to the literal: a fly has
come / the day of disaster has come.

This concludes our section on inclusio within the Jeremianic
poems and also the chapter. We have seen that parts of poems
are structured the same way as whole poems. Occasionally same
words are used. For Jeremiah the inclusio is not merely a device
enabling him to repeat himself. It is a tool of argumentation, and
as such becomes something it was not in Deuteronomy. Deuteronomy's audience needed reminding, and occasionally some
gentle admonition. Jeremiah's audience, however, was of a different sort. It required for the most part penetrating arguments
gauged to break the will.

Editorial structures in Jeremiah have been seen to have a
close affinity with the structures of Deuteronomy. In some cases,
e.g., 1–20, the harshness of the original is toned down making
the final compilation more suitable for temple worship. And we
are not thinking of worship in the exilic and post-exilic community. The process of adaptation began immediately. The scroll
which Baruch reads in the temple in 604 B.C. is already modified
in order that it may end with hope instead of despair.

---

94. Read בה for the second בא with 100 Mss., Greek and Syriac.

Chapter 3

Chiasmus

Although a variety of larger chiastic structures have been found in Deuteronomy and the Deuteronomic literature,[1] there appears to be no concentration of the figure in this literary corpus. Lund showed numerous examples of the chiasmus in Leviticus and he found it also in material as early as the Yahwistic account of the Fall (Genesis 3).[2]

Arguments for a chiasmus usually build upon the distribution of key words or what is believed to be a "thought pattern." Lund argued that the chiasmus was a thought pattern[3] though it is true that most of his structures had key words for undergirding. When these were not present the chiasmus became infinitely more difficult to objectify. While it may be conceded that an author can deliver a concept without using the key word for that concept, e.g., a passage written about love need not have the word "love" in it, nevertheless the possibility that the author had another basic concept in mind or perhaps more than one concept is always present. The danger then is that an outline, if based *only* upon a "thought pattern," all too easily becomes the creation of the modern scholar who imposes on the text something that was never intended to be there in the first place. Numerous discoveries of chiasmi fail because of this and they must be judged no less severely than the so-called genres about which we spoke earlier.

---

1. For a chiastic structure in 2 Kings 1–2 see my article "Elijah's Chariot Ride," *JJS* 24 (1973), 39–50.

2. *Chiasmus in the New Testament*, 59.

3. Ibid., 44.

In our present study we will require that speeches have at least some key words before a chiasmus of thought is proposed. In the larger editorial structures too, key words can almost always be found which make the chiasmus more certain. We would like to know more about ancient Hebrew thought patterns, but this much we do know, that verbal association was widely used in all levels of discourse, and we are therefore well advised to stay close to the specific vocabulary of the text in attempting to find our rhetorical structures.

Another kind of chiasmus not recognized by Lund has been observed by Lohfink, and significantly for us it appears in Deuteronomy. This is a chiasmus of *speaker.* In Deut 1:20–31, Moses narrates in the first person, introducing the *direct address* of each of the participants in a discussion—including himself—in chiastic fashion:[4]

> A   Moses speaks (20–21)
>   B   People speak (22)
>   C   Explorers speak (25)
>   B′ People speak (27–28)
> A′ Moses speaks (29–31)

Lohfink of course does not consider this order fortuitous. Structures in Deuteronomy are intended by their authors to be auditory signals for a people who must listen to material being read to them aloud.[5] We will see this same type of chiasmus in Jeremiah where it becomes almost as important as the key-word type in structuring the Jeremianic speech.

Chiasmus within the Jeremianic Poems

In Hebrew poetry chiasmus is a syntactic structure at base which inverts normal word order. It works especially well in a poetry which makes use of parallelism. Holladay says it serves to "vary the steady drumbeat of the normal [i.e., parallel] pattern."[6] Syntactic chiasmus is commonly found in all Old Testament poetry so we need not make too much of its existence in Jeremiah. But since we are going to show how Jeremiah expands

---

4. *Lectures in Deuteronomy,* 15.
5. Ibid., 5.
6. "The Recovery of Poetic Passages of Jeremiah," 409.

the figure, it would be well to see how he uses the figure in its
most basic form.

We shall begin with the smallest unit of the poetry, the bi-
colon. The greatest number of syntactic chiasmi in Jeremiah are
bi-cola which position verbs at the extremes:

2:9	Therefore I still contend	לכן עד אריב
	with you	אתכם
	and with your children's children	ואת־בני בניכם
	I will contend	אריב
2:19a	It will chasten you	תיסרך
	your wickedness	רעתך
	and your apostasy	ומשבותיך
	will reprove you	תוכחך
4:5a	Declare	הגידו
	in Judah	ביהודה
	and in Jerusalem	ובירושלם
	proclaim	השמיעו
4:7a	It has gone up	עלה
	a lion from his thicket	אריה מסבכו
	and a destroyer of nations	ומשחית גוים
	has gone forth	נסע
4:9c	And they shall be appalled	ונשמו
	the priests	הכהנים
	and the prophets	והנביאים
	shall be astounded	יתמהו
5:6a	Therefore it will slay them	על־כן הכם
	a lion from the forest	אריה מיער
	and a wolf from the desert	זאב ערבות
	will destroy them	ישדדם
5:12b	It will not come upon us	ולא־תבוא עלינו
	evil	רעה
	and sword and famine	וחרב ורעב
	we will not see	לוא נראה
6:21b	And they shall stumble against them	וכשלו בם
	fathers and sons together	אבות ובנים יחדו
	neighbor and friend	שכן ורעו
	shall perish	יאבדו

6:25a	Do not go forth	אל־תצאי
	into the field	השדה
	and by the way	ובדרך
	do not walk	אל־תלכי

14:2a	She mourns	אבלה
	Judah	יהודה
	her gates	ושעריה
	languish	אמללו

18:23b	Do not forgive	אל־תכפר
	their iniquity	על־עונם
	and their sin from your sight	וחטאתם מלפניך
	do not blot out	אל־תמחי

20:6	You shall go	תלכו
	into captivity	בשבי
	and Babylon	ובבל
	you shall enter	תבוא

30:17a	For I will restore	כי אעלה
	health unto you	ארכה לך
	and from your wounds	וממכותיך
	I will heal you	ארפאך

30:18b	And it shall be built	ונבנתה
	the city upon her mound	עיר על־תלה
	and the palace where it used to be	וארמון על־משפטו
	shall stand	ישב

46:14b	Proclaim	והשמיעו
	in Memphis	בנף
	and in Tahpanhes	ובתהפנחס
	say[7]	אמרו[7]

48:11c	Therefore it remains	על־כן עמד
	his taste in him	טעמו בו
	and his scent	וריחו
	is not changed	לא נמר

48:41a	They will be taken	נלכדה
	the cities	הקריות
	and the strongholds	והמצדות
	will be seized	נתפשה

---

7. No need to omit ובתחפנחס with the Greek; also against Rudolph I take אמרו with the previous colon.

51:58c And they toil   ויגעו
    the peoples for nought   עמים בדי־ריק
    and the nations only for fire   ולאמים בדי־אש
    indeed they weary themselves   ויעפו

Using Lowth's terminology these would all be examples of synonymous parallelism. For Schoettgen they would illustrate the rhetorical device "exergasia" (see Appendix). The repetition functions to embellish the idea and the chiasmus merely adds variation.

In only a few instances does Jeremiah use the small chiastic structure for contrast:

4:22c Wise are they   חכמים המה
    for evil   להרע
    and for good   ולהיטיב
    they do not know   לא ידעו

12:13a They have sown   זרעו
    wheat   חטים
    and thorns   וקצים
    they have reaped   קצרו

In 4:22c Jeremiah was perhaps forced into such a construction because of his desire to create balance with an earlier colon in the stanza.[8]

Lowth would have called these antithetical parallelisms but again that definition is not exhaustive. The sequence of expression in 4:22c is worthy of a closer look because it appears elsewhere in different kinds of parallelistic structures. Jeremiah often in stating things twice first uses *positive* and either *ironic* or *mildly humorous* terms, and second *negative* but *sober* terms.[9]

---

8. See earlier analysis of this verse on p. 72.
9. The following five bi-cola are all of one type and demonstrate the sequence well:

Yet you have *a harlot's brow*   ומצח אשה זונה היה לך
    you refuse to be ashamed (3:3)   מאנת הכלם
They have made *their faces harder than rock*   חזקו פניהם מסלע
    they refuse to repent (5:3)   מאנו לשוב
Behold, *their ears are uncircumcised*   הנה ערלה אזנם
    they cannot listen (6:10)   ולא יוכלו להקשיב

In this line to say that the people are *"wise* for (doing) evil" is humorous, whereas the following remark "and for good they do not know" is brutal frankness, perhaps even sarcasm. But Jeremiah's mind typically works in this sequence and we must be on the lookout for it in other places where it occurs.

In 12:13a we find an element of sequentiality present: sowing and reaping. The combination of sequentiality and contrast sets up incongruity: thorns are reaped where wheat was sown. This type of thinking too, as we have already seen, is characteristically Jeremianic.

Only rarely do we find chiasmi with verbs at the center:

2:36b So by Egypt   גם ממצרים
      you will be shamed   תבושי
      as you were shamed   כאשר־בשת
      by Assyria   מאשור

10:11[10] The gods which the heavens   אלהיא די־שמיא וארקא
              and earth
      did not make   לא עבדו
      shall perish   יאבדו
    from the earth and under   מארעא ומן־תחות שמיא אלה
              the heavens

51:38 Together like lions   יחדו ככפרים
      they shall roar   ישאגו
      they shall growl   נערו
      like lion's whelps   כגורי אריות

Sometimes the use of a "double-duty" subject[11] in the center makes an even more impressive pattern:

They hold fast to deceit	החזיקו בתרמת
they refuse to repent (8:5)	מאנו לשוב
They have loved to wander thus	כן אהבו לנוע
they have not restrained their feet (14:10)	רגליהם לא חשכו

10. This verse is in Aramaic and intends a word-play with עבדו and יאבדו.

11. Dahood uses the term "double-duty" in his *Psalms*; see I, 17 and the index in III; also cf. "A New Metrical Pattern in Biblical Poetry."

4:2b	And they shall bless themselves	והתברכו
	in him	בו
	nations	גוים
	and in him	ובו
	shall they glory	ותהללו
4:30c	They despise	מאסו־
	you	בך
	lovers	עגבים
	your soul	נפשך
	they seek	יבקשו

In one instance Jeremiah manages a word-play:[12]

8:5a	Why then has it turned away	מדוע שובבה
	this people	העם הזה
	Jerusalem	ירושלם
	the 'turncoat' pre-eminent!	משבה נצחת

Particles are also structural indicators in Jeremiah. In 4-cola units they frequently repeat at the beginning of the center cola creating a partial chiasmus:

6:8	Be warned O Jerusalem	הוסרי ירושלם
	lest I be alienated from you	פֶּן־תקע נפשי ממך
	lest I make you a desolation	פֶּן־אשימך שממה
	an uninhabited land	ארץ לוא נושבה
8:13	Gathering I will end them	אסף אסיפם
	no grapes on the vine	אֵין ענבים בגפן
	no figs on the fig tree	וְאֵין תאנים בתאנה
	even the leaves are withered	והעלה נבל
9:21 [9:22]	The dead bodies of men shall fall	ונפלה נבלת האדם
	like dung on the open field	כַּדמן על־פני השדה
	like sheaves after the reaper	וּכְעמיר מאחרי הקצר
	and none shall gather them	ואין מאסף
13:16a	Give glory to Yahweh your God	תנו ליהוה אלהיכם כבוד
	before it grows dark	בטרם יחשך
	before your feet stumble	ובטרם יתנגפו רגליכם
	on the mountains at twilight	על־הרי נשף

---

12. See prior discussion of 8:5a on pp. 73–74.

17:1 The sin of Judah is written   חטאת יהודה כתובה
    with a pen of iron   בְּעֵט בַּרְזֶל
    with a point of diamond   בְּצִפֹּרֶן שָׁמִיר
    it is engraved on the tablet   חֲרוּשָׁה עַל־לוּחַ לִבָּם
        of their heart

A construction of the same type is found in Deut 32:27, which
may perhaps have provided Jeremiah with a prototype.[13]

Deut 32:27   לוּלֵי כַּעַס אוֹיֵב אָגוּר
         פֶּן־יְנַכְּרוּ צָרֵימוֹ
         פֶּן־יֹאמְרוּ יָדֵינוּ רָמָה
         וְלֹא יהוה פָּעַל כָּל־זֹאת

Had I not feared provocation by the enemy
    lest their adversaries should judge amiss
    lest they should say, 'Our hand is triumphant
Yahweh has not wrought all this'

    Key nouns can also come at the end of center cola in partial
chiasmi.

4:19 My bowels, my bowels, I am sick   מֵעַי מֵעַי אוֹחִילָה
    Oh, the walls of *my heart*   קִירוֹת לִבִּי
    a commotion within *my heart*   הֹמֶה־לִי לִבִּי
    I cannot keep silent   לֹא אַחֲרִישׁ

12:10 Many shepherds have destroyed   רֹעִים רַבִּים שִׁחֲתוּ כַרְמִי
        my vineyard
    they have trampled down   בֹּסְסוּ אֶת־חֶלְקָתִי
        my portion
    they have made my   נָתְנוּ אֶת־חֶלְקַת חֶמְדָּתִי
        pleasant *portion*
    a desolate wilderness   לְמִדְבַּר שְׁמָמָה

    These partial chiasmi function to retard movement. The
repetition at the center gives the thought pause for embellishment before it is then carried on to completion in the final colon.
    In 9:3 [Eng. 9:4] key nouns provide balance in all four cola.
This chiasmus was noted long ago by John Forbes.[14]

---

    13. In David's lament over Saul and Jonathan (2 Sam 1:20), two cola
beginning with פֶּן *end* a 4-cola unit.
    14. *The Symmetrical Structure of Scripture*, 37.

9:3 [9:4]   אִישׁ מֵרֵעֵהוּ הִשָּׁמֵרוּ וְעַל־כָּל־אָח אַל־תִּבְטָחוּ
כִּי כָל־אָח עָקוֹב יַעְקֹב וְכָל־רֵעַ רָכִיל יַהֲלֹךְ

Let everyone beware of *his neighbor*
   and put no trust in *any brother*
   for *every brother* is a 'Jacob'
and *every neighbor* goes about as a slanderer

Jeremiah has another characteristic way of using the chiasmus to balance contrasting terms while keeping the thought the same. Holladay first noted this in 14:2.[15]

14:2   Judah mourns   אבלה יהודה
         her gates languish   ושעריה אמללו
            they lament on the ground   קדרו לארץ
         and the cry of Jerusalem goes up   וצוחת ירושלם עלתה

As Holladay points out the recognition of a chiasmus here clears up finally the subject of the third colon. It is not "people," which the RSV supplies as a bonus, but "gates." Jeremiah is speaking figuratively of "gates lamenting on the ground."[16] The middle cola are then parallel. Holladay also calls attention to Jeremiah's play on the vertical. Cola 1–3 depict people and gates lying *down* while colon 4 speaks of the cry of the people going *up*. Nevertheless 1 and 4 convey the same idea making the whole a chiasmus.

A similar structure occurs in 20:14, which opens the poem in which Jeremiah curses his birth:

20:14 Cursed be the day   ארור היום
         on which I was born   אשר ילדתי בו
            the day when my mother   יום אשר־ילדתני אמי
               bore me
         let it not be blessed   אל־יהי ברוך

Like 14:2, the center cola balance and colon 4 repeats colon 1 only casting the thought in the negative. The contrast is seen in the beginning and ending words "cursed/blessed," which, if taken alone, make an inclusio. We therefore think that the unit

---

15. "Style, Irony and Authenticity in Jeremiah," 51–52.
16. The gates *lift up* their heads in Ps 24:7, 9.

is self-contained making a stanza within the poem. The next cluster of four cola (20:15) is similar with the terms ארור (cursed) and שמח שמחהו (making him very glad) appearing in the same collocations. This we take to be a second stanza in the poem. With these two stanzas thus delimited we can therefore propose a 2:2:2:2:2 structure, which is how we took the poem earlier.[17]

The preceding opens up yet another line of research for the Jeremianic speeches. Because 14:2 and 20:14 are both regarded as beginning their respective poems in addition to their being similarly structured, we should not seem to be going too far amiss if we suggest that perhaps the poems *en toto* were written alike. It seems that such is the case. Like 20:14–18, 14:2–6 is easily delimited. Verse 2 is preceded by a superscription and chapter number in v. 1, and the lower limit is fixed at v. 6 because of the liturgy isolated in vv. 7–9.[18] Now if 14:2 is also a stanza of two lines as it appears, we can break down the remaining verses into stanzas of two lines each, which then results in 14:2–6 being a 2:2:2:2:2 structure just like 20:14–18.[19] The implications of this should be obvious. For the first time we are now able to see Jeremiah the poet writing at least two of his poems alike, i.e., with similar beginnings and the same number of 2-line stanzas. We know that modern poets and song-writers allow structures to repeat from one work to another, and it should come as a surprise to no one that the same obtained with the ancients. As we increase our understanding of Hebrew poetic structure we will probably find even more structures which repeat from poem to poem.

---

17. See p. 65.

18. We looked at 14:7–9 earlier; see p. 65.

19. I would divide up 14:2–6 as follows:

2 אבלה יהודה ושעריה אמללו
קדרו לארץ וצוחת ירושלם עלתה

3 ואדריהם שלחו צעוריהם למים באו על־גבים
לא־מצאו מים שבו כליהם ריקם

בשו והכלמו וחפו ראשם
4 בעבור האדמה חתה כי לא־היה גשם בארץ

בשו אכרים חפו ראשם
5 כי גם־אילת בשדה ילדה ועזוב כי לא־היה דשא

6 ופראים עמדו על־שפים שאפו רוח כתנים
כלו עיניהם כי־אין עשב

We will now look at a few instances where Jeremiah creates
a chiasmus by assonance. Assonance is a major stylistic feature
in Jeremiah, but when it provides poetry with balance it becomes a structural feature as well.

5:22   האותי לא־תיראו נאם־יהוה אם מפני לא תָחִילוּ
אשר־שמתי חול גבול לים חק־עולם ולא יעברנהו

6:1c–2a   כי רעה נשקפה מִצָּפוֹן ושבר גדול
הנוה והמענגה דמיתי בַּת־צִיּוֹן

20:11   ויהוה אותי כגבור עריץ על־כן רדפי יִכָּשְׁלוּ ולא יֻכָלוּ
בשו מאד כי־לא הִשְׂכִּילוּ כלמת עולם לא תשכח

48:3–4   קול צְעָקָה מחרונים שד וָשֶׁבֶר גדול
נִשְׁבְּרָה מואב השמיעו זְעָקָה צעוריה

Our two final examples of chiasmus within the Jeremianic
poem are slightly larger. Here we begin to see how balanced
terms throughout the unit create a pattern that is commonly
found in whole poems. Chiasmus is now more than syntactic re-
versals or inversion patterns within the 2-line stanza; it becomes
a structure by which large panels are ordered.

2:27b–28a   ובעת רעתם יאמרו
קוּמָה והושיענו
ואיה אלהיך אשר עשית לך
יקוּמוּ אם־יוֹשִׁיעוּךָ
בעת רעתך

But *in the time of their trouble* they say
    '*arise* and *save us*'
        but where are your gods which you made for yourselves?
    let them *arise* if they can *save* you
in your time of trouble

Here Yahweh takes the people's own words to use against them.
But the climax is still in the center where the people are given a
"loaded question" which they cannot answer without first ad-
mitting their guilt.

The chiastic structure in 4:19c–21 also appears to delimit a
stanza within a poem. Since 4:19–22 is generally taken to be a
unit (so Condamin and Bright) and we have earlier isolated both

19ab and 22,[20] our poem thus becomes a 2:4:3 structure, which again should warn us not to be overly predisposed to finding stanzas of equal length.

4:19c–21

כי <u>קול שופר שמעתי</u>
נפשי <u>תרועת</u> מלחמה
שבר על־שבר נקרא
כי <u>שדדה</u> כל־הארץ
פתאם <u>שדדו</u> אהלי
רגע יריעתי
עד־מתי אראה־<u>נס</u>
<u>אשמעה קול שופר</u>

For the *sound of the trumpet* / you have *heard* [21]
   O my soil, the *alarm* of battle
      disaster comes hard on disaster
         for the whole land is *laid waste*
         suddenly my tents are *laid waste*
      in a moment my curtains
   how long must I see the *standard*
must I *hear* / the *sound of the trumpet*?

Here Jeremiah is in conversation with himself. Key terms at the extremes and in the center make the chiasmus, with an added feature being the inversion of terms in the final colon. We may also have a fixed pair in תרועת (alarm) and נס (standard).

These examples should suffice to show how Jeremiah uses the chiasmus in building smaller portions of the prophetic speech. We will now go on to whole poems where the chiasmus becomes the controlling structure.

Chiastic Poems in Jeremiah

Two criteria can be used to identify chiastic poems in Jeremiah: (1) key words and (2) speaker. If either alternate to form an ABA' or expanded type arrangement, we call this a chiasmus. Some poems have only key word balance while others only a

---

20. On 19ab see p. 89; on 22 see p. 72.
21. Against the RSV, we read the MT which preserves the archaic 2fs form שמעתי "you have heard"; Jeremiah is in conversation with himself (cf. 3:19; 5:4–5).

balance of speaker. But many have both working simulta-
neously to create coterminous stanzas. The one then becomes a
control for the other giving added support for the divisions
made. We will look at 12 chiastic poems in all.

2:5–9

We begin with a poem that has been unsuccessfully modeled by
form-critics on the lawsuit genre. It might have been analyzed
form-critically as a "letter" since it has *both* the opening and
closing messenger formulas, but form-critics generally ignore
these. Actually there is no agreement on how the material in
chapter 2 is to be delimited. Volz takes 1–19 as a unit, Rudolph
2–13. Bright ends at 13 but considers 2–3 separate. As we mentioned earlier, Meek isolated 2–3 because they are also framed
by opening and closing formulas.[22] We will argue, however, that
5–9 is an independent poem since its controlling structure is a
chiasmus, both of key words and of speaker.[23]

כה אמר יהוה   5

A   מה־מצאו <u>אבותיכם</u> בי עול כי רהקו מעלי
<u>וילכו אחרי ההבל</u> ויהבלו

B 6   <u>ולא אמרו איה יהוה</u> המעלה אתנו מארץ מצרים[24]
בארץ ערבה ושוחה בארץ ציה וצלמות[25]

C 7   <u>ואביא אתכם אל־ארץ</u> הכרמל לאכל פריה וטובה
ותבאו ותטמאו <u>את־ארצי</u> ונחלתי שמתם לתועבה

B' 8   הכהנים <u>לא אמרו איה יהוה</u> ותפשי התורה לא ידעוני
והרעים פשעו בי והנביאים נבאו בבעל

A'   <u>ואחרי לא־יועלו הלכו</u>
לכן עד אריב אתכם נאם־יהוה ואת־<u>בני בניכם</u> אריב 9

---

22. See p. 23.

23. Some but not all of the key words are noted by Condamin.

24. Delete המוליך אתנו במדבר as an explanatory gloss. Its function is to
clarify the ב of the following בארץ. Without it not only is the transition
from Egypt to the Wilderness abrupt, but there could also be ambiguity
about which *land* is being talked of, the *land of Egypt* or the *land of the Wilderness*. The gloss clears this up: the land of desert and pits, drought and
death-shadows is the Wilderness. The gloss appears to be a conflation of
לכתך אחרי במדבר בארץ . . . in 2:2 (part of which is lacking in the LXX but

5   Thus says Yahweh

      What wrong did *your fathers* find in me
          that they wandered far from me?

A

      They went/ after worthlessness
        and became worthless

6   *They did not say, 'Where is Yahweh*
           who brought us up from the land of Egypt[24]

B

        Into a land of deserts and pits
           into a land of drought and death shadows'[25]

7   And *I brought you into* a garden *land*
             to enjoy its fruits and its good things

C

          But when *you came in* you defiled *my land*
             and made my heritage an abomination

8   The priests *did not say, 'Where is Yahweh?'*
           those who handle the law did not know me

B′

      The shepherds transgressed against me
        the prophets prophesied by Baal

    And *after what does not profit / they went*
      [. . . . . ?]

9   A′   Therefore I still contend with you—oracle of Yahweh
      and with *your children's children* I will contend

The key words give the structure of the poem in outline. Let us look at them. In A "your fathers" balances "your children's children" in A′.[26] Jeremiah uses the extremes here to state the prevailing theology that the sins of the fathers are meted out on their children (but see later 31:29–30 where the Jeremianic theology changes). Also in AA′ our stanzas are balanced by the verb הלך with אחרי and different expressions meaning "worthlessness": הבל and לא־יועלו. The inverted syntax is also nice. We saw this frequently in the inclusio and it works in the chiastic

---

which is nevertheless genuine) and בעת מוליכך בדרך in 2:17 (which is absent in the LXX and is definitely itself a gloss). The H Stem of הלך is here the mark of an editor. For a more complete explanation of this expansion see the discussion to follow.

25. Delete בארץ לא־עבר בה איש ולא־ישב אדם שם as more expansion perhaps intended to fill out a standard liturgical confession; see the discussion to follow and cf. n. 85 for a similar expansion following ארץ ציה וערבה in 51:43.

26. A few Mss. and the Vulgate omit בני.

return as well. B′ repeats "they did not say 'Where is Yahweh?' "
from B. The center (C) has its own internal balance repeating בוא
and ארץ.

The stanza division rests thus far upon the distribution of
key words. Breaking down stanzas in this way would perhaps
seem a bit unjustified were it not known that stanzas in Lamentations 1–2 also contain key words arranged chiastically.[27]
But there an acrostic form provides us with a welcome control.
In Jeremiah there are no acrostics—at least so far as we know—
yet we have a control of another kind. That control is a coexist-
ing chiasmus of speaker. It can work one of two ways. If a single
speaker is narrating throughout, the direct address of various
speakers is introduced in balancing stanzas making the whole a
chiasmus. This is what we have here in 2:5–9. Yahweh is the
narrator. In B he introduces the direct speech of the fathers and
in B′ the direct speech of the priests. Thus Yahweh speaks in A;
the fathers in B; Yahweh in C; the priests (= the fathers) in B′;
and Yahweh concludes in A′. This chiasmus of speaker is very
similar to the one in Deut 1:20–31 which Moses narrated. In
these instances the chiasmus of speaker is not always coterminous with the stanza divisions delimited by key words. This is
most noticeable in B′ where Yahweh narrates the rest of the
stanza (and in B Yahweh also begins with "They did not say").
But we can say that here as well as in other poems where the
same occurs, the quotes of the various speakers never violate
stanza divisions, and in most cases they balance each other
within the poem rather nicely. The second way a chiasmus of
speaker can work is in dialogue poems where two or three par-
ties are in conversation—sometimes with each other, sometimes
with an audience who does not participate—in which cases the
chiasmus of speaker *is coterminous* with the key-word divisions.
Here then we have an excellent control every bit as good as the
acrostic for our division of poems into stanzas.

Now a word about the poem's original form. It will be noted
that without the proposed deletions B would be more than three
full lines. Since the remaining stanzas are all two lines it is reasonable to suppose that B has been expanded. The deletions we

---

27. Condamin, "Symmetrical Repetitions in *Lamentations* Chapters I
and II"; cf. n. 181 on p. 35.

propose appear to us to be scribal glosses added either for purposes of clarification or because an expanded form of the confession was desired at a later time in worship. This is discussed
more fully in the notes. The poem in its original form was then
2:2:2:2:2:2 just like 14:2–6 and 20:14–18.[28]

Finally we must see how structure affects meaning. Jeremiah begins by asking a question about the "fathers." Who are
they? Are they fathers of those present in Jeremiah's audience?
Or are they fathers from the distant past, say the fathers of the
Exodus? We don't know. The second stanza narrows it down
some by saying that these fathers did not remember Yahweh
who brought Israel out of Egypt. The fathers must then be at
least "post-Exodus."

The third stanza (C) brings us up to the Conquest. This is
when things began to go bad and the center of the chiasmus un-
derscores the turning point. Yahweh brought the people into a
"garden land" but in due time they ravaged it. B′ returns to pick
up the thought of B and expands upon it. It also identifies the
fathers. They are the nation's leaders, i.e., the priests, scribes,
kings (= shepherds) and prophets. *All* can be faulted in one way
or another for not asking "Where is Yahweh?" The identification
is made more sure by the words of A′: ואחרי לא־יועלו הלכו. A′
contains judgment which is both contemporary and futuristic.
Yahweh will judge those listening as well as their children for
the sins of Israel's "fathers."

If the audience was made up of ordinary citizens they
would realize, but only at the poem's end, that judgment was
aimed at *them.* The part about the fathers, the nation's leaders,
was foil. The last line is the cap. Jeremiah wants most of all to
say that judgment is to come to the common people. These
would no doubt support Jeremiah as he flayed the nation's leaders, because if the leaders can be blamed for the nation's ills the
rest of the people can rest secure in their innocence. But Jeremiah counters this with "Therefore I still contend with *you*—
oracle of Yahweh—and with *your children's children* I will contend." We saw this same strategy employed in 5:26–31.[29] The

---

28. See pp. 90–91.
29. See p. 59.

real "twist" is saved for the very end, and even then, only those with ears to hear are likely to perceive it.

One final point before leaving this poem. A comparison of key phrases with phrases in the poem that precedes and the poem that follows shows how three poems have been linked into a chain. The line . . . לכתך אחרי במדבר בארץ (2:2) is a link to וילכו אחרי ההבל (2:5) making a chain of 2:2–3 and 2:5–9. The second link is made by the phrases לא־יועלו (2:8) and בלוא יועיל (2:11). These make a chain of 2:5–9 and 2:10–13.[30] Such links can best be explained as mnemonic devices which Jeremiah used to keep these early poems together (for 23 years; cf. 25:3; 36:2). Otherwise we must suppose that someone else created a chain of poems for an early period of oral transmission.

2:33–37

Commentators are likewise not in agreement on the literary unit here. The conclusion of the poem is fairly well established because v. 37 ends the chapter. Bright takes 29–37 as a unit which follows the Massoretic division, but says that this is composed of two parts each having a separate origin. One of these is 33–37.[31] Condamin also takes 33–37 as a unit and even notices some of its balancing terms, but he characteristically misses the proper structure because of his strophic biases.[32] Actually, upon close examination this poem can be shown to be one of the most fully and intricately balanced in the book. It breaks down into three unequal but proportioned stanzas with the center stanza one half the length of the stanzas on either side. The poem is then 4:2:4, and enlarged form of a rhythmic pattern discovered by Dahood in the bi-colon.[33]

---

30. Verses 10–13 must be a separate poem since v. 14 begins a new poem extending to v. 19 (so Gunkel and others; cf. p. 15).

31. Bright, *Jeremiah*, 18: "Finally, in vv. 29–37 there is a further unit of two parts (vv. 29–32, 33–36 [sic]), which were probably of separate origin . . ."

32. Condamin, *Le Livre de Jérémie*, 20.

33. In his article, "A New Metrical Pattern in Biblical Poetry," Dahood notes how a term doing "double-duty" can make a short center for the bi-colon. Dahood is counting syllables, but in most cases the center is about *one-half* of what remains on either side.

מַה־תֵּיטְבִי <u>דַּרְכֵּךְ</u> לְבַקֵּשׁ אַהֲבָה   33

לָכֵן <u>גַּם</u> אֶת־הָרָעוֹת לִמַּדְתְּ אֶת־דְּרָכָיִךְ

<u>גַּם</u> בִּכְנָפַיִךְ נִמְצְאוּ דַּם נַפְשׁוֹת אֶבְיוֹנִים נְקִיִּים   A

<u>לֹא</u>־בַמַּחְתֶּרֶת מְצָאתִים <u>כִּי</u> עַל־כָּל־אֵלֶּה   34

<u>וַתֹּאמְרִי</u> כִּי נִקֵּיתִי אַךְ שָׁב אַפּוֹ מִמֶּנִּי   35

הִנְנִי נִשְׁפָּט אוֹתָךְ עַל־<u>אָמְרֵךְ</u> לֹא חָטָאתִי   B

מַה־תֵּזְלִי מְאֹד <u>לְשַׁנּוֹת אֶת־דַּרְכֵּךְ</u>   36

<u>גַּם</u> מִמִּצְרַיִם תֵּבוֹשִׁי כַּאֲשֶׁר־בֹּשְׁתְּ מֵאַשּׁוּר

<u>גַּם</u> מֵאֵת זֶה תֵּצְאִי וְיָדַיִךְ עַל־רֹאשֵׁךְ   A'

<u>כִּי</u>־מָאַס יְהוָה בְּמִבְטַחַיִךְ <u>וְלֹא</u> תַצְלִיחִי לָהֶם   37

33   *How* well you direct *your way*
      to seek love
      So *even* to wicked women
       you have taught your ways
34   A   *Even* on your skirts is found
       the blood of innocent men[34]
      Not breaking in you found them
       for yet in spite of all these things

35   *You say*, 'For I am innocent
        surely his anger has turned from me'
   B   Behold I will sentence you
        for *your saying* 'I have not sinned'

36   *How* lightly you gad about
       to change *your way*
      Even by Egypt you will be shamed
       as you were shamed by Assyria
37   A'   *Even* from this you will come away
       with your hands upon your head
      For Yahweh has rejected your 'trusted ones'
       not letting you prosper by them

The poem literally teems with balanced terms. AA' both begin their first lines ... לְ .... מַה, and alternate the position of דרך. Each second and third line begins with גם except line 2 of A which modifies to לכן גם. Then stanza 1 ends with

---

34. LXX omits אביונים; Bright and *JB* follow.

. . . . . . כִּי . . . . . לֹא, while stanza 3 inverts to . . . . . וְלֹא . . . . . כִּי. The center (B) is framed nicely by the repetition of אמר in the first and last cola. Also in the center we have another *speaker* introduced: Yahweh quotes the people who twice protest innocence, first in positive then in negative terms.

This poem begins by ironically applauding Israel's efforts to find a 'love.' She was apparently successful although we are not told at the beginning who the lover or lovers might be. Bright thinks they are the fertility gods[35] which is likely enough since idolatry is the major theme of chapter 2. But the structure of the poem forces a connection between A and A' suggesting that Israel's love affair is with Egypt. All the echoes of A in A' help make the connection. The affair with Assyria is over and Egypt is the new lover. But Jeremiah says the new love will end just as the old one did—in shame. Yahweh's sentence of judgment comes in the center, but the audience is not lost because the lover is yet to be named. After the identification the poem ends much the way it began, ironically mentioning Israel's "trusted ones" (מבטחיך).

<u>5:1–8</u>

This poem is rather easily delimited. The chapter division marks the upper limit while the Massoretes close a section at the end of v. 9. Since v. 9 is that stereotyped verse found elsewhere in 5:29 and 9:8, we take it as a later addition. The structure of this poem is seen correctly if not in detail at least in broad outline by both Condamin and Bright. Condamin notes some of the key terms, and Bright recognizes also that the phrase "Why should I forgive you" in v. 7 resumes a theme stated in v. 1. Bright also recognizes that a dialogue is going on between Yahweh and Jeremiah.[36] Jeremiah is faced with the challenge of finding a righteous man in Jerusalem much in the same way Abraham was challenged when Sodom's fate was in the balance (Gen 18:22–33). Both precede Diogenes in Athens, yet Jeremiah by a mere 250 years.

---

35. Bright, *Jeremiah*, 16.
36. Ibid., 41.

שוטטו בחוצות ירושלם וראו־נא ודעו 1

ובקשו ברחובותיה אם־תמצאו **איש**

A

אם־יש עשה משפט מבקש אמונה <u>ואסלה לה</u>

ואם חי־יהוה יאמרו לכן לשקר <u>ישבעו</u> 2

יהוה עיניך הלוא לאמונה 3

<u>הכיתה אתם</u> ולא־חלו כליתם מאנו קחת מוסר B

חזקו פניהם מסלע מאנו לשוב

ואני אמרתי אך־<u>דלים</u> הם נואלו 4

<u>כי לא ידעו דרך יהוה משפט אלהיהם</u>

C

אלכה־לי אל־<u>הגדלים</u> ואדברה אותם 5

<u>כי המה ידעו דרך יהוה משפט אלהיהם</u>

אך המה יחדו שברו על נתקו מוסרות 6

על־כן <u>הכם</u> אריה מיער זאב ערבות ישדדם B'

נמר שקד על־עריהם כל־היוצא מהנה יטרף

כי רבו פשעיהם עצמו משבותיהם

אי לזאת <u>אסלוח־לך</u> בניך עזבוני <u>וישבעו</u> בלא אלהים 7

ואשבע אותם וינאפו ובית זונה יתגדדו A'

סוסים מיזנים משכים היו **איש** אל־אשת רעהו יצהלו 8

1 Run back and forth in the streets of Jerusalem
  look please and take note
  Search in her squares (to see)
  A   if you can find a *man*
  If one exists who does justice
  searching for truth, that *I may pardon her*
2 For if they say, 'As Yahweh lives'
  surely in vain *they swear*

3 O Yahweh, your eyes
  do they not look for truth?
  You have smitten them, but they felt no anguish
  B   you annihilated them, but they refused to
  take correction
  They have made their faces harder than rock
  they refuse to repent

4   Then I thought, but these are the *poor*
               they have no sense
           For they know not Yahweh's way
      C   *the law of their God*
5   I will go to the *great*
               and I will speak to them
           For they know Yahweh's way
               the law of their God

          But both alike had broken the yoke
               they had burst the bonds
6   Therefore *it will smite them*, a lion from the forest
      B'   and a wolf from the desert will devour them
          A leopard is watching over their cities
               anyone going out from them will be torn apart
          For their crimes are many
               their regressions great

7   How then can I *pardon you*?
               your sons have forsaken me
               and *have sworn* by 'no gods'
      A'   When I fed them to the full they fornicated
               and to whore-houses they trooped
8   They were well-fed lusty stallions
               each *man* neighing for his neighbor's wife

This emerges as a nicely formed 5-stanza poem with a
4:3:4:4:3 structure. Here we see the key word and speaker chiasmi coinciding perfectly, the latter clearing up what has otherwise been a speaker problem in the poem.[37] Yahweh is the
speaker in A and A' and Jeremiah the speaker in B, C and B'. The
audience varies but for the most part can be quite easily
identified. Yahweh speaks to Jeremiah in A, although the plural
imperatives, שוטטו . . . וראו־נא ודעו etc. indicate that Jeremiah
must be part of a larger search company. In B Jeremiah addresses Yahweh: in C he is in conversation with himself; and in
B' he is either addressing Yahweh again or speaking in a non-

---

37. Rudolph in *BH*[3] suggested we delete ואסלח לה from 5:1 (*propheta
loquitur* in 1–6), but in the new *BHS* this suggestion is given up in favor of
another which would allow Yahweh to be the speaker in v. 1. He now proposes that at the end of v. 1 we add נאם־יהוה. Neither change is necessary.
The chiastic structure to be shown makes it clear that Yahweh is the
speaker in vv. 1–2.

direct way to the people. Yahweh concludes the poem by speaking to the people in A'. The use of the second person "you" in "How can I pardon you?" makes the final words very direct. We see again a type of rhetoric that begins at a distance but comes in close at the end.

The people presumably know the Yahweh-Abraham dialogue (Gen 18:22–33), and knowing also the outcome they may perhaps wonder if history will not be repeated. Yet the dialogue unfolds in its own unique way. The answer and added subtleties of interpretation come gradually. The repetition at the center marks the turning point even if it does not contain the actual judgment. The poor have been examined and now also the great, which means that *everyone* has been seen. The indictment and judgment follow swiftly in B'. The key word נכה (smite) in B' creates and added subtlety. Yahweh has *smitten* the people previously (B) but now Jeremiah uses metaphors (lion, wolf and leopard) to speak of the enemy poised for attack on Jerusalem. The enemy thus remains unnamed, but if we associate B' with B as Jeremiah intends, it then becomes clear that *Yahweh* is the one *coming again to smite*; he is the enemy even more than the bands of marauders or the Babylonian army.[38] Jeremiah thus understands full well the theology of the Sodom and Gomorrah incident (Gen 19:24).[39]

The key words in the final stanza force an association with stanza 1 making the judgment certain. Yet the final word from Yahweh is a question, "How then can I pardon you?" to which

---

38. Much discussion has been generated about the identity of the "Foe from the North" (1:13ff.), whether it refers to roving bands of marauders (Jer 18:22; 2 Kgs 24:2), the Scythians mentioned by Herodotus in his *Histories* (Book I, 105), or the Babylonian army. For a balanced discussion of the problem, see H. H. Rowley, "The Early Prophecies of Jeremiah in Their Setting," *BJRL* 45 (1962–63), 206ff.

39. In Genesis 18–19 the Yahwist has reworked an earlier version of the story. Note the different designations for the arsonists. They are called אנשים (men) in 18:2, 16, 22; 19:5, 8, 12, 16; and מלאכים (messengers/angels) in 19:1, 15. In 19:18 Lot addresses them as אדני (lords), and if it is to one of them that Abraham speaks in 18:23–33, then we have three additional occurrences of אדני in vv. 30–32. These strands of saga show a gradual progression of theological understanding. In the beginning it was *men* who set the city on fire. But such were later perceived not as ordinary but as divine men, thus the designation "messengers." In the final version, which is the work of the Yahwist, *Yahweh* is the one who destroys Sodom and Gomorrah (19:24).

the people must supply an answer. If they concede that a righteous man has not been found they can only answer "No" to this question. But the audience is still left with a choice—even though it is not really much of a choice—and this is what distinguishes the Jeremianic speeches from those which are dogmatically judgmental. Dialogue is open to the very end—and even after the end.

This poem has a center very much like 2:5–9. In both the normal kind of alternating parallelism acts as a hinge upon which the whole poem can swing. This would seem to support Lund who made a definite point about the centers of chiastic structures being pivot points.[40]

6:1–7

This poem and the one following (6:8–12) have the same number of lines and both are 4:4:4. They also have same words and sounds in identical collocations, besides containing a chiasmus of speaker. We are justified then in calling them companion poems. Not only were they written alike, but it appears that because of their similarities they were also grouped together in the collection process. After we have analyzed each poem separately we will discuss the two together.

The beginning of this poem is marked correctly by the chapter division, but most commentators break after v. 8 because of the introductory formula כה אמר יהוה צבאות beginning v. 9. This suggests that 9ff. is a new poem which it is not. After we have outlined 8–12 this will become clear. For now let us look at 1–7.

1		העזו בני בנימן מקרב ירושלם
	A	ובתקוע תקעו שופר ועל־בית הכרם שאו משאת
		כי רעה נשקפה מצפון ושבר גדול
2		הנוה והמענגה דמיתי בת־ציון
3		תקעו עליה אהלים סביב רעו איש את־ידו[41]
4	B	קדשו עליה מלחמה קומו ונעלה בצהרים
		אוי לנו כי־פנה היום כי ינטו צללי־ערב
5		קומו ונעלה בלילה ונשחיתה ארמנותיה

----

40. Law 1 says that "The centre is always the turning point"; cf. *Chiasmus in the New Testament*, 40ff.

41. Omit אליה יבאו רעים ועדריהם as an explanatory gloss providing the subject for תקעו.

⁴²כרתו עצה ושפכו　על־<u>ירושלם</u> סללה　　6

היא העיר הפקד　כלה עשק <u>בקרבה</u>

כהקיר בור מימיה　כן הקרה רעתה　　A'　7

חמס ושד ישמע בה　על־פני תמיד הלי ומכה

1　Flee for safety, O people of Benjamin
　　from the midst of Jerusalem
　Blow the trumpet in Tekoa
A′　and on Beth-hak-kerem raise a signal
　For evil looms out of the north
　　and great destruction
2　The comely and delicately bred I will destroy
　　the daughter of Zion

3　⁴¹They shall pitch their tents around her
　　they shall pasture, each in his place
4　'Sanctify war against her
　　up, and let us attack at noon'
B　'Woe to us, for the day declines
　　for the shadows of evening lengthen'
5　'*Up, and let us attack* by night
　　and destroy her palaces'

6　⁴² Cut down her trees and pour up
　　against *Jerusalem* a siege mound
　This is the city to be punished
A′　there is nothing but oppression *in her midst*
7　As a well keeps its water fresh
　　so she keeps fresh her wickedness
　Violence and destruction are heard within her
　　before me continually, sickness and wounds

Antiphony of speaker in vv. 4–5 has been noticed by Robert
Gordis who cited this as an example of how the speaker can
change without there being any obvious notations in the text.[43]
Lines 2 and 4 of B are the words of the enemy while line 3 articulates the cry of the frightened people inside Jerusalem. Yahweh is otherwise the narrator throughout ("I will destroy" in
v. 2; "before me continually" in v. 7). Jeremiah does not interject

---

42. Omit כי כה אמר יהוה צבאות as editorial similar to v. 9; cf. n. 45.

43. Robert Gordis, "Quotations as a Literary Usage in Biblical, Oriental and Rabbinic Literature," *HUCA* 22 (1949), 177.

himself at all into the poem unless we take him to be the voice of the people in the center ("Woe to us . . .").

Jeremiah's audience here appears to be the country folk from Benjamin who are living in Jerusalem. These are some of Jeremiah's own people (cf. 1:1) and Yahweh tells them to flee because the wealthy elite (הנוה והמענגה cf. Deut 28:54–56) are about to be destroyed. There is no argument here, no subtlety, no wait until the end to see who is really being addressed. The poem from beginning to end is very straightforward. The key words in A' merely break up the construct chain of A for variation.[44] We are thus looking at a different use of chiasmus. It functions not for argument but mainly for the sake of reinforcement.

6:8–12

In this poem we must argue for beginning and end. Verse 8 is not normally included because of the introductory formula כה אמר יהוה צבאות placed before v. 9. And because v. 12 is similar in content to 8:10a, and also because both introduce a stereotyped unit immediately following (6:13–15 = 8:10b–12), commentators take these verses as variants of a common original. Rudolph, for example, proposes that we delete the last line in v. 12 since it is not present in 8:10. In *BH³* his reason was that "propheta loquitur," but this is dropped in the new *BHS.* Our structure however will argue for the inclusion of both vv. 8 and 12.

הוסרי ירושלם פן־תקע נפשי ממך		8
פן־אשימך שממה ארץ לוא נושבה	A	
עוללו יעוללו כגפן שארית ישראל[45]		9
השב ידך כבוצר על־סלסלות		
על־מי אדברה ואעידה וישמעו		10
הנה ערלה אזנם ולא יוכלו להקשיב	B	
הנה דבר־יהוה היה להם לחרפה לא יחפצו־בו		
ואת חמת יהוה מלאתי נלאיתי הכיל		11

---

44. Recall the break-up of "cedars of Lebanon" in 22:6–7 (cf. pp. 67–68). An excellent article has been published on this phenomenon by Ezra Zion Melamed entitled, "Break-up of Stereotype Phrases as an Artistic Device in Biblical Poetry," in *ScrHier* 8 (1961), 115–53.

שפך על־עולל בחוץ ועל סוד בחורים יחדו
כי־גם־איש עם־אשה ילכדו זקן עם־מלא ימים
ונסבו בתיהם לאחרים שדות ונשים יחדו
כי־אטה את־ידי על־ישבי הארץ נאם־יהוה

A′ 12

8   Be warned O Jerusalem
        lest I be alienated from you
     Lest I make you a desolation
        an *uninhibited land*
9 A Glean thoroughly as a vine[45]
        the remnant of Israel
     Like a grape-gatherer pass *your hand* again
        over its branches

10   To whom shall I speak and give warning
            that they may hear?
         Behold, their ears are uncircumcised
            they cannot listen
      B *Behold*, the word of Yahweh is to them
            an object of scorn, they take no pleasure in it
11   Therefore I am full of the wrath of Yahweh
            I am weary of holding it in

     Pour it out upon the children in the street
        and upon the gatherings of young men also
     Both husband and wife shall be taken
        the old folk and the very aged
12 A′ Their houses shall be turned over to others
        their fields and wives together
     For I will stretch out *my hand*
        against the *inhabitants of the land*—oracle of Yahweh

So arranged this poem is 4:4:4 with key word and speaker chiasmi coinciding. The phrase ארץ לוא נושבה in A balances ישבי הארץ in A′. The other key word is יד (hand). In A it is the hand of the enemy and in A′ the hand of Yahweh. In the center הנה repeats as anaphora making this the pivot point of the poem.

Bright recognizes that a dialogue is going on, and so it turns out that the speakers break precisely where the stanzas break.

---

45. Omit כה אמר יהוה צבאות as editorial; cf. n. 42. Also read עֹלֵל for יְעוֹלְלוּ with Rudolph and most commentators.

Yahweh speaks in A and A′, Jeremiah in B. Yahweh shifts his audience however in A: he addresses the people in v. 8 and the enemy (not Jeremiah) in v. 9. The נאם־יהוה formula belongs right where it is at the end of v. 12, this time confirming the poem's end.

We must now look at 1–7 and 8–12 together. Both are 12 lines and 4:4:4. Both have chiastic structures based on key words and both have a chiasmus of speaker. In each case Yahweh begins and ends the dialogue with Jeremiah speaking in the center. Certain key words—in some cases those making the chiasmus, in other cases different words entirely—appear in identical collocations. "Jerusalem" is mentioned in the first line of each poem (in 1–7 it helped form the chiasmus). Next we note that the third stanza of each poem begins with the verb שפך (pour out/up). Equally impressive are plays on the same sounds.[46] First the verbs תקע and יקע. In 1–7 the second line of the poem begins וּבְתָקוֹעַ תִּקְעוּ creating a word-play on תקע acknowledged by all. This same verb begins in the next stanza (v. 3) only the meaning there is different making then another word-play. In 8–12 the first stanza opens with פֶּן־תֵּקַע נַפְשִׁי מִמֵּךְ. Here we have the similar sounding verb יקע. Now if we can presuppose some sophistication on the part of Jeremiah's audience, it is possible that the audience would hear not only word-plays within a specific poem, but would also recognize when similar sounds are repeated from poem to poem. There are more parallels. Throughout both poems the עַ and עוֹל sounds reverberate. The preposition עַל occurs no fewer than five times in each. A look at the final stanza of each poem will show also that it is this preposition which gives the stanza its own internal balance. Finally we have וְנַעֲלֶה repeated twice in 6:4, 5, and עוֹלֵל עוֹלָל (or עוֹלֵל יְעוֹלְלוּ if one can make sense out of the MT) in 6:9 balancing עַל־עוֹלָל in 6:11b. It becomes quite obvious then that these poems had a much greater impact on the ancient ear than they have on the modern eye.

What do these similarities tell us? Were the poems delivered together, i.e., did they have a common *Sitz im Leben*? Possibly, but not necessarily so. Because of their juxtaposition in the text it seems safe to conclude that they were *collected* together. Their similarities in structure would make them a pair for mnemonic

---

46. Cf. n. 89 on p. 78 regarding the sound balance in Jer 17:5–8.

reasons. But we must not pass over lightly the fact that two poems *were written alike*. We have been saying all along that Jeremiah wrote poems with fixed structures, e.g., 4:4:4, 4:2:4; etc.,
but we now realize in addition that vocabulary and even certain
sounds can remain constant from poem to poem.

8:13–17

The limits of this poem are easily established. The preceding
unit (8:10–12) is found elsewhere in 6:13–15 which argues for
its independence. We also have both opening and closing formulas.[47] Bright takes these verses as a unit but says they are
composite. Volz and Condamin reflect the same opinion relocating all or parts of vv. 14–15. We see no reason for relocating v. 14,
but v. 15 could be independent since it is found again in 14:19
where it functions as the transitional verse of a liturgical unit. It
fits here, as our analysis will show, so we had best reserve judgment as to whether it is original to the poem or editorially inserted. The poem is 2:3:1:3:2 and nicely balanced by key words
and change of speaker. All point to a controlling chiasmus. One
single theme is reiterated: destruction is coming. And like 6:1–
7 we hear it discussed from both sides: Yahweh (the enemy) on
one side, and the people of Judah on the other.

אסף אסיפם נאם־יהוה אֵין ענבים בנפן
וְאֵין תאנים בתאנה והעלה נבל ואתן להם יעברום[48] A 13

על־מה אנחנו ישבים האספו
וְנבוא אל־עָרֵי המבצר ונדמה־שם B 14
כי יהוה אלהינו הדמנו וישקנו מי־ראש כי חטאנו
ליהוה[49]

קוה לשלום וְאֵין טוב לעת מרפה והנה בעתה C 15

מדן נשמע נחרת סוסיו
מקול מצהלות אביריו רעשה כל־הארץ B′ 16
וְיבואו ויאכלו ארץ ומלואה עִיר וישבי בה

כי הנני משלח בכם נחשים צפענים
אשר אֵין־להם לחש ונשכו אתכם נאם־יהוה A′ 17

---

47. The closing formula is lacking in the Greek, but we need not
delete with Rudolph.

13   Gathering I will end them
                oracle of Yahweh
    A   there is *nothing* on the grape vine (16)
            And *nothing* on the fig tree
                even the leaves are withered
                    and what I gave them has passed away from
                                                            them[48] (23)

14   Why do we sit still?
                gather together (12)
            And let us *enter* the fortified *cities*
    B   and be silent there (14)
            For Yahweh our God has silenced us
                given us poisoned water to drink
                    because we have sinned against Yahweh[49] (23)

15   C   We looked for peace, but *nothing* good came
                for a time of healing, but behold, terror (18)

16   From Dan is heard
                the snorting of their horses (8)
    B′   At the sound of their neighing stallions
                the whole land quakes (15)
            They enter to devour the land and all that fills it
                the *city* and those who dwell in it (19)

17   For behold I am sending among you
                poisonous serpents (14)
    A′ *Nothing* you do can charm them
            and they shall bite you
                oracle of Yahweh (16)

Stanzas 1 and 2 of this poem have long final lines which may
indicate expansion. The final colon of stanza 1 is lacking in the
Greek, and the final colon in stanza 2 sounds prosaic (cf. 3:25).
Yet a syllable count shows that all the stanzas have crescendo
which means that at minimum the long final lines fit the poem
in its final form.

---

48. Greek omits ואתן להם יעברום and Rudolph suggests we delete.
Bright (*Jeremiah*, 61) does not translate. Our earlier analysis (p. 88) would
seem to indicate that a nicely balanced 4-cola unit has been expanded.
49. The final colon sounds prosaic (cf. 3:25) and perhaps should be
deleted; see discussion following.

Key words and antiphony of speaker delimit the stanzas.
Yahweh is the speaker in A and A'. BB' and C are the people, or
more probably Jeremiah for the people. The particle of negation
אֵין is a key word in AA' and C, and I have exercised more than
the usual amount of freedom in translation in order to keep this
term constant. If the center stanza is original to the poem, then
Lund would be supported in his contention that key words
of chiastic structures frequently appear at the extremes *and at
the center.*[50] We also noted earlier[51] that אֵין together with אסף
formed an inclusio for the complex 8:13–9:21. In BB' we have
the verb בוא (to go, enter) and the noun עיר (city). And as we
have seen happen before, one stanza breaks up the terms of the
other. This is becoming a common feature now in the Jeremianic poems.

This poem is really one of despair. Jeremiah is advising the
people to return to the city, but with the knowledge that the se-
curity it ordinarily affords will not be enough to save them. His
remark in v. 14 ונדמה־שם (let us be silent there) is thus para-
phrastic (RSV translates "perish"). In case B does not make it
clear that Jeremiah has given up hope, B' does. The repetition of
עיר forces the conclusion that the *cities*—to which they are flee-
ing—will not be spared. The metaphors of A and A' do not co-
alesce, but the repetition of אֵין brings the argument together:
since Yahweh found *nothing* when he went to harvest his crop,
there is now *nothing* the people can do to escape the enemy come
to destroy. Note too the shift from "them" in A to "you" in A'
making Yahweh's word more direct.

8:18–21

The beginning of this poem is not seriously in doubt. It follows
the poem just discussed and most commentators take v. 18 as
the beginning. Only the first word is emended by some and
placed with the final line of the previous poem (so Bright following the LXX). This however is unnecessary. Agreement does
not exist on where the poem ends. Bright following the German

---

50. See Lund's third law of chiastic structures in *Chiasmus in the New
Testament*, 41. Lund refers in this law to *ideas* instead of key words, nevertheless most all his chiastic structures are based on the distribution of key
words.

51. In chapter II; see pp. 44–45.

commentators extends through v. 23 [Eng. 9:1].[52] The RSV breaks
after v. 21 which we take to be correct. The poem is 5 lines, which
is another fixed type used more than once by Jeremiah.

מבליגיתי עלי יגון עלי לבי דוי   A   18

הנה־קול[53] היהוה אין בציון אם־מלכה אין בה   B   19

מדוע הכעסוני בפסליהם בהבלי נכר   C

עבר קציר כלה קיץ ואנחנו לוא נושענו   B′   20

על־שבר בת־עמי השברתי קדרתי שמה החזקתני   A′   21

18   My joy is gone
A   grief is upon me
              my heart is sick (14)

19   Hark a cry[53]
B   'Is Yahweh not in Zion?
                        Is her King not in her?' (15)

                                Why then have they provoked me to
C   anger with their images
                              and with their foreign idols? (16)

20   The harvest is past
B′   the summer is ended
                          and we are not saved (18)

21   For the wound of the daughter of my people I
                                                      am wounded
A′   I mourn
              dismay has taken hold of me (20/21)

The controlling structure here is a chiasmus of speaker:
Jeremiah speaks in A; the people in B; Yahweh in C;[54] the people
again in B′; and Jeremiah finally in A′.

Two text problems merit attention. First the phrase מבליגיתי
עלי beginning the poem. Unsuccessful attempts to translate this

---

52. This view goes back to Duhm (*Jeremia*, 92), who is followed by
Rudolph (*Jeremia*, 64–65) and Volz (*Der Prophet Jeremia*, 110–12).

53. Delete שועת בת־עמי מארץ מרחקים as a gloss; see discussion to follow.

54. Volz, Rudolph and Hyatt all excised C (19b) as a gloss. Holladay,
however, has rightly argued for its genuineness; cf. "The So-called 'Deuteronomic Gloss' in Jeremiah VIII 19b," *VT* 12 (1962), 494–98.

go back at least to the LXX. The noun מבליגיתי is a *hapax legomenon* but comes from an attested verb בלג, which means "to smile" or "to look cheerful."[55] One can thus translate מבליגיתי "my cheerfulness," or as I have rendered it, "my joy." The problematic term is actually the following עלי. Rudolph says we should take this to be the verb עלה but emend to either עָלָה or יַעֲלֶה. A better suggestion comes from Professor Freedman who says that עלי could be the archaic form of the infinitive absolute (normally עָלֹה). This would obviate the need to emend and would also preserve what appears to be a word-play between this term and another עלי two words hence. That עלי is the preposition with its suffix, עָלַי, "upon me." The line is thus a tricolon instead of a bi-colon. For that matter all the lines except the one in the center are tri-cola. Jeremiah is here playing with *space* in the first two cola as he did in 8:4 and 14:2. He says, "My joy has gone *up*,[56] grief is upon me," i.e., come *down* upon me.

The second problem of text comes in line 2. The phrase מארץ מרחקים (from a land far off) is frequently taken as a gloss because it makes what otherwise appears to be a poem uttered in Judah sound exilic.[57] When the people say "Is Yahweh not in Zion? Is her King not in her?" they are expressing the commonly held idea that Zion was Yahweh's eternal dwelling place. Ever since the deliverance of Jerusalem during the reign of Hezekiah it had become dogma that Yahweh's temple was inviolable.[58] Jeremiah of course refutes this dogma in his Temple Sermon (Jeremiah 7, 26), and it is refuted here by Yahweh's interruption in C. I would propose only one change, and that is that we take all of שועת בת־עמי מארץ מרחקים as the gloss. The proper place to break is between קול and שועת since the two terms are redundant together. This has the added advantage of further reducing the length of the line so a crescendo can be seen in the poem as a whole. The syllable count will show this.

---

55. So *BDB* 114; *KBH* 40.

56. עלה can also have the meaning "to go away" (1 Kgs 15:19).

57. Bright following the RSV translates "far and wide through the land" (*Jeremiah*, 62, 64), but Volz "aus fernem Land" with the following comment: "Da die Leute im Land sind und die Worte nicht bedeuten können 'im Lande weit und breit' müssen die Worte als Glosse (oder als aus 8,14–17 versprengt) ausgeschieden werden"; cf. *Der Prophet Jeremia*, 111.

58. See Roland de Vaux, *Jerusalem and the Prophets* (Cincinnati: Hebrew Union College Press, 1965); also *Ancient Israel* II (New York: McGraw-Hill Book Co., 1965), 327.

To find crescendo here in a 5-line poem is significant since Holladay observed gradation in *another 5-line poem*, 4:23–26, only it was not crescendo but diminution.[59]

This poem is a well-structured chiasmus without the help of key words.[60] The center is clearly the climax. There Yahweh interrupts to answer the people's questions with one of his own. The break-up of the . . . מדוע . . . אם . . . . ה formula, which Holladay has called a "signature" of Jeremiah,[61] makes this clear. The people ask the first two rhetorical questions and Yahweh finishes with the third. Judgment is not given, but if the audience answers Yahweh's question they will be forced into making judgment themselves. Jeremiah meanwhile stands outside the argument and grieves. We hear from him at the beginning and again at the end. But in remaining outside he is not an onlooker, as A' makes perfectly clear: "For the wound of the daughter of my people I am wounded."

9:2–5 [Eng. 9:3–6]

Since the text here is troubled with various problems, the commentaries give us no help in delimiting this poem even though both vv. 2 and 5 have concluding formulas.[62] In their own way these adequately mark the limits of the poem. This has not been sufficiently recognized but will become clear after our analysis is completed. There is, however, some uncertainty about stanza formation. If we take the text as it stands the poem would divide 3:3:3. Yet we propose an original 3:2:2:3 because it seems as if a line has fallen out. Verse 3 was found earlier to be chiastic,[63] so we are inclined to take it as an independent stanza. This decision is not however crucial since in either case we have a chiastic structure; in one case it is ABA', in the other ABB'A'. The

---

59. "The Recovery of Poetic Passages of Jeremiah," 404–6.

60. One is tempted to leave בת־עמי (daughter of my people) in v. 19a since the term appears again in v. 21. But 19a is definitely a gloss; also we will see another poem, 17:13–16a (ahead, pp. 116–18), which has a chiasmus of speaker but *no* key word balance.

61. "Style, Irony and Authenticity in Jeremiah," 48. S. R. Driver pointed it out too as one of Jeremiah's characteristic expressions; cf. Driver, *An Introduction to the Literature of the Old Testament* (Cleveland and New York: World Publishing Co., 1967), 275.

62. Both are lacking in the Greek and Rudolph suggests we delete. Our analysis however will argue for their retention.

63. See p. 90.

poem has no obvious chiasmus of speaker; balanced vocabulary
alone shows the poem's structure in outline.

וידרכו את־לשונם קשתם שקר 2
ולא לאמונה גברו בארץ A
כי מרעה אל־רעה יצאו ואתי לא־ידעו נאם־יהוה

איש מרעהו השמרו ועל־כל־אח אל־תבטחו 3
כי כל־אח עקוב יעקב וכל־רע רכיל יהלך B

ואיש ברעהו יהתלו ואמת לא ידברו 4
[. . . .] B′

למדו לשונם דבר־שקר 5
העוה נלאו שבתך בתוך A′
מרמה במרמה מאנו דעת־אותי נאם־יהוה

2   They bend *their tongue*
      their bow is a *lie*[64]
   A   And not for truth
      are they mighty in the land
    For *from evil to evil* they go
      me/they do not know—oracle of Yahweh

3   *Each man* beware of his *neighbor*
       and put no trust in any brother
    B   For every brother is a 'Jacob'
       and every neighbor goes about as a slanderer

4   *Each man* deceives his *neighbor*
       and no one speaks the truth
   B′   [. . . .
      . . . .]

    They have taught their *tongues*
      to speak *lies*
   A′   Iniquity they commit
5   (. . . . ?)[65]
    More evil on more evil
      refusing to know/me—oracle of Yahweh

---

64. This translation is Professor Holladay's and came to me in a letter dated Nov. 18, 1966. See discussion to follow.

65. Hebrew unintelligible; all versions and commentaries follow the
Greek.

Since the Hebrew text is difficult most modern versions seek help from the Greek. Yet for a number of reasons we believe the Hebrew text to be more original even if it is more corrupt. Let us begin at the beginning. The translation of line 1 in A is Holladay's. He recognized that "bow" and "tongue" were meant to be synonyms and that the line is to be read as a partial chiasmus. Thus we do not need to follow the Greek which presupposes כקשת (like a bow). Jeremiah has broken up two very straightforward expressions: "they bend their bow" and "their tongue is a lie." The result is that *bow* becomes a metaphor for *tongue*. A' contains something of an echo: "They have taught their tongues to speak lies." This movement from the figurative to the literal is what we now expect from Jeremiah. So the translators must not be unduly faulted for their imprecise renderings. There were probably many in Jeremiah's original audience who also missed line 1. Actually the LXX translator did realize that the bent tongue was like a bent bow, and so he preserved the essential meaning. Unfortunately we cannot say more about the connection between A and A' because the text in A' is also in poor condition. There is a reference to "your house" which is unclear. Is this Yahweh's house? Perhaps the verse contained something too offensive for later scribes to let stand. In 23:11 wickedness in Yahweh's house is mentioned. In any event the poem is primarily concerned with the mistrust between persons who are normally very close to each other: neighbor and brother. Some malicious talk was evidently circulating among the clergy which Jeremiah interpreted as evidence of a real lack of the knowledge of Yahweh on their part.

The poem is well supplied with balancing terms, and we should note too how the final colon in A' reverses the key words from A. We said earlier that there was no obvious alternation of speaker. The נאם־יהוה formulas ending A and A' indicate that Yahweh speaks at beginning and end (against Rudolph and Bright), and he is probably the speaker throughout. But if Jeremiah be the speaker in BB', then we also have a chiasmus of speaker. The content gives no clue either way, so we offer this only as a suggestion.

17:13–16a

Here is another 5-line poem with chiasmus of speaker only. It is similar to 8:18–21 just discussed. The commentaries give us no help in delimiting the poem. Bright says the whole chapter could have come from Jeremiah's miscellaneous file or else from some cupboard in the editor's home where odds and ends were stored.[66] Verses 12–13 are taken to be one fragment and 14–18 is thought to be one of Jeremiah's *bona fide* confessions. We think, however, that the basic confession is 13–16a which has then been expanded at a later time to include 16b–18. Verse 12 then becomes another fragment. Let us now look at the confession in 13–16a.

מקוה ישראל יהוה כל־עזביך יבשו A 13

יסורי בארץ יכתבו כי עזבו מקור מים־חיים[67] B

רפאני יהוה וארפא הושיעני ואושעה כי תהלתי אתה C 14

הנה־המה אמרים אלי איה דבר־יהוה יבוא נא B' 15

ואני לא־אצתי מרעה אחריך ויום אנוש לא התאויתי A' 16

13 A O Yahweh, the hope of Israel
    all who forsake you shall be put to shame

B Those who turn away from me shall be
       written in the earth
   for they have forsaken the fountain of living
        water[67]

14 C Heal me O Yahweh and I shall be healed
    save me and I shall be saved
    for you are my praise

15 B' Behold they say to me
    'Where is the word of Yahweh, let it come'

16 A' I have not pressed you to send evil
    and the day of disaster I have not desired

Commentators have long been troubled by the first person suffix on יסורי in line 2.[68] But if we take Yahweh to be the speaker of this line the problem disappears. Jeremiah narrates the whole

---

66. Bright, *Jeremiah*, 119.
67. Delete את־יהוה; see discussion to follow.
68. Qere form is וְסוּרַי; Rudolph proposes וְסוּרֶיךָ in the new *BHS* (in *BH*[3], וְסוּרֵי). RSV emends to 2nd p. suffix. For another reading of lines 1–2, see Dahood, "The Metaphor in Jeremiah 17,13," *Biblica* 48 (1967), 109–10.

speaking in A, C and A'. Then in B he speaks for Yahweh and in B' his opponents are quoted. This also enables us to take את־יהוה at the end of line 2 as a gloss.[69] It has in fact created the confusion in the first place by making Yahweh object as well as subject. Perhaps the gloss originally sought to explain the metaphor מקור מים־חיים (fountain of living water).

The poem proceeds much in the way we would expect. Jeremiah tells Yahweh in A that the infidels will be shamed. We don't yet know who the infidels are; we only know that their future is none too bright. In B Yahweh echoes Jeremiah saying the same thing again only in different words. In C Jeremiah asks to be delivered. This is the climax and is Jeremiah's preferred subject. What follows now is like what followed after the climax of 8:18–21, viz., embellishment of what has already been said. The taunt of the opponents is quoted in B' and if we knew who said these words we would know the identity of the infidels. A' is merely supportive argument used by Jeremiah in his defense before Yahweh. The climax has passed and Yahweh's promise of 1:19 was no doubt foremost in his mind at the time.

23:18, 21–22

The structure of this poem is marred by expansion and textual problems, yet we can see its original shape quite nicely after removing vv. 19–20. These verses occur elsewhere as a unit (30:23–24) and we take them here to be a later insertion.[70] There is no reason to rearrange the text as Volz does. The poem is 2:2:2 with good balance throughout.

18	A	כי מי עמד בסוד יהוה וירא את־דברו[71] מי־הקשיב דברי וישמע
21	B	לא־שלחתי את־הנבאים והם רצו לא־דברתי אליהם והם נבאו
22	A'	ואם־עמדו בסודי וישמעו דברי את־עמי וישבום מדרכם הרע ומרע מעלליהם

---

69. Rudolph now agrees in *BHS*; in *BH*[3] he was not sure.

70. Both Hyatt (*Jeremiah*, 993) and Bright (*Jeremiah*, 152) are aware of this possibility but prefer to leave them in.

18   For who has *stood in the council* of Yahweh
        and seen *his word*?[71]
A
        Who has hearkened to *his word*[72]
        and *listened*?

21   *I did not send the prophets*
            yet they ran
B
        I did not speak to them
        yet they prophesied

22   Now if they had *stood in my council*
        and *listened* to my *word* to my people
A′ Then they would have turned them from their
                            evil way
      and from the evil of their doings

There is no problem with the center. The text is fine and the parallelism makes this compare nicely with other centers we have seen, e.g., 2:7; 5:4–5; 6:3–5; 6:10–11. A and A′ are also meant to balance each other. In the poem's original form Yahweh was probably the speaker throughout which means that the Kethib דברי in v. 18 is original.

Yahweh begins by asking whether any have stood in his council. In B he says that prophets were quick enough to run but they were not sent. Then in the return (A′), assuming that his original question remains unanswered, Yahweh goes on to tell what would have happened had the prophets been present in council. The wicked people would then have been turned around. Who might the audience have been? If Jeremiah was speaking directly to the prophets his attack is admittedly brutal. But since the prophets are referred to in the third person it is

---

71. Delete וישמע with the Greek as a gloss. A problem was apparently created by the use of ראה (to see) with את־דברו (his word). Yet we take this to be the original reading. In 2:31 we also have ראו דבר־יהוה. Professor Freedman calls my attention to Exod 20:18: וכל־העם ראים את־הקולת ואת הלפידם ואת קול השפך . . . , and to this we can add Amos 1:1: אשר . . . דברי חזה. Yahweh's word was often received by vision as we know from Jeremiah 1 and 24, but visions were later disparaged in light of Jeremiah's comments in 23:23ff.

72. Reading here the Qere with all modern versions so as to harmonize with את־דברו in the previous colon. The Kethib, however, is probably original; see discussion to follow.

likely that Jeremiah is here addressing the ordinary people. If so, there is subtle judgment for *them* at the end making all but the last line foil and the last line cap. Ordinary people may not have minded an attack on the false prophets, but they would hardly be receptive to the suggestion that they constitute an un-redeemed populace, whether because of the negligence of the prophets or for some other reason.

51:20–23

Here is a catalogue poem which gives Jeremiah the perfect opportunity to use a chiastic structure. And use it he did. The poem is easily delimited from its context. The Massoretes mark the end of v. 19 as a closed section making the upper limit secure. They also close a section at the end of v. 24. Verse 24 is generally considered to be prose expansion so we are left with 20–23. Even without this help we could most likely conclude from content alone that 20–23 is independent. Probably no other poem which we have looked at, with the possible exception of 2:33–37, is so carefully done.

מפץ־אתה לי כלי מלחמה   20

ונפצתי בך <u>גוים</u> והשחתי בך <u>ממלכות</u>
ונפצתי בך <u>סוס ורכבו</u>   A   21
ונפצתי בך <u>רכב ורכבו</u>

ונפצתי בך <u>איש ואשה</u>   22
ונפצתי בך <u>זקן ונער</u>   B
ונפצתי בך <u>בחור ובתולה</u>

ונפצתי בך <u>רעה ועדרו</u>   23
ונפצתי בך <u>אכר וצמדו</u>   A′
ונפצתי בך <u>פחות וסגנים</u>

	20	You are my hammer and weapon of war:
A		I shatter with you *nations*, and I destroy with you *kingdoms*
	21	I shatter with you *horse* and *its rider*
		I shatter with you *chariot* and *charioteer*
	22	I shatter with you *man* and *woman*
B		I shatter with you *old* and *young*
		I shatter with you *young man* and *maiden*

23   I shatter with you *shepherd* and *his flock*
A' I shatter with you *farmer* and *his team*
      I shatter with you *governors* and *commanders*

Repetition and variation here work together for the poet. The repeated ונפצתי at the beginning of each successive line creates the sound of the hammer, which, according to the introduction (v. 20), Jeremiah is himself supposed to be. It is then not only with words but also by his rhetoric that Jeremiah *shatters* the people. A variation in the pattern occurs at the beginning where line 1 is expanded to include והשחתי בך. It is hard to know whether this is original or due to expansion. The verb שחת (to destroy) links this poem into a chain with three others.[73] The verb could thus have been added for such a purpose or else it could be original, in which case the chain was created because it was already there. We will leave והשחתי בך in because while Hebrew poetry is fond of repetition it is also fond of variation,[74] and examples of the latter are not wanting elsewhere in the poetry of Jeremiah.[75]

The real variation of the poem, however, comes in the distribution of its key words. We begin at the center. The Greek omits the center line but that can be attributed to haplography.[76] Its key words זקן (old) and נער (young) make it a pivot point for

---

73. The first poem in the chain is 51:1–10, marked by the chapter division at one end and delimited at the other by the independence of vv. 11–14 (see pp. 69–70). This poem begins הנני מעיר על בבל . . . רוח משחית, "Behold, I will stir up against Babylon . . . the spirit of a *destroyer*." The first verse of 51:11–14 also contains שחת: כי־על־בבל מזמתו להשחיתה, "because concerning Babylon his purpose is to *destroy* it." This appears to be editorial comment which would indicate that 11–14 has been expanded to fit into the chain. We skip over 51:15–19 since it is a duplication of 10:12–16 and is probably a later interpolation into the text. 51:20–23 is the poem just analyzed. The next poem, beginning in 51:25 (so Massoretic divisions), begins הנני אליך הר המשחית, "Behold, I am against you O *destroying* mountain . . ." Again שחת. In all there are four poems which either begin with שחת or have the verb supplied at the beginning.

74. Professor Freedman has called my attention to a number of deliberate variations made in sequences of repeated terms, all of them in poetry. In Amos 1–2 שלחתי אש occurs six times (1:4, 7, 10, 12; 2:2, 5) and הצתי אש once (1:14). Gen 49:25–26 has ויברכך and then five repetitions of ברכת followed by תאות. In Deut 33:13–16 ממגד occurs five times and מראש once.

75. In Jer 50:35–38 the variation is primarily for sound effect: five repetitions of חֶרֶב and at the end חֹרֶב.

76. Janzen, *Studies in the Text of Jeremiah*, 118.

B, distinguishing those persons in the previous line from those in the line following. The איש is the old man and the בחור is the young; the אשה is the old woman and the בתולה the young.[77] The Greek also transposes lines 1 and 3, but with such a structure there is no net loss. The same kind of transposition occurs in the liturgies found in Deut 6:6–9 and 11:18–20[78] and it is attested elsewhere in Scripture.[79] Perhaps the centers of chiastic structures enjoyed a measure of *fluidity* before the written tradition became fixed.

The key terms of A and A' are not necessarily fixed pairs, but we notice some deliberate inversions being made. In A the human figures, i.e., the rider of the horse, and the rider of the chariot, come *second*. In A' they come *first* (shepherd and farmer). The reverse is of course true for the non-human figures. The opening and closing lines of the poem break up a standard bicolon and make an inclusio: the *governors* and *commanders* (A') are the leaders of the *nations* and *kingdoms* (A). Here there is inversion also. Jeremiah chooses terms which make their plurals in ים. and ות, and switches them around. All in all a perfectly balanced poem.

The chiasmus here seems to be mainly for the sake of variation. And it also shows artistry. But there is no argument going on. The repetitions and variations all contribute to an impression of total destruction which Jeremiah means to convey. No person will be spared regardless of age, sex or social status. Even the animals will be destroyed.[80]

---

77. For the translation of בתולה with a meaning broader than "virgin," see G. J. Wenham, "Bᵉtûlāh 'A Girl of Marriageable Age'," *VT* 22 (1972), 326–48.

78. In 6:6–9 the unit beginning "And you shall teach them diligently to your children" and ending "when you lie down and when you rise" comes before the unit "And you shall bind them as a sign upon your hand, and they shall be as frontlets between your eyes." In 11:18–20 these units are *reversed*.

79. When Peter quotes the prophecy from Joel 3:1–2 [Eng. 2:28–29] at Pentecost (Acts 2:17–18) he inverts the two center lines. Since the Hebrew and Greek texts of Joel are the same we must attribute the inversion to Peter.

80. Jer 5:17 has a similar distribution of terms:

They shall eat up your *harvest* and your *food*
They shall eat up your *sons* and your *daughters*
They shall eat up your *flocks* and your *herds*
They shall eat up your *vines* and your *fig trees*

51:34–45

No commentator has yet seen this as an independent poem
Bright following Volz takes the verses as smaller units,[81] and
Condamin, who usually notices key words, misses the structure
completely. The poem is a long 20 lines which divide up
4:4:4:4:4. Key words in each stanza form the chiasmus while the
center has its own peculiar balance. Of special interest is the
נאם־יהוה formula in the center. We are used to seeing messenger
formulas at the beginning or end—and this particular formula
at the end—but here for the first time it occurs in the center.
Since there is no reason for omitting it we can take this to be its
original position. Yahweh is speaker in all stanzas but the first,
so as the poem now stands there is no chiasmus of speaker. Yet
the very *direct* words at the end of A and A' give the whole an
antiphonal effect. In A the people articulate the curse to be
hurled at Babylon and in A' an urgent call is sent throughout
Babylon telling Yahweh's people to flee.

אכלנו ⁸²המַמנו נבוכדראצר מלך בבל הציגנו כלי ריק		34
בלענו כתנין מלא כרשו מעדני הדיחנו	A	
חמסי ושארי על־בבל תאמר ישבת ציון		35
ודמי אל־ישבי כשדים תאמר ירושלם		
⁸³הנני־רב את־ריבך ונקמתי את־נקמתך		36
והחרבתי את־ימה והבשתי את־מקורה	B	
והיתה בבל לגלים מעון־תנים		37
שמה ושרקה מאין יושב		
יחדו ככפרים ישאגו נערו כגורי אריות		38
בחמם אשית את־משתיהם והשכרתים למען יעלזו	C	39
וישנו שנת־עולם ולא יקיצו נאם־יהוה		
אורידם ככרים לטבוח כאילים עם־עתודים		40

The terms at the extremes are all produce, whereas the center terms are
people and animals, which are normally grouped together in the OT.

81. Bright (*Jeremiah*, 359) takes as three separate poems: (1) 34–37;
(2) 38–40; and (3) 41–45, but he acknowledges that the divisions are difficult to make.

82. Reading the Qere here and throughout the verse with all modern
versions.

83. Delete לכן כה אמר יהוה as expansion.

איך נלכדה ששך 84   ותתפש תהלת כל־הארץ   41

איך היתה ל<u>שמה</u>   בבל בגוים

עלה על־בבל ה<u>ים</u>   בהמון <u>גליו</u> נכסתה   B′   42

היו עריה ל<u>שמה</u>   ארץ ציה וערבה 85   43

ופקדתי על־<u>בל בבבל</u>   והצאתי את־<u>בלעו</u> מפיו   44

ולא־ינהרו אליו   עוד גוים   A′   45*

גם־חומת בבל נפלה   *צאו מתוכה עמי

ומלטו איש את־נפשו   מחרון אף־יהוה

34   He has eaten me,[82] he has crushed me
      Nebuchadrezzar, king of Babylon
       he has made me an empty vessel
     He has swallowed me like a monster
A   he filled his belly
       from my luxuries he rinsed me out
35   'My broken flesh be upon Babylon'
     let the inhabitant of Zion say
    'And my blood on Chaldea's inhabitants'
     let Jerusalem say

36   [83]Behold, I will plead your cause
  '   and take vengeance for you
     I will drain her *sea*
B   I will dry up her fountain
37   Babylon will become a *heap*
     a lair for jackals
    A *horror* and a hissing
     without inhabitant

38   Together *like* lions they shall roar
     they shall growl *like* lions' whelps
39   While they fret I'll prepare them a feast
C   I'll make them drunk till they talk loudly
    They'll sleep a perpetual sleep
     they will not waken—oracle of Yahweh
40   I will bring them down *like* lambs to the slaughter
     like rams and he goats

41   How Babylon[84] is taken
           the praise of the whole earth is seized
        How she has become a *horror*
      B′   Babylon among the nations
42   The *sea* has come up upon Babylon
           with its noisy *heaps*, she is covered
43   Her cities have become a *horror*
           a land of drought and desert[85]

44   So I will punish *Bel* in *Babylon*
        and take out what *he swallowed* in his mouth
      They shall not flow to him
    A′   the nations any longer
      Even the wall of Babylon has fallen
45   'Go out from her midst, my people
      Let everyone save his life
      from the fierce anger of Yahweh'

The Greek omits "Bel" at the beginning of v. 44 and in addition the remainder of this verse and the verse following. "Bel" belongs in the text but Rudolph is probably correct in thinking that "Nebuchadrezzar" in v. 34 is added. In the poem's original form the subject of v. 34 was not revealed until v. 44. *Bel was the king in Babylon.* The poem is really telling us about the future cosmic battle about to take place between Yahweh and Bel, otherwise known as the Babylonian god Marduk (cf. Isa 51:9–11).

The chiasmus is well marked by key words. In A and A′ the balancing verb is בלע (to swallow). The king of Babylon, who like a sea monster has swallowed Israel (A), will soon be forced to disgorge what he has swallowed (A′). B and B′ tell of the future "horror" in store for Babylon. Babylon's own "sea" will be drained (B) but another "sea" will come up and inundate her (B′). The noun גל (heap) is also used in BB′ with different meanings. In B Jeremiah speaks of a heap of dry rubble while in B′ the heap is a heap of water, i.e., waves. The center of the structure has its own internal contrast signaled by the 4-fold use of the preposition כ (like). The enemy will cry out like the fiercest of

---

84. ששך is an Athbash for בבל.

85. Delete ולא־יעבר בהן בן־אדם ‏ ארץ לא־ישב בהו כל־איש as expansion (see also the expansion of 2:6 in n. 25).

animals but Yahweh will bring her down as if she were the most docile. The chiastic structure then, carries well Jeremiah's message, i.e., that the future promises to be a complete *turn-around* of the past.

We have now completed our look at the chiastic speeches in Jeremiah. We have seen that like the inclusio, the chiasmus allows Jeremiah to withhold key information until the end and also on occasion to set up a foil for his preferred subject. But the chiasmus does more. Because movement is directed both towards and away from the center, the center becomes a kind of hinge on which the whole poem swings. Not infrequently it is the place of *climax*. But the chiasmus can be used in non-argumentative poems for the simple purpose of providing variation, e.g., 51:20–23, and together with other patterns of repetition, it helps to achieve the Hebrew desire for totality.

The key word chiasmi in Jeremianic poems are most like those found in Lamentations 1–2, while certain speaker chiasmi appear to have their affinity with the chiasmus in Deut 1:20–31. Thus we find that our best comparative material is to be dated about the same time as Jeremiah, which must mean that such structures were well known in the 7th and 6th centuries B.C. and appreciated at that time by the people who heard them.

We concluded earlier that Jeremiah was a prophet of dialogue, and the chiastic structures have only confirmed this conclusion all the more. The many changes of speaker show that he was as much a dramatist as he was a speaker. Yahweh, Jeremiah and the people are continually talking to each other. On occasion the enemy is even heard from. Jeremiah is thus a true mediator between Yahweh and the people because he converses with Yahweh. Yahweh for Jeremiah is someone approachable and in conversations with him Jeremiah is alarmingly frank. He is frequently compared along with Job to the Greek Prometheus.[86] With the people he is no different. He is frank but he is also open. Jeremiah is not a prophet who simply calls out the divine word. He is a person willing to discuss—indeed to argue—with the people. But his aim is not to overpower. There is always the opportunity for rebuttal, and if the audience keeps silent it

---

86. Sheldon H. Blank, "Men Against God: The Promethean Element in Biblical Prayer," *JBL* 72 (1953), 1–13.

is because they have nothing to say. This strategy of course paid off, because by allowing the people to *participate* in the dialogue, the people were thereby helped to live finally with the difficult answers that inevitably had to be given.

Chiasmus in the Larger Book of Jeremiah

In this section we will see how chiastic structures control material larger than the Jeremianic speech. The examples will be varied. Some are collections of more than one poem. Others are prose compilations. We will look at Jeremiah's Letters to the Exiles (chap. 29) and finally at two clusters of biographical prose in chaps. 24ff.

We begin with the chapter that opens the book, the chapter that records Jeremiah's call.

1: Jeremiah's Call

This chapter is usually taken as a compilation of separate fragments, yet a unity of the whole is recognized. The final verses (17–19) pick up the second person "you" from vv. 4–10, making it appear that they are an extension of the call.[87] These are all personal words of Yahweh to Jeremiah. In the center are two visions. The first is the vision of the almond rod (11–12). Everyone recognizes the play on שָׁקֵד and שֹׁקֵד, but to my knowledge no one is quite sure what the vision really means or how it relates to the rest of the chapter. The explanation of Bright is common: "This [vision] suggests that Jeremiah had already been active for some time, and had begun to be troubled about the fulfillment of the word (of judgment) that he was proclaiming."[88] The second vision begins at v. 13 and is customarily extended to v. 16. This vision and its interpretation speak of the judgment to come upon Judah by the Foe from the North.

So arranged a basic continuity is recognized within the chapter. I would agree that the vision of the boiling pot (13–14) leads into the explanation of judgment which follows, and also that the end of the chapter has continuity with the beginning. But the structure is much more than this.

---

87. Bright, *Jeremiah*, 6–7.
88. Ibid., 7.

Let us begin by proposing a slightly different outline which will do more justice to the content and can be more easily defended. There are four basic parts to the chapter: (1) Jeremiah's call (4–10); (2) the vision of the almond rod (11–12); (3) the vision of the boiling pot (13–14); and (4) a further promise to Jeremiah (15–19). No one disputes the call of 4–10. Neither is there any difficulty isolating the vision of the almond rod (11–12). But from this point on a reconstruction is necessary. The second vision we limit to 13–14. Although not containing a word-play quite like the almond rod vision, it is nevertheless tied together by key words: the boiling pot tipped "away from the north" (מפני צפונה)[89] refers metaphorically to the enemy who will come "from the north" (מצפון). It is true that this vision leads into what follows, but we must first show how 15–19 holds together before discussing the connection. Scholars are not correct in breaking after v. 16. *All of 15–19* contains the promise to Jeremiah. These verses set up an important contrast between Jeremiah and the men of Judah which cannot be put aside. A close look at the text will make this clear.

In the promise Yahweh tells Jeremiah that the enemy will come

(ו)על כל־חומתיה סביב
(ו)על כל־ערי יהודה

against all its *walls* round about
against all the *cities* of Judah (v. 15)

Yet Yahweh will make Jeremiah a "fortified *city*" (לעיר מבצר) "and bronze *walls*" (ולחמות נחשת) to protect him from his enemies (v. 18). The key words here point up the contrast very well and one will note also that they are nicely inverted when repeated. The coming of the Foe from the North will set off a chain reaction. The people of Jerusalem will try to defend the city against the enemy but in the end will fail. They in turn will fight against Jeremiah who is announcing their defeat. But to Jeremiah Yahweh promises what he does not promise to the others:

---

89. The Hebrew as it now stands is not precise. The locative *he* on צָפוֹנָה would render the term "towards the north," yet מפני means "from." But common sense tells us that the pot must be tipped *away* from the north if the metaphor is to refer to the Foe from the North.

salvation. The section closes with Yahweh repeating the words given earlier to Jeremiah at the time of his call (v. 19; cf. v. 8).

Now that we have shown the unity of 15–19 we can return to the vision of the boiling pot to see how it relates to the promise. As we mentioned before, scholars have always recognized a link between the vision and vv. 15–16. Actually vv. 15–16 do little more than expand upon 14 giving us the judgment in more detail. But there is also a word-play which connects the two. In the vision the verb פתח (to open) is used so awkwardly that the English versions are unable to translate it literally. The Hebrew reads, "Out of the north evil will *open* upon all the inhabitants of the land" (v. 14). But we see why this verb is used when we read on into the promise: thrones are going to be placed by the enemy at the *opening* (פתח) of the gates of Jerusalem (v. 15). Thus we agree that the second vision is firmly linked to the promise, but the promise we take to be all of 15–19.

We now return to the first vision and the call. Our thesis here is that this vision looks *back* to the call of 4–10 and is to be taken as part of that call. To my knowledge no commentator has recognized this. The word-play within the vision has all but obscured the link that exists between the vision and the call. The link is a key word: דבר. In the vision Yahweh is said to be watching over his דבר to perform it (v. 12). What is this word? It is more than a general word of judgment (so Bright). The answer lies in the verses above where the entire focus is upon the verb דבר (to speak) and the noun דבר (word). Jeremiah complains like Moses before him that he is unable to speak.[90] He says, הנה לא־ ידעתי דבר, "Behold, I do not know how to *speak*" (v. 6). But Yahweh answers, ואת כל־אשר אצוך תדבר, "Whatever I command you, you shall *speak*" (v. 7b), and says further in v. 9: הנה נתתי דברי בפיך, "Behold, I have put my *words* in your mouth." Jeremiah will be able to speak because Yahweh will provide the דבר. The *word* then that Yahweh is watching over becomes the *words* placed in Jeremiah's mouth. The vision and the call are one event. This appears to be corroborated even by the introductory formulas. Verses 4 and 11 begin ויהי דבר־יהוה אלי לאמר whereas v. 13 begins ויהי דבר־יהוה אלי שנית לאמר, "And the word of Yahweh came to me *a second time* saying . . ." There are thus only *two*

---

90. Exod 4:10ff.

events in chapter 1: a call and a subsequent promise. But were accompanied by visions, but because visions contain messages that are terse and opaque they need a more complete articulation. And in each case this articulation is given, only we have all been misled because in the call the normal order of the material is inverted. If it were arranged the same way the promise is arranged, the almond rod vision would come just prior to v. 4. Instead it comes after v. 10.

Chapter 1 is then built into a chiasmus:

> A   Articulation of the Call (4–10)
> B   Vision of the Call (11–12)
> B′ Vision of the Promise (13–14)
> A′ Articulation of the Promise (15–19)

The structure in this case is done for a definite reason. We showed earlier how the opening verses of the call were used to make an inclusio with 20:18. The chiastic structure now makes that possible. If the almond rod vision were placed first the inclusio could not be made. So by inverting the order of the call material, Baruch or Jeremiah created two rhetorical structures, a chiasmus in chapter 1 and an inclusio for 1–20.

One final point. We realize now for the first time that Jeremiah's call came with a vision, which is how the calls of both Isaiah and Ezekiel were received (Isaiah 6; Ezekiel 1–3).

8:22–9:10 [Eng. 9:11]

Two of the poems in this complex have already been examined, 9:2–5 and 9:9b–10. There are two more. One is a nicely balanced poem which we have not discussed (8:22–9:1).[91] The other is a fragment in 9:6–7 to which has been attached the stereotyped v. 8. Taken together these four poems with their supplements are built into a chiasmus based upon key words. The center poems are about lying *tongues* (לשׁון). As we noted earlier the tongue in 9:2 was compared to a bent bow; in 9:7 it is a "deadly arrow." The outer poems in the complex are about *weeping*. In 8:23 Jeremiah says,

---

91. This poem was analyzed in my earlier study, "Patterns of Poetic Balance in the Book of Jeremiah," 51–53.

> Oh that my head were waters
> and my eyes a fountain of tears
> That I might *weep* day and night (ואבכה)
> for the slain of the daughter of my people

The companion poem (9:9b–10) says nothing about weeping, but an introductory line has been prefixed to the poem (9a)[92] which reads:

> I will take up *weeping* and wailing (אשא בכי ונהי)
> for the mountains[93]
> and a lamentation for the pastures
> of the wilderness

It is now possible to explain why 9a was prefixed to 9b–10. This line contains the key word enabling 9–10 to be balanced with the first poem in 8:22–9:1. The cluster as a whole can be outlined as follows:

A   Jeremiah *weeping* for the slain people (8:22–9:1)
  B   Jeremiah warning about evil *tongues* (9:2–5)
  B′   Jeremiah warning about evil *tongues* (9:6–8)
A′   Jeremiah *weeping* for the entire creation (9:9–10)

Since the cluster is within 1–20 we are no doubt looking at a structure created by Jeremiah as a mnemonic device when he kept the early poems together in his head.

11:18–20; 12:1–3

These poems together with intervening commentary (11:21–23) and what follows in 12:4–6 have been the subject of much discussion. Following Cornill, some commentators propose that 12:1–6 be placed before 11:18–23.[94] That however is unnecessary. Upon close examination we see that two poems have been deliberately placed end to end to make another inversion. Both

---

92. See p. 60.
93. No reason to read an imperative here with the Greek and Syriac (so RSV); Hebrew text is correct.
94. See H. H. Rowley, "The Text and Interpretation of Jer 11:18–12:6," *AJSLL* 42 (1926), 219ff.; cf. Bright, *Jeremiah*, 89.

are 2:2:2 and written very much alike, the main difference being
that one begins where the other ends and vice versa. Earlier we
noted that two poems, 6:1–7 and 6:8–12, contained key words
in identical collocations and were even juxtaposed in the collection process, and we called these "companion poems." The two
poems here appear also to be companion poems, the only difference being the inversion which is created.

18	A	ויהוה הודיעני ואדעה אז הראיתני מעלליהם
19		ואני ככבש אלוף יובל לטבוח ולא־ידעתי כי־עלי
	B	חשבו מחשבות נשחיתה עץ בלחמו
		ונכרתנו מארץ חיים ושמו לא־יזכר עוד
20	C	ויהוה צבאות שפט צדק בחן כליות ולב
		אראה נקמתך מהם כי אליך גליתי את־ריבי
1	C'	צדיק אתה יהוה כי אריב אליך אך משפטים אדבר אותך
		מדוע דרך רשעים צלחה שלו כל־בגדי בגד
2	B'	נטעתם גם־שרשו ילכו גם־עשו פרי
		קרוב אתה בפיהם ורהוק מכליותיהם
3	A	ואתה יהוה ידעתני תראני ובחנת לבי אתך
		התקם כצאן לטבחה והקדשם ליום הרגה

18   *Yahweh made it known to me,* and *I knew*
      A   then *you made me see* their evil deeds
19   For I was *like* a gentle *ram* led to the *slaughter*
          For *I did not know* it was against me

          They devised schemes (saying)
       B   'Let us destroy the tree with *its yield*
          Let us cut him off from the land of the living
          that his name be remembered no more'

20   But O *Yahweh* of Hosts, who *judges*
                        righteously
       C   who tries the heart and the mind
          Let me see your vengeance upon them
          for to you I have committed *my suit*

1   *Righteous* are you O *Yahweh, yet I bring*
                               suit to you[95]

     C′   yet I speak *judgment* against you
             Why does the way of the wicked prosper?
             why do all who are treacherous thrive?

2   You plant them, and they take root
    B′   they grow and bring forth *fruit*
        You are near in their mouth
        but far from their heart

3   But you O *Yahweh know me* and *see me*
    A′   and try my mind toward yourself
      Pull them out *like sheep* for the *slaughter*
      and sanctify them for the day of the killing

As one can see the two poems literally swarm with balanced vocabulary. To what we have underlined could be added בחן כליות ולב in v. 20 which has counterparts in ורחוק מכליותיהם of v. 2 and ובחנת לבי אתך of v. 3. Verse 20 is repeated almost verbatim in 20:12. Whether it is original there or not we cannot say, but it certainly must be kept in this context. So also must התקם כצאן לטבחה of v. 3 which is lacking in Greek.

Together the poems argue a single point, viz., that Yahweh in his righteousness should judge Jeremiah's enemies in a way that will suit their wrongdoing. In other words their punishment should fit the crime. This view of justice was common in antiquity as we know from Judg 1:6–7 and especially II Maccabees (4:26, 38; 5:9–10; 8:33; 9:5–6; 13:3–8).

22:6–23

In the previous chapter we established the outer limits of the collection of speeches to kings.[96] In its final form this collection contained an inclusio which contrasted the future messianic king to Zedekiah. Now we will look at the center of the collection where a chiastic structure in the poetry isolates the core This core is made up of three major poems, and two fragments directed to

---

95. For the translation of this line, see Holladay, "Jeremiah's Lawsuit with God," 280–87.
96. See pp. 45–47.

Kings Shallum (Jehoahaz) and Jehoiakim. Two of the major
poems, 22:6–7 and 22:20–23, were analyzed fully in the previous
chapter,[97] so we will present the core in skeleton form only:

You are as Gilead to me
    as the summit of *Lebanon* (הלבנון)

· ·

A   ·

And they shall cut down your choicest *cedars* (ארזיך)
    and cast them into the fire
                        (22:6–7)

        Weep not for him who is dead . . . [i.e., Josiah]
B   but weep bitterly for him who goes away
         · [Jehoahaz]
                        (22:10)

        Woe to him who builds his house . . .

        ·
        He cuts for it windows, paneling it
                            in cedar (בארז)
    C   Do you think you are a king because you
                        complete *in cedar*? (בארז)

        ·
        and for practicing oppression and violence
                        (22:13–17)

        They shall not lament for him
    B′   · [Jehoiakim]
                        (22:18–19)

Go up to *Lebanon* and cry out (הלבנון)
    and lift up your voice in Bashan

· ·

A′ O inhabitants of *Lebanon* (בלבנון)
    nested *in the cedars* (בארזים)

· ·
                        (22:20–23)

    The core is a well-balanced ABCB′A′ structure. Three main
poems are placed at the beginning, middle and end, with frag-

---

97. See pp. 67–69.

ments on either side of the center poem filling out the whole. Our prior analysis of poems A and A' showed their preoccupation with the "cedars of Lebanon," i.e., the wooded structures of Jerusalem. Both had inclusios which used "cedars" and "Lebanon" as key terms. Now we see that the center poem (C) is another which rebukes one of Judah's kings (Jehoiakim?) for his lavish use of cedar. But here the repetition of בארז comes at the center making then the poem a pivot for the whole.

The two fragments directed to Jehoahaz and Jehoiakim are words of lament—or non-lament—as the case may be. Here the introductory formulas, כה־אמר יהוה אל־, are nicely inverted. In the word to Jehoiakim (18–19) the formula is placed at the *beginning* whereas in the word to Jehoahaz (10–12) it is placed at the *end* together with additional comment. This might be a trite observation were it not now known that Deuteronomic scribes took pleasure in doing this very thing.

We conclude then that 22:6–23 constitutes the core of the King Collection and that at one time this was an independent composition. We have other evidence too which shows that the King Collection ended originally with 22:20–23. This latter poem is linked by a catchword to the poem beginning the Prophet Collection (23:9–40). We noted earlier that *opening key words* were used to link poems in chapter 51 into a chain,[98] and we see now the exact same thing being done here. The final "king poem" begins:

> Go up to Lebanon and cry out
> > and lift up your voice in Bashan
> Cry from Abarim
> > for all your lovers *are broken*   כי <u>נשברו</u> כל־מאהביך
> > > (22:20)

And the first "prophet poem" begins:

> My heart *is broken* within me   <u>נשבר</u> לבי בקרבי
> > all my bones shake
> > > (23:9)

We thus conclude that all of 22:24–23:8 is an expansion of the core just as 21:1–22:5 is expansion. We see also how Hebrew

---

98. See p. 121.

literature tends *to grow out in both directions* from the center instead of accumulating in sequential fashion only.

Having now identified the core our attempt to date it is greatly assisted by the fact that datable kings are referred to both inside the core and outside. The word to Jeconiah (22:24–30) lies outside which means that the core was probably put together sometime before his brief reign of three months. This gives us a *terminus ad quem* of 597 B.C. The *terminus a quo* is not far away. In 22:18–19 Jehoiakim's ignoble death is predicted, which is probably Jeremiah's response to Jehoiakim's poor foreign and domestic policies after 604–603 B.C. This gives us very narrow limits—a mere 6–7 years—and it puts the composition of the core at a time immediately following the time when the *Urrolle*—which we take to be 1–20—was written down. That was 605 B.C. (the fourth year of Jehoiakim according to Jeremiah 36). Since the core (along with a portion of the Prophet Collection to which it is linked) immediately follows 1–20 in the present order of the book, we are justified in calling this an early appendix to the *Urrolle* for Jer 36:32 specifically states: "and many similar words were added to them." This was done when Jeremiah and Baruch were in hiding (Jer 36:19). Then after Jehoiakim died and the young Jehoiachin (= Jeconiah) was taken off to exile, the lament over Jehoiachin was added. It lay outside the core but still followed the earlier laments/non-laments in chronological order. It was only in the final stage of the collection's growth that chronology was broken, and that was done in order to make the inclusio contrasting Zedekiah to the messianic king, which framed the whole.

For what purpose was this chiastic structure made? If it had been created earlier we might consider it to be another mnemonic aid for Jeremiah. But since it comes from a time when Baruch was helping Jeremiah bring things together—and also since it follows the creation of 1–20—we think that its function was probably the same as the function of 1–20, i.e., to make the material suitable for use in worship. If Jeremiah was too modest to suggest it himself, Baruch convinced him that one day his speeches would be heard again by the descendants of those who were presently his enemies. And Baruch, being a scribe schooled in the Deuteronomic tradition, saw to it that the material was compiled in such a way that its future use would be facilitated.

29: Jeremiah's Letters to the Exiles

This chapter is not without its problems, the most serious being (1) the omission of vv. 16–20 in the Greek (except Lucian); and (2) how one is to properly interpret vv. 24–28. Verses 16–20 are words of judgment against the "bad figs" left in Jerusalem (cf. chap. 24), and are usually taken to be a late insertion,[99] although Peake admittedly finds it difficult to explain what interest the post-exilic community would have in such an addition.[100]

The other problem concerns the end of the letter. Verse 29 begins a narrative which relates a subsequent discussion that took place between Jeremiah and Zephaniah the priest. This could make v. 28 the conclusion of the letter except for the fact that this verse quotes Jeremiah's words from the same letter (v. 5). Bright therefore takes v. 23 as the conclusion of the letter,[101] and we believe this to be correct. That means that vv. 24–28—which are directed specifically to a certain Shemaiah in Babylon—must constitute another letter or more probably a *fragment* from some other letter which was appended to the original letter at a later time. We will return to discuss the fragment but let us first look at the main letter.

The main letter is contained in vv. 4–23, 1–3 being introductory and beginning in typical Deuteronomic fashion: ואלה דברי, "And these are the words . . ." (cf. Deut 1:1; 28:69). It breaks down into four sections which make another chiasmus. And a count of the lines in MT shows that each section is of approximately the same length. Verse 15 is out of place however in the MT, so we take it along with Lucian to belong prior to 21–23 which it is mean to introduce. The letter breaks down as follows:

A   Welfare of *Babylon* (4–9)—9 lines of MT
 B   Welfare of *Jerusalem* (10–14)—9 lines of MT
 B'   Judgment in *Jerusalem* (16–20)—9+ lines of MT
A'   Judgment in *Babylon* (15, 21–23)—8 lines of MT

The first half of the letter is about שלום (welfare), first the שלום of Babylon (v. 7), and second the eventual שלום of Jerusalem (v. 11). The remainder of the letter is judgment. But in

---

99. So Bright, *Jeremiah*, 211; cf. A. S. Peake, *Jeremiah and Lamentations* II (New York: Henry Frowde, 1911), 60–61.

100. Ibid.

101. *Jeremiah*, 211.

apportioning the judgment Jeremiah reverses the order which
he used in the שלום part of the letter. The remnant in Jerusalem
is judged first (16–20), and second those prophets in Babylon
who give false hopes for a speedy return from exile (15, 21–23).
We thus argue for the inclusion of 16–20 which the Greek omits.
It most certainly belongs and is to be deleted only at the expense
of what is deliberately intended to be a rhetorical structure.

We return now to the fragment. Bright takes vv. 24–28 along
with the narrative in 29ff. as "repercussions of the letter,"[102] still
assuming that we have only one letter from Jeremiah. But this
cannot be. Verses 24–28 constitute a fragment from another letter sent by Jeremiah to Babylon, and the introductory "To Shemaiah of Nehelam you shall say:" (v. 24) is a directive from
Jeremiah to the recipient of the letter in Babylon. It is not a directive from Yahweh to Jeremiah (so Bright).[103] We say too that
this is a *fragment* rather than a whole letter because, as scholars
have long noted, the ending is abrupt.[104] Jeremiah recounts
what Shemaiah has said in his letters and then says no more. We
anticipate something additional—a word of judgment perhaps—but that does not come until later when Jeremiah writes
his third letter. Now it may be that Jeremiah was acting in his
usual cautious manner waiting to hear Shemaiah's letter to
Zephaniah before cursing him.[105] But if the letter is seeking
some kind of explanation from Shemaiah, which is what appears to be the case, should we not hear more than a mere summary of what Shemaiah has said? It would seem so, and thus we
are compelled, I believe, to see this as only a fragment of what
was originally a much longer letter. Also, we must remember
that letters in antiquity were often semi-public containing messages for more than one person. Jeremiah's third letter containing the curse on Shemaiah (v. 31) was sent "to all the exiles in
Babylon." Since letters had a wider audience we can assume

---

102. Ibid., 206–7; 211–12.

103. Ibid., 212.

104. Peake, *Jeremiah and Lamentations* II, 64–65; Bright (ibid.) speaks
of an oracle to Shemaiah which is interrupted and never resumed.

105. The caution which Jeremiah displayed in dealing with Hananiah (chap. 28) is instructive. After their first encounter, which ended
without the dispute being resolved, we are told that Jeremiah "went his
way" (v. 11). Only later did he return to curse Hananiah (vv. 12ff.).

that only certain portions were selected for inclusion into the biblical text. Other parts of the letter containing material not deemed important the compiler edited out.

We can now proceed to a reconstruction of the events as they took place. Jeremiah began by writing a letter to the exiles in Babylon, which we have perhaps in full in vv. 4–23. In this letter he told the exiles to build houses and have families because the exile would be long. Shemaiah, most likely a prophet (v. 31: יען אשר נבא לכם שמעיה) exiled in Babylon, then wrote a number of letters[106] back to people in Jerusalem objecting to what Jeremiah had said. In his letter to Zephaniah the priest (and perhaps in some of the other letters as well) he demanded that Jeremiah be censured. Jeremiah had not yet heard the letter sent to Zephaniah, but on the basis of either the other letters or perhaps from reports which came to him about the letter to Zephaniah, he sent a second letter to Babylon. This conveyed the substance of Shemaiah's letter/letters and apparently sought to find out from Shemaiah what was going on. The fragment in vv. 24–28 is from that letter. Now Zephaniah is finally confronted by Jeremiah and is forced to read his letter.[107] Jeremiah hears this letter for the first time and after hearing it dictates another letter to Babylon cursing Shemaiah (vv. 31–32). This letter is the *third* sent by Jeremiah to Babylon and it is not extant.

We are now ready to look at the main letter and the fragment together. The "abrupt ending" of the fragment as we noted earlier is a quotation from the main letter. More than that it is a quotation from the *very beginning* of that letter. The original letter begins:

29:5	Build houses and live in them;	בנו בתים ושבו
	plant gardens and eat their	ונטעו גנות ואכלו
	produce . . .	את־פרין

---

106. Bright argues that the plural "letters" can refer to just one letter (*Jeremiah*, 206); so also Volz (*Der Prophet Jeremiah*, 276). This is forced and we see no reason to so read the text.

107. The interpretation here hangs on the antecedent of "this letter" (את־הספר־הזה) in v. 29. The Greek omits הזה too which does not help. But Bright is undoubtedly correct in taking this letter to be the letter sent by Shemaiah to Zephaniah about Jeremiah; cf. *Jeremiah*, 212.

And the fragment ends:

29:28	Build houses and live in them;	בנו בתים ושבו
	plant gardens and eat their	ונטעו גנות ואכלו
	produce.	את־פריהן

The end of one is made to match the beginning of the other, and the result is an inclusio. Together the two make a rhetorical whole which is meant to convey a single point: "Settle down and accept the exile as a thing which you must bear for a time." And it is not unlikely that this expanded form of Jeremiah's Letters to the Exiles was tailored as was other material for the ongoing worship life in exile.

The Jehoiakim Cluster: 25, 26, 35, and 36

These four chapters are the only dated narrative from Jehoiakim's reign except for 45 which is Baruch's autobiographical postscript. They appear interspersed with dated narrative from Zedekiah's reign, together lending support to the "disarray theory." But we should note that this interspersion takes place only in chapters 24–36. Chapters 37–44, which conclude the reign of Zedekiah, follow in perfect chronological order.

Our main concern is with the chapters out of chronological order, viz., 24–36. The present arrangement is of course the final one, and while this arrangement cannot be understood as the one that was originally intended, it can be satisfactorily explained once we know something of the materials' pre-history. Other structures more carefully designed existed prior to this one, and it is these that we now want to show. The key which unlocks the pre-history is found by *extracting the Jehoiakim chapters from the rest and looking at them separately.* When we do this we see that these chapters form a cluster arranged into a chiasmus. Here our primary criterion is the *date* which is found in each of the superscriptions. Five dates are given in all, four appearing at the beginnings of chapters 25, 26, 35 and 36, and a fifth coming in 36:9. The date in 36:9 marks what we believe to be an expansion of 36:1–8, but more about that in a moment. Let us look first at the cluster. The four chapters with their dates are as follows:

A   Chap. 25—4th year of Jehoiakim
   B   Chap. 26—the beginning of Jehoiakim's reign
   B'   Chap. 35—in the days of Jehoiakim
A'   Chap. 36—4th year of Jehoiakim

Chapters 26, 35 and 36 all appear to be in chronological order. Chapter 26 dates from the "beginning" (בראשית) of Jehoiakim's reign and is generally given a date of ca. 609–608 B.C.[108] Chapter 35 can also fit into the period prior to 605 B.C., although this is still debated.[109] Only chapter 25 is manifestly out of chronological order, but again, we believe this to be deliberate. As was the case with 21:1–23:8, so here too chronology is broken in order to make the beginning balance the end.

Were date the *sole* criterion for the identification of this rhetorical structure we would have to call our structure an inclusio. A and A' balance nicely but the descriptions of date in B and B' are different. Nevertheless we note that 26 and 35 are *both* accounts of Jeremiah in the *temple*, suggesting that the center of the structure was probably meant to be in balance as well. Thus we take B and B' as genuine counterparts and the whole as a chiasmus.

A word now about the superscription in 36:9. Since our chiasmus builds primarily on dated superscriptions it becomes necessary to explain the one remaining superscription not used in the structure. In our judgment 36 was originally only 36:1–8. Verses 9–32 are later expansion as one can easily tell when

---

108. Bright, *Jeremiah*, 169.

109. Bright dates chap. 35 ca. 599/598 B.C. which I believe is too late. A date prior to 605 B.C. is historically defensible since Nebuchadnezzar made his first campaign into Palestine in 604 B.C. On this occasion he destroyed Ashkelon; see Bright, *A History of Israel*, 2nd ed. (Philadelphia: Westminster Press, 1972), 325–26. This date easily satisfies the military threat implied in 35:11, which is the basis on which Bright proposes his date (*Jeremiah*, 189–90). More important, a date prior to 605 would avoid our having to ask the obvious question of how Jeremiah could be in the temple (in 599/598 according to Bright) after he was debarred in 605 (so 36:5). It is not only unlikely that Jeremiah went into the temple from 604 to 598, but it is unlikely that he (and Baruch) *went anywhere at all* during this period. We know the fate of another prophet less able to avoid the grasp of King Jehoiakim (cf. 26:20–23), which indicates that this was the only course to follow so long as Jehoiakim was still alive.

reading from verses 8 to 9. Verse 8 tells in summary fashion that Baruch did what Jeremiah commanded him to do, i.e., go to the temple and read the scroll the two of them had prepared. It says nothing more. But in 9ff. we get a *detailed account* of what actually took place when Baruch went. Thus it appears that Baruch decided sometime later to expand upon what he had said very summarily in v. 8. And when he added this he introduced it with a superscription telling us that the reading took place in the 5th year of Jehoiakim, the ninth month (36:9). But the Jehoiakim Cluster originally concluded with 36:1–8, not with all 32 verses now found in our present chapter.

We can now proceed to explain Baruch's rationale in creating the chiasmus the way he did, which in turn will enable us to perceive the original function of 36:1–8. We realize that Baruch broke chronology to make the chiasmus, but why 25 first and 36:1–8 last? He could have reversed the two with no net loss. Let us look at 36:1–8 first since its position is easiest to explain. If one looks closely at this passage he will see that Baruch figures prominently just as he does in 45. He is in fact the key figure. *He* takes Jeremiah's dictation and *he* it is who reads the scroll before the temple audience. Thus we believe that at this earlier time Baruch wanted 36:1–8 to be *his signature* just as he later wanted 45 to be the signature of the book when completed. In his own way Jeremiah identified himself in 1–20; now Baruch writes a partially concealed colophon for that which is *his* creation.

Why Baruch placed 25 at the beginning is not so obvious. Since in his collection this chapter introduced the Oracles to Foreign Nations, it may be that he desired to place the Oracles to Foreign Nations *first* instead of last. It is true they are last in the MT but that is only because of Seraiah's relocation. We see in Amos that they are first, although admittedly they were placed there for rhetorical reasons of a different sort.[110]

We conclude then that the Jehoiakim Cluster was originally an independent collection of prose narrative written and arranged by Baruch. Since also it contained part if not all of the

---

110. The deliberate judgment of nations leading up to Israel in Amos 1–2 has long been recognized; see Lund, *Chiasmus in the New Testament*, 87–88; A. Bentzen, "The Ritual Background of Amos i 2–ii 16," *OS* 8 (1950), 85–99.

Oracles to Foreign Nations, it is probably the "this book" (בספר הזה) referred to in 25:13.[111] Eventually it would be added to earlier collections for the purpose of expanding what was rapidly becoming *a book* of Jeremiah. If the *Urrolle* (1–20) be the first edition, and the second edition be the *Urrolle* plus an early version of the King and Prophet Collection, then the third edition would contain the two collections of the second edition plus the Jehoiakim Cluster. The date here must be just prior to 597 B.C. when Jeremiah and Baruch were still in hiding.

The Zedekiah Cluster: 24, 27, 28, and 29

We proceed in our analysis of the pre-history of chapters 24–36 by looking at what is left after the Jehoiakim Cluster has been taken out. What we find is another cluster—four chapters of dated Zedekiah prose prior to the Book of Comfort (30–33)—and it too is structured into a chiasmus! The chapters in this cluster are 24, 27, 28 and 29. The criteria here for the chiasmus are just exactly what they were for the Jehoiakim Cluster. The primary criterion is *date*; the secondary criterion the *subject matter* of the center units. Let us look now at the Zedekiah Cluster:

A   Chap. 24—after the exile of Jeconiah
   B   Chap. 27—beginning of Zedekiah's reign [4th year][112]
   B'   Chap. 28—beginning of Zedekiah's reign (4th year)
A'   Chap. 29—after the exile of Jeconiah

As one can see the similarity to the other cluster is almost unbelievable. A and A' are dated at the same time, and so also are B and B' despite the textual problems in 27:1. But similar subject matter in B and B' makes the chiasmus certain. In both 27 and 28 Jeremiah gives his object lesson using the yoke-bar. Perhaps even more interesting is a look at how the clusters differ. We

---

111. Numerous scholars take 25:13 to be the conclusion to the first collection of Jeremiah's prophecies; cf. Eissfeldt, *The Old Testament: An Introduction*, 350–51; Bright, *Jeremiah*, lvii, 162–63.

112. The 4th year is derived from the superscription in 28:1 which reads, ויהי בשנה ההיא, "In that same year . . ." The entire verse is problematic. The LXX omits, while the MT reads "Jehoiakim," which cannot be correct. On the basis of a few Mss., the Syriac and Arabic, all modern English versions (RSV, NEB, JB) correct to "Zedekiah."

noted that in the Jehoiakim Cluster A was out of chronological order. This cluster, however, breaks chronology in precisely the *opposite* way: the chapter out of order is A'. Thus we see again that Baruch enjoyed inversions every bit as much as Jeremiah.

It is not clear why 29 should come at the end, but 24 is a suitable beginning to this cluster because of its similarity to chapter 1 opening the book. These two chapters, 1 and 24, are the only chapters which record Jeremiah's visions, and in 24:3 Jeremiah is addressed with the same words appearing in 1:11 and 13: מה־אתה ראה ירמיהו, "What do you see Jeremiah?" With such balance and consistency we believe that Baruch must have chosen material very carefully for his collections. No doubt there was much else to tell but because it didn't fit into the scheme it was left out.

We might assume that the Zedekiah Cluster was added to the Jehoiakim Cluster to make an enlarged fourth edition. But here we are not at all certain how the book looked ca. 593 B.C. because very soon after the Zedekiah Cluster was completed it was interspersed with the Jehoiakim Cluster. It is to this problem that we now turn since we must explain how clusters so deliberately conceived were then broken up leaving us with the disorder now prevailing. Why was not the Zedekiah Cluster placed immediately behind the Jehoiakim Cluster? The answer is perhaps one which we will never know for certain, but an explanation can be given, and it is one that squares with all we have thus far learned about Baruch's compositional methods. We suggested earlier that Baruch had certain ideas about what made appropriate beginnings and what made appropriate conclusions. In the Jehoiakim Cluster the autobiographical passage had to be last, and in the Zedekiah Cluster the chapter with Jeremiah's vision had to be first. Now one will quickly see that any attempt to put these two together necessitates a compromise. If Baruch placed the Zedekiah Cluster immediately after the Jehoiakim Cluster, 36 would no longer be the conclusion. Nor would 24 be at the beginning. He could conceivably have placed the entire Zedekiah Cluster ahead of the Jehoiakim Cluster and kept both his chosen beginning and conclusion, but this would have manifest a complete disregard for chronology and apparently Baruch ruled that out too. The only other option was to intersperse the two and this is the option he chose. Chapter 24 became the new beginning and 36 remained as the conclusion. Chronology in the final stage was partially broken but that could not be helped. Also we recall that in 21:1–23:8 chronology likewise remained intact until the final stage when it was then broken.

We can now pick up a few loose ends and conclude our discussion of 24–36. The Book of Comfort is of course an independent collection as we have already seen. It was expanded with the addition of two chapters of Zedekiah prose (32–33) in the course of time, but we do not know exactly when this was or why the whole collection is where it is in the present text. The only chapter not yet accounted for is 34. Chronologically it fits just prior to 37, but as I have shown on another occasion, it was displaced in order to set up a contrast between Zedekiah and the Rechabites (35).[113]

The final stage of the book saw the addition of chapters 37–44, all of which are in chronological order and describe the events leading up to Jerusalem's fall. This added material now makes a fifth edition perhaps and the book is all but in its final form. For the first time 36 is no longer the conclusion, being replaced by 45. This is Baruch's final book and it is the book from which the LXX was translated. There is thus no longer any good reason to believe that composition and major editing of the book went on well into the exile. Seraiah's text was fluid slightly longer than the text of Baruch, but the fact that Seraiah keeps Baruch's text intact except for the relocation of the Oracles to Foreign Nations argues strongly for the fixing of Baruch's text very soon after the fall of Jerusalem.

One final comment. With the explanation of how chapters 24–36 came into their present state, and also with our earlier and now later discussions of the prose material on both sides, it should perhaps be pointed out that we have accounted for *all* the biographical prose in chapters 21–45, and we have done so *without any rearranging of the present text*!

This concludes the chapter and also the substance of our research. We have seen that Jeremiah and Baruch both make use

---

113. This was in a paper entitled "Scribal Contributions to Old Testament Theology: Composition by Contrast" given at the International Congress of Learned Societies in the Field of Religion, Los Angeles, September, 1972; forthcoming in the *Festschrift for Frederick C. Holmgren* (eds. Paul Koptak and Bradley Bergfalk; Chicago: Covenant Publications, 1997).

of the chiasmus to structure their respective compositions. To this extent they both reflect a common rhetorical tradition. This cannot be overemphasized because Jeremiah is still too often set over against the Deuteronomic institution of his day. That he stood opposed to much for which that institution stood is clear enough. But like so many others who are forced to leave home, there was something from home that he took along with him. This was his rhetoric, for the rhetoric of Jeremiah is clearly the rhetoric of Deuteronomy, which was also the prevailing rhetoric of the Deuteronomic institution in his day.

Chapter 4

Conclusion

The Rhetoric of Jeremiah

The preceding pages have been filled with numerous observations about the Jeremianic speech and they cannot all be reiterated here. Only the most important points will be drawn together for the purpose of making a statement on the rhetoric of Jeremiah.

We have gone to the poetry to find the Jeremianic speeches, and consider it established that Jeremiah used rhetorical structures to control both parts and the whole of speeches. We chose only two structures, the inclusio and the chiasmus, but even so a significant amount of material was covered. A rough count of poetic lines in the MT shows that out of approximately 1000 lines, we dealt in one way or another with over 300, which is slightly under one-third. And much of what we left aside, while not making use of either the inclusio or chiasmus, is nevertheless very well balanced, e.g., 2:14–19; 6:16–21; 17:5–8; 31:10–14; 49:28b–33a; 51:47–48, 52–53; etc. If one were to use our data as a control in working elsewhere in the poetry, he would no doubt come up with additional insight into the Jeremianic speeches. This in turn could be compared with the present research to see if the conclusions we are about to draw are valid for the speeches as a whole.

We have seen that the Jeremianic speeches are controlled not by fixed genre structures, i.e., the letter, lawsuit, hymn, lament, judgment speech, or whatever, but by structures that were dictated by canons of Hebrew rhetoric in the 8th–6th centuries B.C. Jeremiah drew upon the rhetorical tradition that first manifested itself in Deuteronomy. Heretofore it has been difficult if not impossible to compare the Jeremianic *speeches* with the speeches in Deuteronomy because the Jeremianic speeches are in poetry.

Previous studies compared only the prose of Jeremiah with the prose of Deuteronomy. But now we see that even the poetic speeches of Jeremiah have an affinity with Deuteronomy, and that affinity is one of structure.

If then Jeremiah took over rhetorical structures already in use, how did he use them? We can begin by stating the obvious. He used the inclusio and the chiasmus as homiletical devices to aid him in preaching. Jeremiah's rhetoric is thus *a preacher's rhetoric*. These devices were known to his audience and no doubt appreciated by them. They were used with frequency in the temple, and for all we know the temple may have been where Jeremiah learned them in the first place. In non-argumentative poems Jeremiah achieves the same ends as the Deuteronomic preacher. Structures alert the audience to where the preacher is going, sometimes functioning to restore focus, other times to give the necessary emphasis—whether in the middle or at the end. In the case of the chiasmus, variation is sometimes necessary when the speech builds heavily upon repetition. And for the listeners, the inclusio and chiasmus are mnemonic devices aiding them in retention. The audiences of Jeremiah were conditioned to this rhetoric and they responded to it. Despite then all his protestations to the contrary, Jeremiah *was* heard by his audience and his speeches *were* remembered.

Secondly, Jeremiah's rhetoric is *a rhetoric of totality*. The structures of Jeremiah were used to present a total thought, only it came forth in fragmented form. This was done deliberately and is what made possible the subtleties and added meanings Jeremiah conveyed beyond words. But even normal parallelism functions this way. A though is broken up and given in segments instead of all at one time. Schoettgen in his *Exergasia Sacra* saw this more clearly than Lowth. Jeremiah was also able to create anticipation by breaking up his thoughts. The audience frequently knew it must wait for something and when that something came the desire for totality was satisfied. Muilenburg is then correct when he says that this sense of totality "is as apparent in Israel's rhetoric as in her psychology."[1]

The importance of this cannot be overstated especially in the interest of proper exegetical and theological understanding.

---

1. "A Study in Hebrew Rhetoric: Repetition and Style," 99; cf. Appendix.

What we are saying in essence is that one cannot properly understand the parts of the Jeremianic speech unless he first understands the whole. Structure is a key to meaning and interpretation. The Jeremianic speeches contain theological statements which are hidden from view when the structure is not perceived. This should then be a warning to those who apply a purely philological or text-critical methodology to the text. The structural method is a necessary control for these other methods and future scholars will be better exegetes and theologians if they pay this heed.

Jeremiah's rhetoric is *a rhetoric of argumentation*. We have long known that Jeremiah was a prophet of dialogue and we have also known that he was a man of contention (15:10). But we have not realized the extent to which he was argumentative because we have heretofore not been able to get from his speeches a picture of the prophet *vis à vis* his audience. Now that has all changed and we are able to see Jeremiah in quite a new light.

This perhaps more than anything else is what makes Jeremiah's rhetoric different from the rhetoric of Deuteronomy. In Deuteronomy, judgment (and reward too) is stated in conditional terms: "If you do good you will be rewarded, and if you do bad you will be punished." Thus unless the hearer was unusually sensitive to being issued a warning, he would not likely feel alienated. But Jeremiah had moved beyond Deuteronomy. It was no longer an "if/then" situation. Israel *had* broken the covenant, therefore she *would* be punished. Such a message is hard to deliver and it is no wonder that Jeremiah had an argument on his hands much of the time. His audience is surely alienated in a way that it would not be alienated by the message of Deuteronomy.

Our recognition of the argumentative character of Jeremiah's rhetoric will also force upon us a new estimation of Jeremiah the man. Previously we have been influenced by popular conceptions of the prophets in general, and Jeremiah in particular, and these have not given us a fair picture. The prophets are seen by many as merely dogmatic preachers. They receive a word directly from God and then speak it with boldness. Jotham and Elijah lend support to such a view (Judges 9; 1 Kings 18). One does not enter into conversation with such a man. You either take what he says or leave it, and if he speaks judgment, the latter is usually the case.

Other stereotyped views have obtained with Jeremiah only. He is the "weeping prophet" pictured as one who can do nothing more in a desperate situation than sit and lament. He is even unfairly sought out as a model by the cynic and the complainer. Still others are attracted to Jeremiah because in him they see someone who is greatly misunderstood. Only God can know his plight.

It must certainly be conceded that there is a measure of dogmatism in Jeremiah and also that Jeremiah shows more than the normal amount of pathos. The poem in 51:20–23 shows that he could be bombastic. And he also wept (8:23; 9:9 [Eng. 9:1, 10]). But Jeremiah is primarily a prophet of engagement. He meets his audience on common ground, engages them, and then takes them with him as one does when he takes another for a ride. Only Jeremiah is taking them to an undesired place and they find they must either beg to get off or stay with him. Either way they are caught. A rhetoric of argumentation has this one quality: it does not permit an audience to remain merely as onlookers.

Finally, Jeremiah's rhetoric is *a rhetoric of descent.* We have seen that the Jeremianic argument goes quite consistently in the following directions:

$$\longrightarrow$$

ironic—straightforward
figurative—literal
general—specific
abstract—concrete

It begins at a distance and gradually comes closer until it is right upon you. Throughout the speech Jeremiah *lowers* the level of abstraction and this serves a practical end. An audience is much more easily engaged by irony, generalities, well-known laws, word-plays, unusual metaphors, proverbs and observations from the natural order. Any truth whatever in abstract form gives Jeremiah common ground with his audience. But Jeremiah is delivering a message of judgment and so he must postpone the unveiling of his preferred subject until the very end—and indeed in some instances until after the end has passed. Otherwise his chance will be lost. People rarely sit around and listen for long when the finger is pointed at them.

Now that we have stated the salient features of Jeremiah's rhetoric it might be well to see if our picture squares with the picture of Jeremiah given in the prose, and also with pictures we have of other prophets engaged in controversy. Perhaps the classic confrontation found in the prose comes in chapter 28 where Jeremiah meets Hananiah. Jeremiah is not in agreement with Hananiah about the duration of the exile, nevertheless he begins the conversation by ostensibly agreeing with him: "Amen! May Yahweh do so; may Yahweh make the words which you have prophesied come true, and bring back to this place from Babylon the vessels of the house of Yahweh, and all the exiles" (28:6). Micaiah had spoken the same way to Ahab (1 Kgs 22:15). Jeremiah then follows with his own statement, but it is very general. He doesn't counter Hananiah saying that the exile will be long—which he could have done (cf. 27:7). Instead he sets up the criterion by which a true prophet can be distinguished from a false one. This he gets from Deut 18:22. His lack of directness is no deterrent, however, and the controversy enters a physical stage. Hananiah breaks the yoke-bar off Jeremiah's neck. And what does Jeremiah do? The text tells us very tersely: "But Jeremiah the prophet went his way" (28:11b). Only later does Jeremiah return to curse Hananiah (vv. 12ff.). It took him a while, but over time Jeremiah could become very specific. We concluded the same when Jeremiah had to deal with Shemaiah (29), and there are other instances where the pattern is very much the same, e.g., in 32 where Jeremiah proceeds very cautiously with Yahweh in accepting a message of future hope.

Jeremiah's rhetoric compares in a striking way to the rhetoric of Nathan and Amos. When Nathan convicts David of the crime against Uriah (2 Samuel 12), he begins with a hypothetical case which he knows will "hook" David. Once David gives the desired judgment Nathan can quickly make the analogy and point the finger saying "You are the man!" His move here is from the general to the specific, from the abstract to the concrete. Amos, on the other hand, "hooks" his audience with sweeping worldwide judgments (Amos 1–2). We can almost hear the audience applauding with delight as he flays one nation after another. But in the end Amos reveals his preferred subject, i.e., Israel. All the rest was foil. And by the time Amos comes to his preferred subject the audience is so conditioned by assenting to seven guilty verdicts that the eighth is inescapable.

Jeremiah addresses "the people" this way. He uses prophets, priests and kings as foil, and in the end reveals his preferred subject, which is the people themselves.

We thus conclude that the rhetoric of Jeremiah as revealed in our analysis of the speech material is one that can stand. The inclusio and the chiasmus—with their ability to return the audience to the beginning in particular—were admirably suited for Jeremiah's needs. Despite Jeremiah's protestation that he was unable to speak (1:6), we find on the contrary that he could indeed speak very well.

The Rhetoric of the Book of Jeremiah

We seem to have evidence that the book of Jeremiah developed in two stages: (1) an oral stage, and (2) a written stage. The oral stage we know least about, although structures did emerge in the course of our investigation which point to such a stage prior to 605 B.C. Since we take 1–20 to be the scroll of 605 our predisposition is to consider any structure within that collection a structure created by Jeremiah during the 23 years he collected his own works. This would include the chain of poems in chapter 2 as well as the large inclusio and chiastic structures within 1–20. We are not sure about the chain in chapters 22–23. This early form of the King and Prophet Collection may have circulated orally; then on the other hand it may be the work of a writing scribe. The chain of four poems in chapter 51 is most likely a grouping prepared for a brief period of oral transmission. The entire question needs more research. But from now on we insist that so-called "tradition-complexes" be sought in the poetry, not in the biographical prose. This means 1–20, 22–23, 30–31 and 46–51. And even then corroborating evidence will certainly be necessary in order to keep such studies from becoming overly subjective. As for the current theories about the four great tradition-complexes we can dispense with them entirely. Such simply do not exist. None of the blocks proposed by either Engnell or Rietzschel can any longer be defended, nor is 1:1–25:13 by itself anything at all. The LXX and MT break at 25:13 only because of the relocation of the Oracles to Foreign Nations in the MT. Related to this, of course, is our judgment that the prose in 24–45 is not legend. It is historical biography written down by Baruch very soon after the events themselves took place. Whatever contribution the community made to this material—if it made any at all—was minimal. In any case it is not significant enough for the material to be called legend.

The latter stage is the written stage and about that we know significantly more than previously. The prose commences about the same time as Baruch appears on the scene, i.e., early in Jehoiakim's reign, and from 605 until 586 numerous collections are put together, eventually being joined together into a single book. The inclusio and chiastic structures of these various collections become very useful to us in marking the stages of the book's growth because they delimit units. The history of composition may indeed be more complex than we realize, but at least we can see what took place in broad outline.

Being a Deuteronomic scribe, Baruch was a direct heir to the great rhetorical tradition in Judah of the past century or more. He was certainly familiar with how Deuteronomy was written and compiled, which means that, besides knowing how to use rhetorical structures, he knew the importance of arranging things chronologically and also had some definite ideas on how books should begin and end. We know too that he was capable of writing good biography. Because of him the *book* of Jeremiah is what it is, for it is Baruch more than Jeremiah who creates this work.

We have argued that Baruch tailored the written collections for use in temple worship. This was his main reason for using the inclusio and the chiasmus. We can assume this, because, after writing down the very first scroll from Jeremiah's dictation, he goes to the *temple* to read it. There he finds a gathered congregation, who as far as we know, heard him out in his entirety. This was a congregation accustomed to temple rhetoric, which was still basically the rhetoric of Deuteronomy. Now when they heard a collection of prophecies from Jeremiah it had a familiar ring. At the end of Baruch's reading the audience was brought back to the beginning and Jeremiah's despair was thus tempered with a strong statement of faith. The people could respond to this, not merely because they had heard judgment often enough before—which they had—but because Baruch had come to them using the rhetoric that they had heard many times before.

Now if Baruch tailored his first scroll for use in the temple we can assume that he did the same with subsequent collections.

More and more Jeremiah's words were heard by audiences removed from the audience Jeremiah originally addressed. In this
way the re-presentation of the Jeremianic material began, and in
the process a book took shape that became more and more like
Deuteronomy, which up to that time had been *the book par excellence* in Israel. Deuteronomy re-presented Moses to an audience
removed in time if not in spirit from the Mosaic Age (cf. Deut
5:2–3). Now in the book of Jeremiah it is Jeremiah who becomes
the "new Moses."[2]

One question remains. If Baruch was preparing material for
subsequent use in worship, did either he or Jeremiah have a future temple in mind? The first scroll and perhaps other early
scrolls were prepared for delivery in the existing temple, but
Jeremiah had predicted that temple's destruction. Was there
some hope on the part of either that it would not be destroyed?
On the other hand, if the temple's eventual destruction was
conceded—which is most likely—then we might well assume
that Jeremiah and Baruch looked forward to the day when a
new temple would be built. No doubt both realized that worship in some form would continue on into the exile, temple or
no temple, but the question may still be asked whether they
looked beyond the exile to a restoration back in Jerusalem (cf.
29:10). Any argument either way is of course an argument from
silence, since Jeremiah on no occasion spoke about a future
temple (or lack thereof). He said that the ark would be gone,
that old confessions and proverbs would be replaced by something new, and even that there would be a new covenant. But
about a new temple Jeremiah said nothing. Nevertheless if
structure be a silent witness to things not otherwise uttered, we
may perhaps be allowed the suggestion that Baruch and Jeremiah did indeed envision a new temple. If so, the gap normally
assumed between Jeremiah and Ezekiel is at least partially nar-
rowed.[3] It is only that Jeremiah (and Baruch) say silently what
Ezekiel proclaims loud and clear.

---

2. For the development of this thesis, see Holladay, "The Background
of Jeremiah's Self-Understanding: Moses, Samuel and Psalm 22," *JBL* 83
(1964), 153–64. This thesis was also presented by James Muilenburg in the
unpublished Nils Lund Memorial Lectures (North Park Theological Seminary, 1963) entitled, "The Mediators of the Covenant."

3. For the usual distinctions typically drawn by source-critics
between prophet and priest, see T. J. Meek, "Was Jeremiah a Priest?" *The
Expositor*, 8th series, 25 (1923), 215–22.

Appendix

Christian Schoettgen's Exergasia Sacra

It has been customary to credit Robert Lowth with the discovery of Hebrew parallelism even though we realize that he did not actually discover it.[1] Lowth's primary source was an essay on Hebrew rhythm by Azariah de Rossi, a rabbi from Ferrara, who included this in his larger work *Me³or Enayim* published in 1574.[2]

More recent research has shown that biblical parallelism was widely known by the end of the 17th century. Roman Jakobson has called attention to studies done in Scandinavia 50 years before Lowth which compared Hebrew parallelism with parallelism in Finnish poetry.[3] Among Lowth's other predecessors there were two who defined the phenomenon in rhetorical categories. One was the Italian Alessio Simmaco Mazzocchi, the other a German named Christian Schoettgen. Mazzocchi saw parallelism as "epesegesi," whereas for Schoettgen it was "exergasia." The contributions of both scholars have been relatively unknown, although some years ago Mazzocchi was given his redress.[4] It is now proper, then, to give to Schoettgen what is due him.

---

1. For the most recent article on Lowth see Aelred Baker, "Parallelism: England's Contribution to Biblical Studies," *CBQ* 35 (1973), 429–40.

2. מאור עינים [The Light of the Eyes] (Volna: R. M. Romma Press, 1866); see chapter 60, "Essays in Criticism" (אמרי בינה), 477–85.

3. "Grammatical Parallelism and Its Russian Facet," *Language* 42 (1966), 403.

4. See Ugo Bonamartini, "L'epesegesi nella S. Scrittura," *Biblica* 6 (1925), 424–44; cf. Baker, "Parallelism: England's Contribution to Biblical Studies," 433.

Very little is known about Schoettgen's *Exergasia Sacra*, and even less is known about Schoettgen himself. To make matters worse, what has been passed on about Schoettgen in the English tradition is not entirely correct. The one scholar in the English tradition who seems to have seen Schoettgen's dissertation in *Horae Hebraicae et Talmudicae* was John Jebb, who, like Schoettgen himself, is another scholar not well known.[5] Jebb makes numerous references to the work in his *Sacred Literature*, but he evidently does not know the author. He discusses the *Exergasia Sacra* with other works by Abarbanel and Azariah in a paragraph entitled "Two *or three* rabbinical dissertations" [italics mine].[6] This is cautious, but nevertheless incorrect. Schoettgen was not a rabbi but a Christian scholar living in the 18th century in Germany.

Another erroneous belief has crept into English scholarship, although this is not the responsibility of Jebb. Both Charles Briggs and Theophile Meek have made statements to the effect that Lowth used the earlier work of Schoettgen's.[7] Yet nowhere in either Lowth's *Lectures on the Sacred Poetry of the Hebrews* or *Isaiah* does he even mention Schoettgen. Jebb notes this too.[8] This appears then to be decisive because Jebb knows of no writer (presumably in the English tradition) who has cited Schoettgen when discussing Hebrew poetry,[9] in addition to the fact that both Briggs and Meek appear to be ultimately dependent upon Jebb for their information.[10] Briggs seems to be the one who first made the connection, and unless evidence is forthcoming which shows that he had independent information, we are more correct to assume that Lowth worked independent of Schoettgen and did not use the *Exergasia Sacra* as one of his sources.

---

5. See Frederick Bussby, "Bishop Jebb, A Neglected Biblical Scholar," *ET* 60 (1948–49), 193.

6. *Sacred Literature*, 14–15.

7. Briggs, *ICC: Psalms* I (Edinburgh: T & T Clark, 1952), xxxv; Meek, "The Structure of Hebrew Poetry," *JR* 9 (1929), 528.

8. *Sacred Literature*, 14.

9. Ibid.

10. Briggs' remarks about Schoettgen are immediately followed by a reference to Jebb's *Sacred Literature*. Meek in his discussion then repeats what Briggs says almost verbatim.

It is time now to set the record straight, which we can do with the help of an article on Schoettgen in *Biographie Universelle*.[11] Christian Schoettgen was a philologist born in 1687 at Wurzen in Saxony, not far from Leipzig. His father was a shoemaker, but having had himself a literary education, was in a position to give his son the same. After early training at the gymnasiums, the young Schoettgen matriculated at the University of Leipzig for a course in theology, at which time he also began a study of the oriental languages. Nine years were spent at Leipzig giving lessons and doing literary work of one kind or another. At the request of the local library Schoettgen undertook the revision of a 1667 manuscript by Thomas Reinesius entitled *Eponymologicum*. This was a glossary explaining ancient inscriptions. Schoettgen's teaching career began in 1716 when he was named rector at the gymnasium of Frankfort on the Oder. In 1719 he became professor of literature. Then in 1728 he became rector at one of the gymnasiums at Dresden, where he remained until his death on October 15, 1751. Schoettgen was married and had eight children. He was a much respected teacher and was remembered also for his interest in fellow-citizens and strangers.

Besides being an expert in philology and historical scholarship, Schoettgen mastered to a rare degree the oriental and rabbinic literature. He was often consulted by Jewish scholars who venerated him until they found out about his desire to prove from the Old Testament that Jesus was the Messiah. The second volume of *Horae Hebraicae et Talmudicae* (1742)[12] is taken up almost entirely by a discussion of the Messiah. This work was then followed in 1748 by *Jesus le vrai Messie*.

Schoettgen published many other works. Some were updated editions of works done by earlier scholars, while others were his own. Included among the former were the works of Lambert Bos on the Greek ellipsis and Walter on the Hebrew ellipsis. Schoettgen also published a new edition of Pasor's *Lexique* on the New Testament. In 1746 he published a better lexicon

---

11. Ed. J. Fr. Michaud, 38 (Graz, Austria: Akademische Druck- u. Verlagsanstalt, 1969), 409.

12. In the biographical article in *Biographie Universelle* (see note above), Schoettgen's second volume is given a publication date of 1740. The second volume in my possession is dated 1742.

himself, and a third edition of this with later additions by Krebs and Spohn was considered by Thomas Horne in the 19th century to be the best Greek-Latin lexicon of the New Testament currently available.[13]

The first volume of *Horae Hebraica et Talmudicae* was published in 1733 predating the Lowth Lectures by eight years. It is mostly commentary on the books of the New Testament, with eight dissertations on various subjects at the back. The sixth of these is *Exergasia Sacra*. In this dissertation Schoettgen first gives a general explanation of exergasia equating it with the Latin figure "expolitio." The exergasia had already been thoroughly discussed by Julius Scaliger so the reader is referred to him for further information. Then follows 10 canons of "exergasia sacra," which we now present for the first time in English translation. Each canon is illustrated by three biblical texts, and in two instances—in Canons III and VII—Schoettgen makes some additional comments. The 10 canons are then given further demonstration following their enumeration. Here we will present only the canons and the illustrative texts. After we have looked at them we will conclude with some comparisons to Lowth's doctrine of parallelism as well as to the subsequent restatements that have come more recently.

Canon I.   *Exergasia is complete when each member of the two cola so corresponds to the other that one is neither greater nor less than the other.*

Psalm 33:7:
Gathering together / as in a bottle / the waters of the sea
    and putting / in a storehouse / the abyss

Numbers 24:17:
It comes / a star / out of Jacob
    and it is raised / a scepter / out of Israel

Luke 1:47:
It magnifies / my soul / the Lord
    and it exults / my spirit / in God my savior

---

13. Thomas H. Horne, *An Introduction to the Critical Study and Knowledge of the Holy Scripture*, II, 4th ed. (Philadelphia: E. Littell, 1831), 705–6.

Canon II.   *Sometimes, however, in the second part of the total thought, the subject is not repeated, but by ellipsis is omitted, and by common usage is understood.*

Isaiah 1:18:
If your sins / be as scarlet / they shall be white as snow
   and if - - / red as a berry / they shall be as wool

Proverbs 7:19:
Whereas the husband / is not in his house
   - - / is gone on a distant journey

Psalm 129:3:
Upon my back plowed / the plowers
   cut their furrows long / - -

Canon III.   *Sometimes also, only part of the subject is missing.*

Psalm 37:30:
The mouth of the just / meditates / upon wisdom
   his tongue / speaks / justice

Here only part of the subject is repeated, viz., the suffix "his," not indeed the whole subject.

Psalm 102:29:
Sons of your servants / will dwell
   and their seed / before your face will be

Isaiah 53:3:
And he / was wounded / for our transgressions
   - - / was bruised / for our sins

Canon IV.   *Examples appear, where in the repeated line of the exergasia, the predicate is omitted.*

Numbers 24:5:
How beautiful they are / your tents / O Jacob
   - - / your habitations / O Israel

Psalm 33:12:
Happy / that nation / whose Lord is God
   - - / that people / whom he willed in his inheritance

Psalm 123:4:[14]
It is sated / our soul / with the mockery of the arrogant
    - - / - - / with the contempt of the proud

Canon V. *Sometimes only part of the predicate is missing.*
Psalm 57:10:[15]
I will acknowledge you / among the peoples / O Lord
  I will sing songs / among the nations / - -
Psalm 103:1:
Bless / O my soul / the Lord
  and - / all my innards / the name of his holiness
Psalm 129:7:
So that he does not fill up / his hands / the reaper
  or - - / his fists[16] / the binder of sheaves

Canon VI. *Some elements may be added in one member when not present in the other.*
Number 23:18:
Arise / Balak / and hear
  - - / son of Zippor / give ear to me
Psalm 102:29:
The children of your servants / - - - / shall dwell
  and their seed / before your face / shall be established
Daniel 12:3:
And those who make people wise[17] / - - / shall shine /
               as the brightness of the firmament
  and those who make just / many / - - / as the stars /
                          forever

Canon VII. *Sometimes two propositions treating different things occur, but which, arranged by means of a distribution, can and should be interpreted as one general proposition.*

---

14. Correction; Schoettgen text has 123:6.
15. Correction; Schoettgen text has 57:11.
16. Compare "bosom" in both the Hebrew and the Vulgate. Is he striving after a more exact parallelism with "hands"?
17. Schoettgen supplies *reddunt* to render the Hebrew H Stem (compare modern English versions).

Psalm 94:9:[18]
The one who plants / the ear / does he not hear?
  the one who forms / the eye / does he not see?

Psalm 128:3:
Your wife / as a fruitful vine / in the company of your house
  your sons / as olive plantings / around your table

Sirach 3:16:
As a blasphemer is he / who forsakes / his father
  and cursed by the Lord / who incites to wrath / his mother

No one supposes here, that we believe the 'eye' to be the 'ear,'
or the 'father' to be the 'mother,' etc., for these two propositions refine one generalization. Thus, in the first saying, the
general proposition is this: 'God knows everything'; in the second: 'Fruitful will you be in marriage'; in the third: 'Unhappy
is he who strikes his parents.'

Canon VIII. *Exergasia also occurs when the second proposition ex-
      presses the opposite of the first.*

Proverbs 15:8:
The sacrifice / of the wicked / is an abomination to the Lord
  and the prayers / of the upright / are his good pleasure

Proverbs 14:1:
The wisdom of women / builds a house
  and foolishness within her hands / destroys it

Proverbs 14:11:
The house / of the wicked / will be devastated
  and the tent / of the righteous / will flourish

Canon IX.   *We also have examples of this kind of exergasia where
      whole propositions correspond, although the subject and
      predicate are for the most part not the same.*

Psalm 51:7:
Behold, in iniquity I was brought forth
  and in sin my mother conceived me

---

18. Correction; Schoettgen text has 94:8.

Psalm 119:168:

I have kept your injunctions and your testimonies
  because all my ways are before you

Jeremiah 8:22:

Is there no balm in Gilead, nor a doctor there?
  for why has the daughter of my people not come to health?

Canon X.   *There occur even three-member exergasias.*

Psalm 1:1:

Blessed is the man / who has not gone / in the counsel /
                                         of the wicked
  and - - / - - has not stood / in the way / of sinners
  and - - / - has not sat / in the seat / of scoffers

Psalm 130:5:

I have waited for the Lord
  my soul has waited
  and in his word have I hoped

Psalm 52:9:

Behold the man, who would not make God his help
  and - - - has confided in the multitude of his riches
  and - - - was hardy in his emptiness

Schoettgen's canons cover all Lowth's categories: I–VII and
X are what Lowth calls "synonymous parallelism"; VIII is "antithetical parallelism"; and IX is "synthetic parallelism." And
like Lowth's third category, Canon IX is the weakest: Ps 51:7
may perhaps fit but neither Ps 119:168 nor Jer 8:22 is exergasia.
Schoettgen lists more types of synonymous parallelism and in
so doing anticipates the later refinements of Lowth by G. B.
Gray. In Gray's terminology, Canons II–V would be "incomplete
parallelism without compensation," and Canon VI "incomplete
parallelism with compensation."[19]

But the real importance of Schoettgen's dissertation is that it
emphasizes the rhetorical nature of parallelism. We are shown
how parallelism strives after *totality* (Canon VII), which is what

---

19. *The Forms of Hebrew Poetry*, 74. Lowth has also recognized this,
however; cf. *Lectures on the Sacred Poetry of the Hebrews*, 262–63.

Muilenburg continually stressed.[20] And we see too the *elliptical* quality of Hebrew poetry (Canon II). This latter observation has been made repeatedly by Dahood in his *Psalms I–III* where he shows how all parts of speech and even suffixes can do "double-duty" for more than one colon of poetry.[21]

Schoettgen thus deserves his rightful place alongside Lowth. Not only does his work predate Lowth, but more important, it shows how parallelism *functions* for the Hebrew poet.

---

20. "A Study in Hebrew Rhetoric: Repetition and Style," 99.
21. See especially *Psalms III*, 429–44.

Bibliography

Commentaries

Blayney, Benjamin. *Jeremiah and Lamentations: A New Translation with Notes Critical, Philological, and Explanatory* (Oxford: Clarendon Press, 1784; 3d ed.; London: Thomas Tegg and Son, 1836).

Boadt, Lawrence. *Jeremiah 1–25* (OTM 9; Wilmington, Del.: Michael Glazier, 1982).

_____. *Jeremiah 26–52, Habakkuk, Zephaniah, Nahum* (OTM 10; Wilmington, Del.: Michael Glazier, 1982).

Bright, John. *Jeremiah* (AB 21; Garden City, N.Y.: Doubleday and Co., 1965).

Brueggemann, Walter. *To Pluck Up, To Tear Down: A Commentary on the Book of Jeremiah 1–25.* (ITC; Grand Rapids; Wm. B. Eerdmans Publishing Co., 1988).

_____. *To Build, To Plant: A Commentary on Jeremiah 26–52* (ITC; Grand Rapids: Wm. B. Eerdmans Publishing Co., 1991).

Carroll, Robert P. *The Book of Jeremiah* (OTL; Philadelphia: Westminster Press, 1986).

Condamin, P. Albert. *Le Livre de Jérémie* (3d ed.; Paris: Librairie Victor Lecoffre, 1936). Originally 1920.

Cornill, D. Carl Heinrich. *Das Buch Jeremia* (Leipzig: Chr. Herm. Tauchnitz, 1905).

Craigie, Peter C., *et al. Jeremiah 1–25* (WBC 26; Dallas: Word Books, 1991).

Driver, S. R. *The Book of the Prophet Jeremiah* (2d ed.; London: Hodder & Stoughton, 1908).

Duhm, D. Bernhard. *Das Buch Jeremia* (KHC; Tübingen and Leipzig: J. C. B. Mohr [Paul Siebeck], 1901).

Freedman, Harry. *Jeremiah* (Soncino Books of the Bible; London: Soncino Press, 1949).

Giesebrecht, D. Fredrich. *Das Buch Jeremia* (HKAT; Göttingen: Vandenhoeck und Ruprecht, 1894).

Graf, Karl Heinrich. *Der Prophet Jeremia* (Leipzig: T. O. Weigel, 1862).

Holladay, William L. *Jeremiah I* (Hermeneia; Philadelphia: Fortress Press, 1986).

_____. *Jeremiah II* (Hermeneia; Minneapolis: Augsburg Fortress Press, 1989).

Hyatt, J. Philip. "Jeremiah," in *IB* 5 (ed. George A. Buttrick; New York: Abingdon Press, 1956) 777–1142.

Jones, Douglas Rawlinson. *Jeremiah* (NCBC; Grand Rapids: William B. Eerdmans / London: Marshall Pickering and HarperCollins, 1992).

Keown, Gerald L., *et al. Jeremiah 26–52* (WBC 27; Dallas: Word Books, 1995).

McKane, William. *Jeremiah I* (ICC; Edinburgh: T. & T. Clark, 1986).

_____. *Jeremiah II* (ICC; Edinburgh: T. & T. Clark, 1996).

O'Connor, Kathleen M. "Jeremiah," in *The Women's Bible Commentary* (eds. Carol A. Newsom and Sharon H. Ring; Louisville, KY: Westminster/John Knox Press, 1992) 169–77.

Peake, A. S. *Jeremiah I* (CB; New York: H. Frowde and Edinburgh: T. C. & E. C. Jack, 1910).

_____. *Jeremiah and Lamentations II* (CB; New York: Henry Frowde and Edinburgh: T. C. & E. C. Jack, 1911).

Rosenberg, A. J. *Jeremiah I–II* (New York: Judaica Press, 1985).

Rudolph, Wilhelm. *Jeremia* (HAT; 3d ed.; Tübingen: J. C. B. Mohr [Paul Siebeck], 1968).

Streane, A. W. *The Book of the Prophet Jeremiah together with The Lamentations* (CBSC; Cambridge: Cambridge University Press, 1952). Originally 1913.

Thompson, J. A. *The Book of Jeremiah* (NICOT; Grand Rapids: William B. Eerdmans Publishing Co., 1980).

Volz, D. Paul. *Der Prophet Jeremia* (KAT 10; 2d ed.; Leipzig: A. Deichertsche Verlagsbuchhandlung D. Werner Scholl, 1983). Originally 1928.

Weiser, Artur. *Das Buch Jeremia 1–25,14* (ATD 20; 8th ed.; Göttingen: Vandenhoeck und Ruprecht, 1981). Originally 1952.

_____. *Das Buch Jeremia 25,15–52,34* (ATD 21; 7th ed.; Göttingen: Vandenhoeck und Ruprecht, 1982). Originally 1955.

Books, Monographs, and Articles

Abrams, M. H. *The Mirror and the Lamp: Romantic Theory and the Critical Tradition* (New York: Oxford University Press, 1953).

Achtemeier, Paul. "*Omne verbum sonat*: The New Testament and the Oral Environment of Late Western Antiquity." *JBL* 109 (1990), 3–27.

Ackroyd, Peter R. "Historians and Prophets." *SEÅ* 33 (1968), 18–54.

Albright, William F. "The Old Testament and Canaanite Language and Literature." *CBQ* 7 (1945), 5–31.

_____. "Some Remarks on the Song of Moses in Deuteronomy XXXII." *VT* 9 (1959), 339–46. Repr. Noth, *Essays in Honour of Millar Burrows* (1959), 3–10.

_____. *Yahweh and the Gods of Canaan* (Garden City, N.Y.: Doubleday and Co., 1968). Repr. (Winona Lake, Ind.: Eisenbrauns, 1979).

Alexandre, Manuel Jr. "Rhetorical Argumentation as an Exegetical Technique in Philo of Alexandria," in *Hellenica et Judaica* (Hommage à Valentin Nikiprowetzky; eds. A. Caquot, *et al.*; Leuven/Paris: Éditions Peeters, 1986), 13–27.

Alonso Schökel, Luis. "Die stilistische Analyse bei den Propheten," in *Congress Volume: Oxford, 1959* (VTSupp 7; Leiden: E. J. Brill, 1960), 154–64.

_____. *Estudios de poética hebrea* (Barcelona: Juan Flors, 1963).

_____. *A Manual of Hebrew Poetics* (Rome: Pontifical Biblical Institute, 1988).

Amit, Yairah. "The Multi-Purpose 'Leading Word' and the Problems of Its Usage." *Prooftexts* 9 (1989), 99–114.

Andersen, Francis I. *The Sentence in Biblical Hebrew* (The Hague/Paris: Mouton, 1974). "Surprise Clauses," 94–96; "Chiastic Sentences," 119–40.

Anderson, Bernhard W. "The New Frontier of Rhetorical Criticism," in *Rhetorical Criticism* (eds. Jared J. Jackson and Martin Kessler; Pittsburgh: Pickwick Press, 1974), ix–xviii.

_____. "'The Lord Has Created Something New': A Stylistic Study of Jer 31:15–22." *CBQ* 40 (1978), 463–78. Repr. Perdue and Kovacs, *A Prophet to the Nations* (1984), 367–80; and B. W. Anderson, *From Creation to New Creation* (1994), 179–94.

_____. *From Creation to New Creation* (Minneapolis: Fortress Press, 1994).

Anderson, Bernhard W., and Walter Harrelson (eds.). *Israel's Prophetic Heritage* (In Honor of James Muilenburg; New York: Harper and Bros., 1962).

Anderson, G. W. "Some Aspects of the Uppsala School of Old Testament Study." *HThR* 43 (1950), 239–56.

apRoberts, Ruth. "Old Testament Poetry: The Translatable Structure." *PMLA* 92 (1977), 987–1004.

Aristotle. *The "Art" of Rhetoric* (trans. John Henry Freese; LCL; Cambridge, Mass.: Harvard University Press, 1947).

Arnold, Carroll C. "Rhetoric in America since 1900," in Oliver and Bauer, *Reestablishing the Speech Profession: The First Fifty Years* (1959), 3–7.

Auffret, Pierre. *La sagesse a bati sa maison* (Fribourg: Éditions Universitaires / Göttingen: Vandenhoeck & Ruprecht, 1982).

Baker, Aelred. "Parallelism: England's Contribution to Biblical Studies." *CBQ* 35 (1973), 429–40.

Baker, Sheridan. *The Complete Stylist* (New York: Thomas Y. Crowell Co., 1966).

Baldwin, Charles Sears. *God Unknown: A Study of the Address of St. Paul at Athens* (Milwaukee: Morehouse Publishing Co. and London: A. R. Mowbray & Co., 1920).

_____. *Ancient Rhetoric and Poetic* (Gloucester, Mass.: Peter Smith, 1959). Originally 1924.

Ball, Ivan J. Jr. "The Rhetorical Shape of Zephaniah," in *Perspectives on Language and Text: Essays and Poems in Honor of Francis I. Andersen's Sixtieth Birthday, July 28, 1985* (eds. Edgar W. Conrad and Edward G. Newing; Winona Lake, Ind.: Eisenbrauns, 1987) 155–65.

_____. *Zephaniah: A Rhetorical Study* (Berkeley: Bibal, 1988).

Barré, Lloyd M. *The Rhetoric of Political Persuasion: The Narrative Artistry and Political Intentions of 2 Kings 9–11* (CBQMS 20; Washington, D.C.: Catholic Biblical Association of America, 1988).

Baumgartner, Walter. *Die Klagegedichte des Jeremia* (BZAW 32; Giessen: Alfred Töpelmann, 1917). English: *Jeremiah's Poems of Lament* (trans. David E. Orton; Sheffield: Sheffield Academic Press, 1987).

Bellis, Alice Ogden. *The Structure and Composition of Jeremiah 50:2–51:58* (Lewiston, N.Y.: Mellen Biblical Press, 1995).

Bengel, Joh. Albert. *Gnomon Novi Testamenti* (3d ed.; London and Edinburgh: Williams & Norgate, 1862).

Bentzen, Aage. "The Ritual Background of Amos i 2–ii 16." *OS* 8 (1950), 85–99.

Bercovitch, Sacvan. *The American Jeremiad* (Madison: University of Wisconsin Press, 1978).

Berlin, Adele. "Shared Rhetorical Features in Biblical and Sumerian Literature." *JANES* 10 (1978), 35–42.

_____. *Poetics and Interpretation of Biblical Narrative* (Sheffield: The Almond Press, 1983).

_____. *The Dynamics of Biblical Parallelism* (Bloomington: University of Indiana Press, 1985).

_____. "Azariah de' Rossi on Biblical Poetry." *Prooftexts* 12 (1992), 175–81.

Berridge, John Maclennan. *Prophet, People, and the Word of Yahweh: An Examination of Form and Content in the Proclamation of the Prophet Jeremiah* (Zürich: EVZ-Verlag, 1970).

Bertman, Stephen. "Symmetrical Design in the Book of Ruth." *JBL* 84 (1965), 165–68.

_____. "Structural Symmetry at the End of the *Odyssey.*" *GRBS* 9 (1968), 115–23.

Best, Thomas F. (ed.). *Hearing and Speaking the Word: Selections from the Works of James Muilenburg* (Chico, Calif.: Scholars Press, 1984).

Betz, Hans Dieter. *Der Apostel Paulus und die sokratische Tradition* (BHT 45; Tübingen: J. C. B. Mohr [Paul Siebeck], 1972).

_____. "The Literary Composition and Function of Paul's Letter to the Galatians." *NTS* 21 (1975), 353–79.

_____. *Galatians* (Hermeneia; Philadelphia: Fortress Press, 1979).

_____. *2 Corinthians 8 and 9* (Hermeneia; Philadelphia: Fortress Press, 1985).

Beuken, W. A. "Isaiah Chapters lxv–lxvi: Trito-Isaiah and the Closure of the Book of Isaiah," in *Congress Volume: Leuven, 1989* (VTSupp 43; Leiden: E. J. Brill, 1991), 204–21.

Bevan, Edwyn R. "Rhetoric in the Ancient World," in *Essays in Honor of Gilbert Murray* (eds. J. A. Thomson and A. J. Toynbee; London: George Allen and Unwin, 1936), 189–213.

Bewer, Julius A. "Critical Notes on Old Testament Passages," in *Old Testament and Semitic Studies in Memory of William Rainey Harper II* (Chicago: University of Chicago Press, 1908), 207–26.

Birkeland, Harris. *Zum hebräischen Traditionswesen: Die Komposition der prophetischen Bucher des Alten Testaments* (Oslo: Jacob Dybwad, 1939).

_____. *Jeremia: Profet og dikter* (Oslo: Gyldendal Norsk Forlag, 1950).

Bitzer, Lloyd F. "The Rhetorical Situation." *PhRh* 1 (1968), 1–14. Repr. W. R. Fisher, *Rhetoric: A Tradition in Transition* (1974), 247–60.

Bitzer, Lloyd F., and Edwin Black (eds.). *The Prospect of Rhetoric* (Englewood Cliffs, N.J.: Prentice-Hall, 1971).

Black, C. Clifton II. "The Rhetorical Form of the Hellenistic Jewish and Early Christian Sermon: A Response to Lawrence Wills." *HThR* 81 (1988), 1–18.

_____. "Rhetorical Criticism and Biblical Interpretation." *ET* 100 (1989), 252–58.

Black, Edwin. *Rhetorical Criticism: A Study in Method* (New York: Macmillan Co., 1965).

Blank, Sheldon H. "Men against God: The Promethean Element in Biblical Prayer." *JBL* 72 (1953), 1–13.

_____. "Irony by Way of Attribution." *Semitics* 1 (1970), 1–6.

Blenkinsopp, Joseph. "The Prophetic Reproach." *JBL* 90 (1971), 267–78.

Bliese, Loren F. "Chiastic and Homogeneous Metrical Structures Enhanced by Word Patterns in Obadiah." *JTT* 6 (1993), 210–27.

Bligh, John. *Galatians in Greek* (Detroit: University of Detroit Press, 1966).

Bloomfield, Maurice. *Rig-Veda Repetitions* (HOS 20; Cambridge, Mass.: Harvard University Press, 1916).

Boadt, Lawrence. "The A:B:B:A Chiasm of Identical Roots in Ezekiel." *VT* 25 (1975), 693–99.

_____. "Intentional Alliteration in Second Isaiah." *CBQ* 45 (1983), 353–63.

Boling, Robert G. "'Synonymous' Parallelism in the Psalms." *JSS* 5 (1960), 221–55.

Bonamartini, Ugo. "L'epesegesi nella S. Scrittura." *Biblica* 6 (1925), 424–44.

Booth, Wayne C. "The Revival of Rhetoric," in *New Rhetorics* (ed. Martin Steinmann Jr.; New York: Scribner's, 1967), 2–15.

_____. *A Rhetoric of Irony* (Chicago and London: University of Chicago Press, 1974).

Bowra, C. M. *Ancient Greek Literature* (New York: Oxford University Press, 1960).

Boys, Thomas. *A Key to the Book of Psalms* (London: L. B. Seeley and Son, 1825). Revised and enlarged with an Introduction by E. W. Bullinger (London: St. Paul's Churchyard, 1890).

Bozak, Barbara A. *Life "Anew": A Literary-Theological Study of Jeremiah 30–31* (Rome: Pontifical Biblical Institute, 1991).

Bradley, Pearl G. "A Criticism of the Modes of Persuasion Found in Selected Civil Rights Addresses of John F. Kennedy, 1962–63." Unpublished Ph.D. dissertation (Ohio State University, 1967).

Brandt, William J. *The Rhetoric of Argumentation* (New York: Bobbs-Merrill Co., 1970).

_____. "The Rhetoric of Poetry." Unpublished Manuscript.

Breck, John. "Biblical Chiasmus: Exploring Structure for Meaning." *BTB* 17 (1987), 70–74.

Briggs, Charles A. "Hebrew Poetry." *Hebraica* 2 (1885–86), 164–70.

Briggs, Charles A., and Emile G. Briggs. *A Critical and Exegetical Commentary on the Book of Psalms I–II* (ICC; Edinburgh: T. & T. Clark, 1906–7; 1952).

Bright, John. "The Date of the Prose Sermons of Jeremiah." *JBL* 70 (1951), 15–29. Repr. Perdue and Kovacs, *A Prophet to the Nations* (1984), 193–212.

_____. "The Book of Jeremiah: Its Structure, Its Problems, and Their Significance for the Interpreter." *Int* 9 (1955), 259–78.

_____. "Jeremiah's Complaints: Liturgy, or Expressions of Personal Distress?" in *Proclamation and Presence* (In Honor of G. Henton Davies; eds. John I. Durham and J. R. Porter; Richmond: John Knox Press, 1970), 189–214.

_____. *A History of Israel* (2d ed., Philadelphia: Westminster Press, 1972; 3d ed., 1981).

Brock, Bernard L. and Robert L Scott (eds.). *Methods of Rhetorical Criticism: A Twentieth-Century Perspective* (2d ed.; Detroit: Wayne State University Press, 1980).

Brockriede, Wayne. "Rhetorical Criticism as Argument." *QJS* 60 (1974), 165–74.

Brongers, H. A. "Merismus, Synekdoche und Hendiadys in der Bibel-Hebräischen Sprache." *OS* 14 (1965), 100–114.

Brookhiser, Richard. "Poetry Out Loud." *Atlantic Monthly* 263/2 (1989), 43–45.

Brooks, Keith. *The Communicative Arts and Sciences of Speech* (Columbus: Charles E. Merrill, 1967).

Browne, Robert M. "Rhetorical Analysis and Poetic Structure," in _Rhetoric: Theories for Application_ (ed. Robert M. Gorrell; Champaign, Ill.: National Council of Teachers of English, 1967), 90–98.

Brueggemann, Walter. "Jeremiah's Use of Rhetorical Questions." _JBL_ 92 (1973), 358–74.

Bryant, Donald C. "Rhetoric: Its Function and Scope." _QJS_ 39 (1953), 401–24. Repr. Schwartz and Rycenga, _The Province of Rhetoric_ (1965), 3–36; Natanson and Johnstone, _Philosophy, Rhetoric, and Argumentation_ (1965), 32–62; and W. R. Fisher, _Rhetoric: A Tradition in Transition_ (1974), 195–230.

_____ (ed.). _The Rhetorical Idiom: Essays in Rhetoric, Oratory, Language and Drama_ (Presented to Herbert A. Wichelns; Ithaca, N.Y.: Cornell University Press, 1958).

_____ (ed.). _Papers in Rhetoric and Poetic_ (Iowa City: University of Iowa Press, 1965).

_____. "Uses of Rhetoric in Criticism" in Bryant, _Papers in Rhetoric and Poetic_ (1965), 1–14.

_____. _Rhetorical Dimensions in Criticism_ (Baton Rouge: Louisiana State University Press, 1973).

_____. "Rhetoric: Its Function and Its Scope _Rediviva_," in Bryant, _Rhetorical Dimensions in Criticism_ (1973), 3–23. Repr. W. R. Fisher, _Rhetoric: A Tradition in Transition_ (1974), 231–46.

Buber, Martin. _Good and Evil_ (New York: Charles Scribner's Sons, 1953).

Budde, Karl. "Poetry (Hebrew)," in _HDB_ 4, 2–13.

Bühlmann, Walter and Karl Scherer. _Stilfiguren der Bibel_ (Fribourg: Verlag Schweizerisches Katholisches Bibelwerk, 1973).

Bujard, Walter. _Stilanalytische Untersuchungen zum Kolosserbrief als Beitrag zur Methodik von Sprachvergleichen_ (Göttingen: Vandenhoeck und Ruprecht, 1973).

Bullinger, Ethelbert W. _Figures of Speech Used in the Bible_ (2d ed.; Grand Rapids: Baker Book House, 1969). Originally 1898.

Burney, C. F. _The Poetry of Our Lord_ (Oxford: Clarendon Press, 1925).

Bussby, Fredrick. "Bishop Jebb, a Neglected Biblical Scholar." _ET_ 60 (1948–49), 193.

Butler, B. C. _The Originality of St. Matthew_ (Cambridge: Cambridge University Press, 1951).

Buttenwieser, Moses. _The Prophets of Israel_ (New York: Macmillan Co., 1914).

Buttrey, T. V. "Accident and Design in Euripides' 'Medea.'" _AJP_ 79 (1958), 1–17.

Campbell, Edward F. Jr., and David Noel Freedman (eds.). _The Biblical Archaeologist Reader II_ (Garden City, N.Y.: Doubleday, 1964).

_____. _The Biblical Archaeologist Reader III_ (Garden City, N.Y.: Doubleday, 1970).

_____. _The Biblical Archaeologist Reader IV_ (Sheffield: Almond Press and American Schools of Oriental Research, 1983).

Carleton, James G. "The Idiom of Exaggerated Contrast." _The Expositor_ 4th Series 6 (1892), 365–72.

Carney, T. F. "Plutarch's Style in the _Marius_." _JHS_ 80 (1960), 24–31.

Carpenter, Ronald H. "The Essential Schemes of Syntax: An Analysis of Rhetorical Theory's Recommendations for Uncommon Word Orders." _QJS_ 55 (1969), 161–68.

Carrubba, R. W. "The Technique of the Double Structure in Horace." *Mnemosyne* Series 4, 20 (1967), 68–75.

Casanowicz, Immanuel M. "Paronomasia in the Old Testament." *JBL* 12 (1893), 105–67. Reprinted and expanded (Boston: Norwood Press, 1894).

Casetti, Pierre. *Gibt es ein Leben vor dem Tod? Eine Auslegung von Psalm 49* (Göttingen: Vandenhoeck & Ruprecht, 1982).

Ceresko, Anthony R. "The A:B:B:A Word Pattern in Hebrew and Northwest Semitic with Special Reference to the Book of Job." *UF* 7 (1975), 73–88.

_____. "The Chiastic Word Pattern in Hebrew." *CBQ* 38 (1976), 303–11.

_____. "The Function of Chiasmus in Hebrew Poetry." *CBQ* 40 (1978), 1–10.

_____. "A Poetic Analysis of Ps 105, with Attention to Its Use of Irony." *Biblica* 64 (1983), 20–46.

Cheyne, T. K. "Jeremiah" in *EncB* 11th ed., 15 (1911), 323–25.

Christensen, Duane L. "Anticipatory Paronomasia in Jonah 3:7–8 and Genesis 37:2." *RB* 90 (1983), 261–63.

Church, F. Forrester. "Rhetorical Structure and Design in Paul's Letter to Philemon." *HThR* 71 (1978), 17–33.

[Cicero]. *Rhetorica ad Herennium* (trans. Harry Caplan; LCL; Cambridge, Mass.: Harvard University Press, 1964).

Clark, Donald L. *Rhetoric and Poetry in the Renaissance* (New York: Columbia University Press, 1922).

Clark, Robert C. "Literary and Rhetorical Criticism," in *Essays on Rhetorical Criticism* (ed. Thomas R. Nilsen; New York: Random House, 1968), 64–74.

Clark, W. P. "Ancient Reading." *CJ* 26 (1930–31), 698–700.

Clifford, Richard J. "Style and Purpose in Psalm 105." *Biblica* 60 (1979), 420–27.

_____. *Fair Spoken and Persuading: An Interpretation of Second Isaiah* (New York: Paulist Press, 1984).

Clines, David J. "The Parallelism of Greater Precision," in Follis, *Directions in Biblical Hebrew Poetry* (1987), 77–100.

Cohn, Gabriël H. *Das Buch Jona* (Assen: Van Gorcum and Co., 1969).

Cohn, Robert L. "Form and Perspective in 2 Kings V." *VT* 33 (1983), 171–84.

Collins, John J. "Chiasmus, the 'ABA' Pattern and the Text of Paul," in *Studiorum Paulinorum Congress Internationalis Catholicus II* (Rome: Pontifical Biblical Institute, 1961), 575–83.

Condamin, Albert. "Symmetrical Repetitions in *Lamentations* Chapters I and II." *JThS* Old Series 7 (1905), 137–40.

_____. *Poémes de la Bible* (2d ed.; Paris: Gabriel Beauchesne et ses Fils, 1933).

Conley, Thomas M. "The Enthymeme in Perspective." *QJS* 70 (1984), 168–87.

_____. "Philo's Rhetoric: Argumentation and Style," in *Aufstieg und Niedergang der römischen Welt II* 21:1 (Berlin: Walter de Gruyter, 1984), 343–71.

Connors, Robert J., *et al.* "The Revival of Rhetoric in America," in *Essays on Classical Rhetoric and Modern Discourse* (eds. Robert J. Connors, *et al.*; Carbondale, Ill.: Southern Illinois University Press, 1984), 1–15.

Consigny, Scott. "Rhetoric and Its Situations." *PhRh* 7 (1974), 175–86.

Coogan, Michael David. "A Structural and Literary Analysis of the Song of Deborah." *CBQ* 40 (1978), 143–66.

Cooper, Jerrold S. "Symmetry and Repetition in Akkadian Narrative." *JAOS* 97 (1977), 508–12.

Corbett, Edward P. "Rhetoric and Teachers of English." *QJS* 51 (1965), 375–81.

_____ (ed.). *Rhetorical Analyses of Literary Works* (New York: Oxford University Press, 1969).

_____. *Classical Rhetoric for the Modern Student* (2d ed.; New York: Oxford University Press, 1971).

_____. "The Cornell School of Rhetoric," in *Selected Essays of Edward P. J. Corbett* (ed. Robert J. Connors; Dallas: Southern Methodist University Press, 1989), 290–304.

Cornell Faculty in the Department of Public Speaking. "Some Subjects for Graduate Study Suggested by Members of the Department of Public Speaking of Cornell University." *QJS* 9 (1923), 147–53.

Cornill, Carl Heinrich. *Introduction to the Canonical Books of the Old Testament* (trans. G. H. Box; New York: G. P. Putnam's Sons / London: Williams and Norgate, 1907). German: *Einleitung in das Alte Testament* (Freiburg: J. C. B. Mohr [Paul Siebeck], 1891).

Corvin, William R. "The Rhetorical Practice of Paul Tillich." Unpublished Ph.D. dissertation (University of Oklahoma, 1968).

Cosby, Michael R. "The Rhetorical Composition of Hebrews 11." *JBL* 107 (1988), 257–73.

Craven, Toni. *Artistry and Faith in the Book of Judith* (SBLDS 70; Chico, Calif.: Society of Biblical Literature and Scholars Press, 1983).

Crenshaw, James. "A Living Tradition: The Book of Jeremiah in Current Research," *Int* 37 (1983), 117–29. Repr. Mays and Achtemeier, *Interpreting the Prophets* (1987), 100–112.

Croft, Albert J. "The Functions of Rhetorical Criticism." *QJS* 42 (1956), 283–91. Repr. Schwartz and Rycenga, *The Province of Rhetoric* (1965), 403–14.

Cross, Frank M. Jr. "The History of the Biblical Text in the Light of Discoveries in the Judean Desert." *HThR* 57 (1964), 281–99. Repr. Cross and Talmon, *Qumran and the History of the Biblical Text* (1975), 177–95.

_____. "The Structure of the Deuteronomic History," in *Perspectives in Jewish Learning III* (Chicago: College of Jewish Studies, 1968), 9–24.

Cross, Frank M. Jr., and David Noel Freedman. *Studies in Ancient Yahwistic Poetry* (SBLDS 21; Missoula, Mont.: Society of Biblical Literature and Scholars Press, 1975). Originally 1950.

Cross, Frank M. Jr., and Shemaryahu Talmon (eds.). *Qumran and the History of the Biblical Text* (Cambridge, Mass.: Harvard University Press, 1975).

Crotty, R. B. "Changing Fashions in Biblical Interpretation." *ABR* 33 (1985), 15–30.

Crow, Loren D. "The Rhetoric of Psalm 44." *ZAW* 104 (1992), 394–401.

Cummins, Patrick. "Jeremias Orator." *CBQ* 11 (1949), 191–201.

Cunningham, David S. "Theology as Rhetoric." *TS* 52 (1991), 407–30.

Dahood, Mitchell. "Hebrew-Ugaritic Lexicography I." *Biblica* 44 (1963), 289–303.

_____. *Psalms I–III* (AB 16–17A; Garden City, N.Y.: Doubleday & Co., 1966–1970).

_____. "The Metaphor in Jeremiah 17,13." *Biblica* 48 (1967), 109–10.

_____. "A New Metrical Pattern in Biblical Poetry." *CBQ* 29 (1967), 574–79.

_____. "The Breakup of Stereotyped Phrases: Some New Examples." *JANES* 5 (1973), 83–89.

_____. "Chiasmus in Job: A Text-Critical and Philological Criterion," in *A Light unto My Path* (In Honor of Jacob M. Myers; eds. Howard N. Bream, *et al.*; Philadelphia: Temple University Press, 1974), 119–30.

_____. "Further Instances of the Breakup of Stereotyped Phrases in Hebrew," in *Studi Hierosolymitana II: Studi esegetici* (eds. P. Emmanuele Testa, *et al.*; Jerusalem: Franciscan Press, 1976), 9–19.

_____. "The Chiastic Breakup in Isaiah 58,7." *Biblica* 57 (1976), 105.

_____. "Chiasmus," in *IDBSupp*, 145.

Daniels, Dwight R. "Is There a 'Prophetic Lawsuit' Genre?" *ZAW* 99 (1987), 339–60.

Daube, David. "A Rhetorical Principle in the Gospels." *ET* 54 (1942–43), 305–6.

_____. "Three Questions of Form in Matthew V." *JThS* Old Series 45 (1944), 21–31.

_____. "Rabbinic Methods of Interpretation and Hellenistic Rhetoric." *HUCA* 22 (1949), 239–64. Repr. Alan D. Corré, *Understanding the Talmud* (New York: KTAV, 1975), 275–89.

_____. "Four Types of Questions." *JThS* 2 (1951), 45–48.

_____. "The Extension of a Simile," in *Interpreting the Hebrew Bible* (In Honour of E. I. J. Rosenthal; eds. J. A. Emerton and Stefan C. Reif; Cambridge: Cambridge University Press, 1982), 57–59.

Deeks, David. "The Structure of the Fourth Gospel." *NTS* 15 (1968), 107–29.

DeRoche, Michael. "Structure, Rhetoric and Meaning in Hosea iv 4–10." *VT* 33 (1983), 185–98.

DeVries, Simon. "Biblical Criticism, History of," in *IDB* A–D, 413–18.

Dewey, Joanna. "The Literary Structure of the Controversy Stories in Mark 2:1–3:6." *JBL* 92 (1973), 394–401.

_____. *Markan Public Debate: Literary Technique, Concentric Structure, and Theology in Mark 2:1–3:6* (SBLDS 48; Chico, Calif.: Scholars Press, 1980).

_____. "Oral Methods of Structuring Narrative in Mark." *Int* 43 (1989), 32–44.

Di Marco, Angelico. "Der Chiasmus in der Bibel." *LB* 36 (1975), 21–97; 37 (1976), 49–68; 39 (1976), 37–85.

Dorn, Louis. "The Unexpected as a Speech Device: Shifts of Thematic Expectancy in Jeremiah." *BiTr* 37 (1986), 216–22.

Dorson, Richard M. "Oral Styles of American Folk Narrators," in *Style in Language* (ed. Thomas A. Sebeok; [Cambridge, Mass.]: MIT Press / New York: John Wiley & Sons, 1960), 27–51.

Douglas, Claude C. *Overstatement in the New Testament* (New York: Henry Holt and Co., 1931).

Driver, G. R. "Linguistic and Textual Problems: Jeremiah." *JQR* 28 (1937–38), 97–129.

_____. "Problems and Solutions." *VT* 4 (1954), 225–45. "Paronomasia," 240–45.

_____. *Semitic Writing: From Pictograph to Alphabet* (rev. ed. London: British Academy and Oxford University Press, 1976). Originally 1948.

Driver, S. R. "The Double Text of Jeremiah." *The Expositor* 3d Series 9 (1889), 321–37.

_____. *A Critical and Exegetical Commentary on Deuteronomy* (ICC; 3d ed.; Edinburgh: T. & T. Clark, 1902). Originally 1895.

_____. *An Introduction to the Literature of the Old Testament* (Cleveland and New York: World Publishing Co., 1967). Originally 1891.

Drummond, A. M. "Graduate Work in Public Speaking." *QJS* 9 (1923), 136–47.

_____ (ed.). *Studies in Rhetoric and Public Speaking in Honor of James Albert Winans* (New York: The Century Co., 1925).

Duckworth, George Eckel. *Foreshadowing and Suspense in the Epics of Homer, Apollonius and Vergil* (Princeton: Princeton University Press, 1933).

_____. *Structural Patterns and Proportions in Vergil's Aeneid* (Ann Arbor: University of Michigan Press, 1962).

Duhm, D. Bernhard. *Das Buch Jesaia* (HKAT; 2d rev. ed. Göttingen: Vandenhoeck und Ruprecht, 1902). Originally 1892.

_____. "Poetical Literature" in *EncBib* 3.3793–3804.

Dundes, Alan (ed.). *The Study of Folklore* (Englewood Cliffs, N.J.: Prentice-Hall, 1965).

Eissfeldt, Otto. *The Old Testament: An Introduction* (trans. Peter R. Ackroyd; New York: Harper & Row, 1965).

Eitan, Israel. "La répétition de la racine en hébréu." *JPOS* 1 (1920–21), 171–86.

Emery, V. J. "On the Definition of Some Rhetorical Terms." *AJP* 18 (1897), 206–13.

Engnell, Ivan. *Gamla Testamentet I: En Traditionshistorisk Inledning* (Stockholm: Svenska Kyrkans Diakonistyrelses Bokförlag, 1945).

_____. "Methodological Aspects of Old Testament Study," in *Congress Volume: Oxford, 1959* (VTSupp 7; Leiden: E. J. Brill, 1960), 13–30.

_____. "Jeremias bok," in *SBU* 1.1098–1106.

Exum, J. Cheryl. "A Literary and Structural Analysis of the Song of Songs." *ZAW* 85 (1973), 47–79.

_____. "Of Broken Pots, Fluttering Birds and Visions in the Night: Extended Simile and Poetic Technique in Isaiah." *CBQ* 43 (1981), 331–52.

Exum, J. Cheryl, and Charles Talbert. "The Structure of Paul's Speech to the Ephesian Elders (Acts 20,18–35)." *CBQ* 29 (1967), 233–36.

Farrar, Frederic W. "Rabbinic Exegesis." *The Expositor* 1st Series 5 (1877), 362–78.

_____. *Language and Languages* (London: Longmans, Green and Co., 1878).

_____. "The Rhetoric of St. Paul." *The Expositor* 1st Series 10 (1879), 1–27.

Farrer, Austin. *St. Matthew and St. Mark* (Westminster: Dacre, 1954).

Feldman, Asher. *The Parables and Similes of the Rabbis* (Cambridge: Cambridge University Press, 1924).

Fenton, J. C. "Inclusio and Chiasmus in Matthew," in *Texte und Untersuchungen zur Geschichte der altchristlichen Literatur 73: Studia Evangelica* (ed. Kurt Aland; Berlin: Akademie-Verlag, 1959), 174–79.

Ferrara, A. J. "*Topoi* and Stock-Strophes in Sumerian Literary Tradition: Some Observations, Part I." *JNES* 54 (1995), 81–117.

Filson, Floyd V. "How Much of the New Testament Is Poetry?" *JBL* 67 (1948), 125–34.

Fiorenza, E. Schüssler. "Rhetorical Situation and Historical Reconstruction in 1 Corinthians." *NTS* 33 (1987), 386–403.

Fischel, Henry A. "The Uses of Sorites (Climax, Gradatio) in the Tannaitic Period." *HUCA* 44 (1973), 119–51.

Fishbane, Michael. "Composition and Structure in the Jacob Cycle (Gen 25:19–35:22)."*JJS* 26 (1975), 15–38.

_____. *Text and Texture* (New York: Schocken Books, 1979).

Fisher, L. R. "The Temple Quarter." *JSS* 8 (1963), 34–41.

Fisher, Walter R. (ed.). *Rhetoric: A Tradition in Transition* (In Honor of Donald C. Bryant; East Lansing, Mich.: Michigan State University Press, 1974).

Flight, John W. "The Present State of Studies in the History of Writing in the Near East," in *The Haverford Symposium on Archaeology and the Bible* (New Haven: American Schools of Oriental Research, 1938), 111–35.

Floyd, Michael H. "Prophecy and Writing in Habakkuk 2,1–5." *ZAW* 105 (1993), 462–81.

Fogarty, Daniel. *Roots for a New Rhetoric* (New York: Columbia University Teacher's College, 1959).

Follis, Elaine R. (ed.). *Directions in Biblical Hebrew Poetry* (Sheffield: Sheffield Academic Press, 1987).

Forbes, John. *The Symmetrical Structure of Scripture* (Edinburgh: T. & T. Clark, 1854).

Ford, Desmond. "A Rhetorical Study of Certain Pauline Addresses." Unpublished Ph.D. dissertation (Michigan State University, 1960).

Fordyce, C. J. "Puns on Names in Greek." *CJ* 28 (1932–33), 44–46.

Foresti, Fabrizio. "Il rapimento di Elia al cielo." *RevBib* 31 (1983), 257–72.

Fox, Michael V. "The Rhetoric of Ezekiel's Vision of the Valley of the Bones." *HUCA* 51 (1980), 1–15.

Franke, Chris A. "The Function of the Satiric Lament over Babylon in Second Isaiah (XLVII)." *VT* 41 (1991), 407–18.

_____. *Isaiah 46, 47, and 48: A New Literary-Critical Reading* (Biblical and Judaic Studies 3; Winona Lake, Ind.: Eisenbrauns, 1994).

Fredericks, Daniel C. "Chiasm and Parallel Structure in Qoheleth 5:9–6:9." *JBL* 108 (1989), 17–35.

Freedman, David Noel. "Archaic Forms in Early Hebrew Poetry." *ZAW* 72 (1960), 101–7.

_____. "Pentateuch," in *IDB* K–Q, 711–27.

_____. "On Method in Biblical Studies: The Old Testament." *Int* 17 (1963), 308–18.

_____. "Divine Commitment and Human Obligation." *Int* 18 (1964), 419–31.

_____. "The Structure of Job 3." *Biblica* 49 (1968), 503–8. Repr. Freedman, *Pottery, Poetry, and Prophecy* (1980), 323–28.

_____. "The Structure of Psalm 137," in *Near Eastern Studies in Honor of William Foxwell Albright* (ed. Hans Goedicke; Baltimore: Johns Hopkins University Press, 1971), 187–205. Repr. Freedman, *Pottery, Poetry, and Prophecy* (1980), 303–21.

_____. "Prolegomenon," to Gray, *The Forms of Hebrew Poetry* (1972), vii–lvi.

_____. "Acrostics and Metrics in Hebrew Poetry." *HThR* 65 (1972), 367–92. Repr. Freedman, *Pottery, Poetry, and Prophecy* (1980), 51–76.

_____. *Pottery, Poetry, and Prophecy: Studies in Early Hebrew Poetry* (Winona Lake, Ind.: Eisenbrauns, 1980).

_____. "Acrostic Poems in the Hebrew Bible: Alphabetic and Otherwise." *CBQ* 48 (1986), 408–31.

_____. "Deliberate Deviation from an Established Pattern of Repetition in Hebrew Poetry as a Rhetorical Device," in *Proceedings of the Ninth World Congress of Jewish Studies (Jerusalem, August 4–12, 1985). Division A: The Period of the Bible* (Jerusalem: World Union of Jewish Studies, 1986), 45–52.

_____. "Another Look at Biblical Hebrew Poetry," in Follis, *Directions in Biblical Hebrew Poetry* (1987), 11–28.

_____. "The Structure of Isaiah 40:1–11," in *Perspectives on Language and Text: Essays and Poems in Honor of Francis I. Andersen's Sixtieth Birthday, July 28, 1985* (eds. Edgar W. Conrad and Edward G. Newing; Winona Lake, Ind.: Eisenbrauns, 1987), 167–93.

_____. "The Structure of Psalm 119: Part II." *HAR* 14 (1994), 55–87.

Friedman, Richard Elliott. "The Deuteronomistic School," in *Fortunate the Eyes That See* (In Honor of David Noel Freedman; eds. Astrid B. Beck *et al.*; Grand Rapids: Eerdmans, 1995), 70–80.

Frye, Northrop. "Rhetorical Criticism: Theory of Genres," in Frye, *Anatomy of Criticism* (Princeton: Princeton University Press, 1957), 243–337.

Gaechter, Paul. "Semitic Literary Forms in the Apocalypse and Their Import." *TS* 8 (1947), 547–73.

Gandz, Solomon. "Oral Tradition in the Bible," in *Jewish Studies in Memory of George A. Kohut* (New York: The Alexander Kohut Memorial Foundation, 1935), 248–69.

Garland, D. David. "Exegesis of Jeremiah 2:10–13." *SJT* New Series 2/2 (1959–60), 27–32.

Garsiel, Moshe. "Puns upon Names as a Literary Device in 1 Kings 1–2." *Biblica* 72 (1991), 379–86.

Geller, Stephen A. *Parallelism in Early Biblical Poetry* (HSM 20; Missoula, Mont: Scholars Press, 1979).

_____. "The Dynamics of Parallel Verse: A Poetic Analysis of Deut 32:6–12." *HThR* 75 (1982), 35–56.

Gemser, B. "The 'Rîb' or Controversy-Pattern in Hebrew Mentality," in *Wisdom in Israel and in the Ancient Near East* (eds. M. Noth and D. Winton Thomas; VTSupp 3; Leiden: E. J. Brill, 1955), 120–37.

Gevaryahu, Haim. "Notes on Authors and Books in the Bible" [Hebrew]. *BeitM* 43 (1970), 368–74.

_____. "Limmudim: Scribal Disciples in the Book of Isaiah" [Hebrew]. *BeitM* 47 (1971), 438–56.

_____. "Biblical Colophons: A Source for the 'Biography' of Authors, Texts and Books," in *Congress Volume: Edinburgh, 1974* (VTSupp 28; Leiden: E. J. Brill, 1975), 42–59.

Gevirtz, Stanley. "The Ugaritic Parallel to Jeremiah 8:23." *JNES* 20 (1961), 41–46.

_____. *Patterns in the Early Poetry of Israel* (Chicago: University of Chicago Press, 1963).

_____. "On Canaanite Rhetoric: The Evidence of the Amarna Letters from Tyre." *Orientalia* 42 (1973), 162–77.

Gilliard, Frank D. "More Silent Reading in Antiquity: *Non omne verbum sonabat.*" *JBL* 112 (1993), 689–94.

Gilula, M. "An Egyptian Parallel to Jeremia I 4–5." *VT* 17 (1967), 114.

Ginsberg, H. L. "The Rebellion and Death of Baʿlu." *Orientalia* 5 (1936), 161–98.

_____. "Ugaritic Studies and the Bible." *BA* 8 (1945), 41–58. Repr. Campbell and Freedman, *Biblical Archaeologist Reader II* (1964), 34–50.

Ginsburg, Christian D. *Introduction to the Massoretico-Critical Edition of the Hebrew Bible* (New York: KTAV Publishing House, 1966). Originally 1897.

Gitay, Yehoshua. "Rhetorical Criticism and the Prophetic Discourse," in *Persuasive Artistry: Studies in New Testament Rhetoric in Honor of George A. Kennedy* (ed. Duane F. Watson; Sheffield: Sheffield Academic Press, 1991), 13–24.

_____. "Rhetorical Criticism," in *To Each Its Own Meaning* (eds. Stephen R. Haynes and Steven L. McKenzie; Louisville: Westminster/John Knox Press, 1993), 135–49.

Glasson, T. Francis. "Chiasmus in St. Matthew vii. 6." *ET* 68 (1956–57), 302.

Gonda, J. *Stylistic Repetition in the Veda* (Amsterdam: N. V. Noord-Hollandsche Uitgevers Maatschappij, 1959).

Good, Edwin M. *Irony in the Old Testament* (Philadelphia: Westminster Press, 1965). Repr. (2d ed.; Sheffield: Almond Press, 1981).

_____. "The Composition of Hosea." *SEÅ* 31 (1966), 21–63.

Gordis, Robert. "A Rhetorical Use of Interrogative Sentences in Biblical Hebrew." *AJSLL* 49 (1933), 212–17. Repr. Gordis, *The Word and the Book* (1976), 152–57.

_____. "Quotations in Wisdom Literature." *JQR* 30 (1939–40), 123–47.

_____. "Quotations as a Literary Usage in Biblical, Oriental and Rabbinic Literature." *HUCA* 22 (1949), 157–219. Repr. Gordis, *Poets, Prophets and Sages* (1971), 104–59.

_____. "On Methodology in Biblical Exegesis." *JQR* 61 (1970), 93–118.

_____. "The Structure of Biblical Poetry," in Gordis, *Poets, Prophets and Sages* (1971), 61–94.

_____. *Poets, Prophets and Sages: Essays in Biblical Interpretation* (Bloomington and London: Indiana University Press, 1971).

_____. *The Word and the Book* (New York: KTAV Publishing House, 1976),

Gordon, Alex R. "Pioneers in the Study of the Old Testament Poetry, I: Lowth." *ET* 22 (1910–11), 444–48.

_____. "Pioneers in the Study of the Old Testament Poetry II: Herder." *ET* 24 (1912–13), 227–32.

Gordon, Cyrus H. *Ugaritic Textbook* (Rome: Pontifical Biblical Institute, 1965).

Gottwald, Norman K. *Studies in the Book of Lamentations* (Chicago: Alec R. Allenson / London: SCM Press, 1954).

_____. "Lamentations." *Int* 9 (1955), 320–38.

_____. "Samuel, Book of," in *EJ* 14.788–97.

Goulder, M. D. "The Chiastic Structure of the Lucan Journey," in *Studia Evangelica II* (ed. F. L. Cross; Berlin: Akademie-Verlag, 1964), 195–202.

_____. *Type and History in Acts* (London: SPCK, 1964).

Graves, Richard L. "Symmetrical Form and the Rhetoric of the Sentence," in *Essays on Classical Rhetoric and Modern Discourse* (eds. Robert J. Connors, et al.; Carbondale, Ill.: Southern Illinois University Press, 1984), 170–78.

Gray, George Buchanan. *The Forms of Hebrew Poetry* (Prolegomenon David Noel Freedman; New York: KTAV, 1972). Originally 1915. Repr. of articles in *The Expositor* 8th Series (1913).

Green, H. B. "The Structure of Matthew's Gospel," in *Studia Evangelica IV* (ed. F. L. Cross; Berlin: Akademie-Verlag, 1968), 47–59.

Greenwood, David C. "Rhetorical Criticism and Formgeschichte: Some Methodological Considerations." *JBL* 89 (1970), 418–26.

Gressmann, Hugo. "Die literarische Analyse Deutero-Jesajas." *ZAW* 34 (1914), 254–97.

Grobel, Kendrick. "A Chiastic Retribution-Formula in Romans 2," in *Zeit und Geschichte* (Rudolph Bultmann Festschrift; ed. Erich Dinkler; Tübingen: J. C. B. Mohr [Paul Siebeck], 1964), 255–61.

———. "Form Criticism," in *IDB* E–J, 320–21.

Gross, Karl. *Die literarische Verwandtschaft Jeremias mit Hosea* (Borna and Leipzig: Universitätsverlag von Robert Noske, 1930).

———. "Hoseas Einfluss auf Jeremias Anschauungen." *NKZ* 42 (1931), 241–56, 327–43.

Grossberg, Daniel. "The Disparate Elements of the Inclusio in the Psalms." *HAR* 6 (1982), 97–104.

———. "Pivotal Polysemy in Jeremiah XXV 10–11A." *VT* 36 (1986), 481–85.

Guillaume, D. F. "Paronomasia in the Old Testament." *JSS* 9 (1964), 282–90.

Gunkel, Hermann. *Genesis übersetzt und erklärt* (7th ed.; Göttingen: Vandenhoeck und Ruprecht, 1966). Originally 1901.

———. *The Legends of Genesis* (trans. W. H. Carruth; Introduction by W. F. Albright; New York: Schocken Books, 1966).

———. *Ausgewählte Psalmen übersetzt und erklärt* (3d ed.; Göttingen: Vandenhoeck und Ruprecht, 1911). Originally 1904.

———. "Die Grundprobleme der israelitischen Literaturgeschichte." *DLZ* 29 (1906), 1797–1800; 1861–66.

———. *The History of Religion and Old Testament Criticism* (Berlin-Schöneberg: Protestantischer Schriftenvertrieb / London: Williams and Norgate, 1911). German: "Die Religionsgeschichte und die alttestamentliche Wissenschaft," in *Fünfter Weltkongress für Freies Christentum und Religiösen Fortschritt, Berlin 5. bis 10. August 1910, Protokoll der Verhandlungen* (eds. D. Max Fischer and D. Friedrich Michael Schiele; Berlin: Verlag des Protestantischen Schriftenvertriebs, 1910), 169–80.

———. *Die Propheten* (Göttingen: Vandenhoeck und Ruprecht, 1917).

———. "Schriftstellerei und Formensprache der Propheten," in Gunkel, *Die Propheten* (1917), 104–40.

———. *Das Märchen im Alten Testament* (Tübingen: J. C. B. Mohr [Paul Siebeck], 1921).

———. "Die Propheten als Schriftsteller und Dichter," in *Die Schriften des Alten Testaments II: Die großen Propheten* (ed. D. Hans Schmidt; Göttingen: Vandenhoeck und Ruprecht, 1923), xxxiv–lxx. English: "The Prophets as Writers and Poets," in Petersen, *Prophecy in Israel* (1987), 22–73.

———. "The Secret Experiences of the Prophets." *The Expositor* 9th Series (1924) 1: 356–66; 427–35; 2: 23–32. German: "Die geheimen Erfahrungen der Propheten," in *Die Schriften des Alten Testaments II: Die großen Propheten* (ed. D. Hans Schmidt; Göttingen: Vandenhoeck und Ruprecht, 1923), xvii–xxxiv.

———. *Die Israelitische Literatur* (Darmstadt: Wissenschaftliche Buchgesellschaft, 1963). Originally 1925.

———. "The Poetry of the Psalms: Its Literary History and Its Application to the Dating of the Psalms," in *Old Testament Essays* (ed. D. C. Simpson; London: Charles Griffin & Co., 1927), 118–42.

_____. *What Remains of the Old Testament and Other Essays* (trans. A. K. Dallas; London: George Allen and Unwin / New York: Macmillan Co., 1928).

_____. *The Psalms: A Form-Critical Introduction* (trans. Thomas M. Horner; Introduction James Muilenburg; Facet Books, Biblical Series 19; Philadelphia: Fortress Press, 1967). Originally 1930.

_____. "Propheten: IIB. Propheten Israels seit Amos." *RGG* ² 4 (1930), 1538–54. English: "The Israelite Prophecy from the Time of Amos," in Pelikan, *Twentieth Century Theology in the Making I* (1969), 48–75.

_____. *Einleitung in die Psalmen: Die Gattungen der religiösen Lyrik Israels* (Completed Joachim Begrich; Göttingen: Vandenhoeck und Ruprecht, 1933; 2d ed.; 1966).

Habel, Norman. "The Form and Significance of the Call Narratives." *ZAW* 77 (1965), 297–323.

_____. *Literary Criticism of the Old Testament* (Philadelphia: Fortress Press, 1971).

Hahn, Herbert F. *The Old Testament in Modern Research* (Philadelphia: Fortress Press, 1966).

Hals, Ronald M. "Legend: A Case Study in OT Form-Critical Terminology." *CBQ* 34 (1972), 166–76.

Hamori, Andras. "Notes on Paronomasia in Abu Tammam's Style." *JSS* 12 (1967), 83–90.

Haran, Menahem. "Book-Scrolls in Israel in Pre-Exilic Times." *JJS* 33 (1982), 161–73.

_____. "More concerning Book-Scrolls in Pre-Exilic Times." *JJS* 35 (1984), 84–85.

_____. "Book-Size and the Device of Catch-Lines in the Biblical Canon." *JJS* 36 (1985), 1–11.

_____. "Catch-Lines in Ancient Palaeography and in the Biblical Canon" [Hebrew with English summary], in *Naham Avigad Volume* (eds. B. Mazar and Y. Yadin; Eretz-Israel 18; Jerusalem: Israel Exploration Society and Hebrew University, 1985), 124–29; 69*.

_____. "On the Diffusion of Literacy and Schools in Ancient Israel," in *Congress Volume: Jerusalem, 1986* (VTSupp 40; Leiden: E. J. Brill, 1988), 81–95.

Harvey, Julien. "Le 'Rîb-Pattern': Réquisitoire prophétique sur la rupture de l'alliance." *Biblica* 43 (1962), 172–96.

Hayward, Robert. *The Targum of Jeremiah* (AramB 12; Wilmington, Del.: Michael Glazier, 1987).

Held, Moshe. "The Action-Result (Factitive-Passive) Sequence of Identical Verbs in Biblical Hebrew and Ugaritic." *JBL* 84 (1965), 272–82.

_____. "Rhetorical Questions in Ugaritic and Biblical Hebrew," in *W. F. Albright Volume* (ed. A. Malamat; Eretz-Israel 9; Jerusalem: Israel Exploration Society, 1969), 71–79.

Hendrickson, G. L. "Ancient Reading." *CJ* 25 (1929–30), 182–96.

Hens-Piazza, Gina. "Repetition and Rhetoric in Canaanite Epic." *UF* 24 (1992), 103–12.

Herder, Johann Gottfried von. *The Spirit of Hebrew Poetry I–II* (trans. James Marsh; Burlington, Vt.: Edward Smith, 1833). German: *Vom Geist der Ebräischen Poesie I–II* (3d ed.; Leipzig: Johann Ambrosius Barth, 1825). Originally 1782–83.

Herodotus. *Histories I–II* (trans. A. D. Godley; LCL; Cambridge, Mass.: Harvard University Press, 1946).

Heschel, Abraham J. *The Prophets* (New York and Evanston, Ill.: Harper and Row, 1962).

Hess, Richard S. "Rhetorical Forms in EA 162." *UF* 22 (1990), 137–48.

Hester, James D. "The Rhetorical Structure of Galatians 1:11–2:14." *JBL* 103 (1984), 223–33.

Hiebert, Theodore. "The Use of Inclusion in Habakkuk 3," in Follis, *Directions in Biblical Hebrew Poetry* (1987), 119–40.

Hillers, Delbert R. *Treaty-Curses and the Old Testament Prophets* (Rome: Pontifical Biblical Institute, 1964).

_____. "The Effective Simile in Biblical Literature." *JAOS* 103 (1983) 181–85. Repr. *Studies in Literature from the Ancient Near East* (ed. Jack M. Sasson; New Haven: American Oriental Society, 1984), 181–85.

Hobbs, T. R. "Some Remarks on the Structure and Composition of the Book of Jeremiah." *CBQ* 34 (1972), 257–75. Repr. Perdue and Kovacs, *A Prophet to the Nations* (1984), 175–91.

Hölscher, Gustav. *Die Propheten: Untersuchungen zur Religionsgeschichte Israels* (Leipzig: J. C. Hinrichs'sche Buchhandlung, 1914).

Holladay, William L. *The Root Šûbh in the Old Testament* (Leiden: E. J. Brill, 1958).

_____. "Prototypes and Copies: A New Approach to the Poetry-Prose Problem in the Book of Jeremiah." *JBL* 79 (1960), 351–67.

_____. "The So-Called 'Deuteronomic Gloss' in Jer. VIII 19b." *VT* 12 (1962), 494–98.

_____. "Style, Irony and Authenticity in Jeremiah." *JBL* 81 (1962), 44–54.

_____. "Jeremiah's Lawsuit with God: A Study in Suffering and Meaning." *Int* 17 (1963), 280–87.

_____. "The Background of Jeremiah's Self-Understanding: Moses, Samuel and Psalm 22." *JBL* 83 (1964), 153–64. Repr. Perdue and Kovacs, *A Prophet to the Nations* (1984), 313–24.

_____. " 'The Priests Scrape Out on Their Hands': Jeremiah V 31." *VT* 15 (1965), 111–13.

_____. "Chiasmus, the Key to Hosea XII 3–6." *VT* 16 (1966), 53–64.

_____. "Jeremiah xxxi 22b Reconsidered: The Woman Encompasses the Man." *VT* 16 (1966), 236–39.

_____. "Jeremiah and Moses: Further Observations." *JBL* 85 (1966), 17–27.

_____. "The Recovery of Poetic Passages of Jeremiah." *JBL* 85 (1966), 401–35.

_____. "Form and Word-Play in David's Lament over Saul and Jonathan." *VT* 20 (1970), 153–89.

_____. "The Covenant with the Patriarchs Overturned: Jeremiah's Intention in 'Terror on Every Side' (Jer 20:1–6)." *JBL* 91 (1972), 305–20.

_____. *The Architecture of Jeremiah 1–20* (Lewisburg, Pa.: Bucknell University Press, 1976).

Holman, Jan. "The Structure of Psalm CXXXIX." *VT* 21 (1971), 298–310.

Holmgren, Fredrick. "Chiastic Structure in Isaiah LI 1–11." *VT* 19 (1969), 196–201.

Hommel, Fritz. "A Rhetorical Figure in the Old Testament." *ET* 11 (1899–1900), 439–41.

Honeyman, A. M. "Merismus in Biblical Hebrew." *JBL* 71 (1952), 11–18.

Horne, Thomas Hartwell. *An Introduction to the Critical Study and Knowledge of the Holy Scriptures II* (4th ed.; Philadelphia: E. Littell, 1831).

Horning, Estella B. "Chiasmus, Credal Structure, and Christology in Hebrews 12:1–2." *BiRes* 23 (1978), 37–48.

House, Paul R. (ed.). *Beyond Form Criticism: Essays in Old Testament Literary Criticism* (Sources for Biblical and Theological Study 2; Winona Lake, Ind.: Eisenbrauns, 1992).

Howard, David M. Jr. "Rhetorical Criticism in Old Testament Studies." *BBR* 4 (1994), 87–104.

Howard, George. "Frank Cross and Recensional Criticism." *VT* 21 (1971), 440–50.

_____. "Stylistic Inversion and the Synoptic Tradition." *JBL* 97 (1978), 375–89.

Howell, Wilber Samuel. "Renaissance Rhetoric and Modern Rhetoric: A Study in Change," in Bryant, *The Rhetorial Idiom* (1958), 53–70. Repr. Schwartz and Rycenga, *The Province of Rhetoric* (1965), 292–308.

Howes, Raymond F. (ed.). *Historical Studies of Rhetoric and Rhetoricians* (Ithaca, N.Y.: Cornell University Press, 1961).

Hudson, Hoyt H. "The Field of Rhetoric." *QJS* 9 (1923), 167–80. Repr. Howes, *Historical Studies of Rhetoric and Rhetoricians* (1961), 3–15; and Natanson and Johnstone, *Philosophy, Rhetoric, and Argumentation* (1965), 20–31.

_____. "Rhetoric and Poetry." *QJS* 10 (1924), 143–54. Repr. Howes, *Historical Studies of Rhetoric and Rhetoricians* (1961), 369–79.

_____. " 'Compendium Rhetorices' by Erasmus: A Translation," in Wichelns, *Studies in Speech and Drama* (1944), 326–40.

Huffmon, Herbert B. "The Covenant Lawsuit in the Prophets." *JBL* 78 (1959), 285–95.

_____. "Prophecy in the Mari Letters." *BA* 31 (1968), 101–24. Repr. Campbell and Freedman, *Biblical Archaeologist Reader III* (1970), 199–224.

_____. "The Origins of Prophecy," in *Magnalia Dei: The Mighty Acts of God* (eds. Frank Moore Cross, *et al.*; Garden City, N.Y.: Doubleday & Co., 1976), 171–86.

Humbert, Paul. "La formule hébraïque en *hineni* suivi d'un participe," in Humbert, *Opuscules d'un hébraïsant* (Neuchâtel: Secrétariat de l'Université, 1958), 54–59.

Humphries, Raymond A. "Paul's Rhetoric of Argumentation in 1 Corinthians 1–4." Unpublished Ph.D. dissertation (Graduate Theological Union, 1979).

Hunt, Everett Lee. "The Scientific Spirit in Public Speaking." *QJS* 1 (1915), 185–93.

_____. "Herbert A. Wichelns and the Cornell Tradition of Rhetoric as a Humane Study," in Bryant, *The Rhetorical Idiom* (1958), 1–4.

Hyatt, J. Philip. "The Writing of an Old Testament Book." *BA* 6 (1943), 71–80.

_____. "The Deuteronomic Edition of Jeremiah," in *Vanderbilt Studies in the Humanities* 1 (1951), 71–95. Repr. Perdue and Kovacs, *A Prophet to the Nations* (1984), 247–67.

Immerwahr, Henry R. *Form and Thought in Herodotus* (Cleveland: Western Reserve University Press, 1966).

Irwin, William A. "The Face of the Pot: Jeremiah 1:13b." *AJSLL* 47 (1930–31), 288–89.

Ittmann, N. *Die Konfessionen Jeremias* (WMANT 54; Neukirchen-Vluyn: Neukirchener Verlag, 1981).

Jackson, Jared J., and Martin Kessler (eds.). *Rhetorical Criticism: Essays in Honor of James Muilenburg* (Pittsburgh: Pickwick Press, 1974).

Jacobs, Louis. "The *Qal va-Homer* Argument in the Old Testament." *BSOAS* 35 (1972), 221–27.

_____. *The Talmudic Argument* (Cambridge: Cambridge University Press, 1984).

Jacobsen, Thorkild, and Kirsten Nielsen. "Cursing the Day." *SJOT* 6 (1992), 187–204.

Jakobson, Roman. "Grammatical Parallelism and Its Russian Facet." *Language* 42 (1966), 399–429.

Janzen, J. Gerald. "Double Readings in the Text of Jeremiah." *HThR* 60 (1967), 433–47.

_____. *Studies in the Text of Jeremiah* (Cambridge, Mass.: Harvard University Press, 1973).

Jebb, John. *Sacred Literature* (London: T. Cadell and W. Davies, 1820).

Jeremias, Joachim. "Chiasmus in den Paulusbriefen." *ZNW* 49 (1958), 145–56.

Johnson, Aubrey R. "The Prophet in Israelite Worship." *ET* 47 (1935–36), 312–19.

Johnson, Marshall D. "The Paralysis of Torah in Habakkuk I 4." *VT* 35 (1985), 257–66.

Johnson, Sherman E. "The Preaching to the Dead." *JBL* 79 (1960), 48–51.

Karstetter, Allan B. "Toward a Theory of Rhetorical Irony." *SpeMo* 31 (1964), 162–78.

Kaufman, Stephen A. "Rhetoric, Redaction, and Message in Jeremiah," in *Judaic Perspectives on Ancient Israel* (eds. Jacob Neusner, *et al.*; Philadelphia: Fortress Press, 1987), 63–74.

Kennedy, George. "The Rhetoric of Advocacy in Greece and Rome." *AJP* 89 (1968), 419–36.

_____. *The Art of Rhetoric in the Roman World 300 B.C.–A.D. 300* (Princeton: Princeton University Press, 1972).

_____. *Classical Rhetoric and Its Christian and Secular Tradition from Ancient to Modern Times* (Chapel Hill, N.C.: University of North Carolina Press, 1980)

_____. *New Testament Interpretation through Rhetorical Criticism* (Chapel Hill, N.C.: University of North Carolina Press, 1984).

Kessler, Martin. "A Prophetic Biography: A Form-Critical Study of Jer 26–29, 32–45." Unpublished Ph.D. dissertation (Brandeis University, 1965).

_____. "Form-Critical Suggestions on Jer 36." *CBQ* 28 (1966), 389–401.

_____. "A Methodological Setting for Rhetorical Criticism." *Semitics* 4 (1974), 22–36.

_____. "Inclusio in the Hebrew Bible." *Semitics* 6 (1978), 44–49.

Kikawada, Isaac M. "Some Proposals for the Definition of Rhetorical Criticism." *Semitics* 5 (1977), 67–91.

Kimelman, Reuven. "Psalm 145: Theme, Structure, and Impact." *JBL* 113 (1994), 37–58.

Kittel, Bonnie Pedrotti. *The Hymns of Qumran* (SBLDS 50; Chico, Calif.: Society of Biblical Literature and Scholars Press, 1981).

Klyn, Mark S. "Toward a Pluralistic Rhetorical Criticism," in *Essays on Rhetorical Criticism* (ed. Thomas R. Nilsen; New York: Random House, 1968), 146–57.

Knierim, Rolf. "Old Testament Form Criticism Reconsidered." *Int* 27 (1973), 435–68.

Knox, Bernard M. "Silent Reading in Antiquity." *GRBS* 9 (1968), 421–35.

Koch, Klaus. *The Growth of the Biblical Tradition* (trans. S. M. Cupitt; New York: Charles Scribner's Sons, 1969).

Köhler, Ludwig. *Deuterojesaja (Jesaja 40–55) Stilkritisch Untersucht* (BZAW 37; Giessen: Alfred Töpelmann, 1923).

König, E. *Stilistik, Rhetorik, Poetik in Bezug auf die biblische Literatur* (Leipzig: Dieterich'sche Verlagsbuchhandlung, 1900).

_____. "Style of Scripture," in *HDB Extra Volume* (1904), 156–69.

Kogut, Simcha. "On the Meaning and Syntactical Status of הִנֵּה in Biblical Hebrew," in *Studies in Bible* (ed. Sara Japhet; Jerusalem: Magnes Press, Hebrew University, 1986), 133–54.

Korpel, Marjo C., and Johannes C. de Moor. "Fundamentals of Ugaritic and Hebrew Poetry." *UF* 18 (1986), 173–212.

Kosmala, Hans. "Form and Structure in Ancient Hebrew Poetry." *VT* 14 (1964), 423–45; 16 (1966), 152–80.

Kraft, Charles Franklin. *The Strophic Structure of Hebrew Poetry* (Chicago: University of Chicago Press, 1938).

_____. "Some Further Observations concerning the Strophic Structure of Hebrew Poetry," in *A Stubborn Faith* (In Honor of William Andrew Irwin; ed. Edward C. Hobbs; Dallas: Southern Methodist University Press, 1956), 62–89.

_____. "Poetic Structure in the Qumran Thanksgiving Psalms." *BiRes* 2 (1957), 1–18.

Kramer, Samuel Noah. "Schooldays: A Sumerian Composition Relating to the Education of a Scribe." *JAOS* 69 (1949), 199–215.

_____. "Sumerian Similes: A Panoramic View of Some of Man's Oldest Literary Images." *JAOS* 89 (1969), 1–10.

_____. *The Sacred Marriage Rite* (Bloomington, Ind.: Indiana University Press, 1969), 23–48. Chapter 2: "The Poetry of Sumer: Repetition, Parallelism, Epithet, Simile."

Krašovec, Jože. *Antithetic Structure in Biblical Hebrew Poetry* (VTSupp 35; Leiden: E. J. Brill, 1984).

Kruger, P. A. "Prophetic Imagery: On Metaphors and Similes in the Book of Hosea." *JNSL* 14 (1988), 143–51.

Kselman, John S. "Semantic-Sonant Chiasmus in Biblical Poetry." *Biblica* 58 (1977), 219–23.

_____. "The ABCB Pattern: Further Examples." *VT* 32 (1982), 224–29.

Kugel, James L. *The Idea of Biblical Poetry* (New Haven and London: Yale University Press, 1981).

Kuntz, J. Kenneth. "Psalm 18: A Rhetorical-Critical Analysis." *JSOT* 26 (1983), 3–31.

_____. "King Triumphant: A Rhetorical Study of Psalms 20–21." *HAR* 10 (1986), 157–76.

Kurz, William S. "Hellenistic Rhetoric in the Christological Proof of Luke–Acts." *CBQ* 42 (1980), 171–95.

Laato, Antti. "The Composition of Isaiah 40–55." *JBL* 109 (1990), 207–28.

Labuschagne, C. J. "The Particles הֵן and הִנֵּה." *OS* 18 (1973), 1–14.

Laessøe, J. "Literacy and Oral Tradition in Ancient Mesopotamia," in *Studia Orientalia Ioanni Pedersen . . . Dicta* (ed. Flemming Hvidberg; Copenhagen: Einar Munksgaard, 1953), 205–18.

Lafontaine, René, and Pierre Mourlon Beernaert. "Essai sur la Structure de Marc 8,27–9,13." *RSR* 57 (1969), 543–61.

Lagercrantz, Olof. *August Strindberg* (Stockholm: Wahlström & Widstrand, 1979).

Lambert, W. G. "Ancestors, Authors, and Canonicity." *JCS* 11 (1957), 1–14.

Lampe, Peter. "Theological Wisdom and the 'Word about the Cross': The Rhetorical Scheme in I Corinthians 1–4." *Int* 44 (1990), 117–31.

Lanahan, William F. "The Speaking Voice in the Book of Lamentations." *JBL* 93 (1974), 41–49.

Landsberger, Benno. "Babylonian Scribal Craft and Its Terminology," in *Proceedings of the Twenty-Third International Congress of Orientalists* (ed. Denis Sinor; London: Royal Asiatic Society, 1954), 123–26.

Lanham, Richard A. *A Handlist of Rhetorical Terms* (Berkeley and Los Angeles: University of California Press, 1968).

Lausberg, Heinrich. *Elemente der literarischen Rhetorik* (Munich: Max Hueber, 1967). Originally 1949.

Leichty, Erle. "The Colophon," in *Studies Presented to A. Leo Oppenheim* (Chicago: Oriental Institute of the University of Chicago, 1964), 147–54.

Lenchak, Timothy A. *"Choose Life!" A Rhetorical-Critical Investigation of Deuteronomy 28,69–30,20* (Rome: Pontifical Biblical Institute, 1993).

Léon-Dufour, Xavier. "Trois chiasmes johanniques." *NTS* 7 (1960–61), 249–55.

Levy, S. "Azariah dei Rossi." *The Jewish Annual* (1940–1941), 59–72.

Lewin, Ellen Davis. "Arguing for Authority: A Rhetorical Study of Jeremiah 1.4–19 and 20.7–18." *JSOT* 32 (1985), 105–19.

Lewis, Ralph Loren. "The Persuasive Style and Appeals of the Minor Prophets Amos, Hosea and Micah." Unpublished Ph.D. dissertation (University of Michigan, 1958).

Ley, Julius. *Grundzüge des Rhythmus des Vers- und Strophenbaues in der hebräischen Poesie* (Halle: Verlag der Buchhandlung des Waisenhauses, 1875).

————. *Leitfaden der Metrik der hebräischen Poesie* (Halle: Verlag der Buchhandlung des Waisenhauses, 1887).

Licht, Jacob. "Time and Eschatology in Apocalyptic Literature and in Qumran." *JJS* 16 (1965), 177–82.

————. "An Analysis of the Treatise of the Two Spirits in DSD," in *Scripta Hierosolymitana, IV: Aspects of the Dead Sea Scrolls* (2d ed.; eds. C. Rabin and Y. Yadin; Jerusalem: Hebrew University and Magnes Press, 1965), 88–100.

Lichtenstein, Murray H. "Chiasm and Symmetry in Proverbs 31." *CBQ* 44 (1982), 202–11.

Liebreich, Leon J. "The Compilation of the Book of Isaiah." *JQR* 46 (1956), 259–77; 47 (1956), 114–38.

Limburg, James. "The Root ריב and the Prophetic Lawsuit Speeches." *JBL* 88 (1969), 291–304.

Lincoln, Andrew T. " 'Stand, Therefore . , .': Ephesians 6:10–20 as *Peroratio*." *BiInt* 3 (1995), 99–114.

Lindblom, Johannes. *Die literarische Gattung der prophetischen Literatur* (UUÅ 1924:1; Uppsala: A.-B. Lundequistska Bokhandeln, 1924).

_____. "Ecstasy in Scandinavian Christianity." *ET* 57 (1945–46), 236–41.

_____. *Prophecy in Ancient Israel* (Philadelphia: Fortress Press, 1965).

Lipiński, Edward. "Jeremiah" in *EJ* 9.1345–59.

_____. "Royal and State Scribes in Ancient Israel," in *Congress Volume: Jerusalem, 1986* (VTSupp 40; Leiden: E. J. Brill, 1988), 157–64.

Loewenstamm, Samuel E. "The Expanded Colon in Ugaritic and Biblical Verse." *JSS* 14 (1969), 176–96.

_____. "The Expanded Colon, Reconsidered." *UF* 7 (1975), 261–64.

_____. "Observations on Chiastic Structures in the Bible," in Loewenstamm, *From Babylon to Canaan* (Jerusalem: Magnes Press, Hebrew University of Jerusalem, 1992), 1–5.

Lohfink, Norbert. "Darstellungskunst und Theologie in Dtn 1,6–3,29." *Biblica* 41 (1960), 105–34. Repr. Lohfink, *Studien zum Deuteronomium und zur deuteronomistischen Literatur I* (1990), 15–44.

_____. *Das Hauptgebot: Eine Untersuchung literarischer Einleitungsfragen zu Dtn 5–11* (Rome: Pontifical Biblical Institute, 1963).

_____. *Lectures in Deuteronomy* (trans. S. McEvenue; Rome: Pontifical Biblical Institute, 1968).

_____. *Studien zum Deuteronomium und zur deuteronomistischen Literatur I* (Stuttgart: Verlag Katholisches Bibelwerk, 1990).

_____. *Studien zum Deuteronomium und zur deuteronomistischen Literatur II* (Stuttgart: Verlag Katholisches Bibelwerk, 1991).

Lohr, Charles H. "Oral Techniques in the Gospel of Matthew." *CBQ* 23 (1961), 403–35.

Lord, Albert Bates. "Composition by Theme in Homer and Southslavic Epos." *TAPA* 82 (1951), 71–80.

_____. *The Singer of Tales* (New York: Atheneum, 1968).

Loretz, Oswald. "Die Sprüche Jeremias in Jer 1,17–9,25." *UF* 2 (1970), 109–30.

_____. "Jer 8,23 und KTU 1.16 I 26–28," in *Mélanges bibliques et orientaux en l'honneur de M. Henri Cazelles* (eds. A. Caquot and M. Delcor; Neukirchen-Vluyn: Neukirchener Verlag, 1981), 297–99.

Lowth, Robert. *Lectures on the Sacred Poetry of the Hebrews* (trans. G. Gregory; Boston: Joseph T. Buckingham, 1815). Latin: *De Sacra Poesi Hebraeorum Praelectiones* (Oxford: Clarendon Press, 1753).

_____. *Isaiah: Preliminary Dissertation and Notes* (10th ed. London: T. T. & J. Tegg, 1833). English summary of Azariah de Rossi's Chapter 60 on Hebrew poetry in *Me'or Enayim* (pp. xxxiiiff.).

Ludwig, Theodore M. "The Shape of Hope: Jeremiah's Book of Consolation." *CTM* 39 (1968), 526–41.

Lugt, Pieter van der. *Rhetorical Criticism and the Poetry of the Book of Job* (OS 32; Leiden: E. J. Brill, 1995).

Lund, Nils W. "The Presence of Chiasmus in the Old Testament." *AJSLL* 46 (1930), 104–26.

_____. "The Presence of Chiasmus in the New Testament." *JR* 10 (1930), 74–93.

_____. "The Literary Structure of Paul's Hymn to Love." _JBL_ 50 (1931), 266–76.

_____. "The Influence of Chiasmus upon the Structure of the Gospels." _AThR_ 13 (1931), 27–48.

_____. "The Influence of Chiasmus upon the Structure of the Gospel according to Matthew." _AThR_ 13 (1931), 405–33.

_____. "Chiasmus in the Psalms." _AJSLL_ 49 (1933), 281–312.

_____. _Outline Studies in the Book of Revelation_ (Chicago: Covenant Book Concern, 1935).

_____. _Chiasmus in the New Testament_ (Chapel Hill, N.C.: University of North Carolina Press, 1942). Repr. (Peabody, Mass.: Hendrickson Publishers, 1992).

_____. "The Significance of Chiasmus for Interpretation." _CroQ_ 20 (1943), 105–23.

_____. "Chiasmus i nya Testamentet." _STK_ 25 (1949), 299–320.

_____. _Studies in the Book of Revelation_ (Chicago: Covenant Press, 1955).

Lundbom, Jack R. "Patterns of Poetic Balance in the Book of Jeremiah." Unpublished B.D. thesis (North Park Theological Seminary, 1967).

_____. "Elijah's Chariot Ride." _JJS_ 24 (1973), 39–50.

_____. "Response" to Luis Alonso-Schökel's "Narrative Structures in the Book of Judith," in _Protocol Series of the Colloquies of the Center for Hermeneutical Studies in Hellenistic and Modern Culture, Colloquy 11_ (ed. Wilhelm Wuellner; Berkeley: Center for Hermeneutical Studies, 1974), 36–37.

_____. "Double-Duty Subject in Hosea VIII 5." _VT_ 25 (1975), 228–30.

_____. _Jeremiah: A Study in Ancient Hebrew Rhetoric_ (SBLDS 18; Missoula, Mont.: Society of Biblical Literature and Scholars Press, 1975).

_____. "The Lawbook of the Josianic Reform." _CBQ_ 38 (1976), 293–302.

_____. "God's Use of the _Idem per Idem_ to Terminate Debate." _HThR_ 71 (1978), 193–201.

_____. "Poetic Structure and Prophetic Rhetoric in Hosea." _VT_ 29 (1979), 300–308.

_____. "The Double Curse in Jeremiah 20:14–18." _JBL_ 104 (1985), 589–600.

_____. "Baruch, Seraiah, and Expanded Colophons in the Book of Jeremiah." _JSOT_ 36 (1986), 89–114.

_____. "Contentious Priests and Contentious People in Hosea IV 1–10." _VT_ 36 (1986), 52–70.

_____. "Scribal Colophons and Scribal Rhetoric in Deuteronomy 31–34," in _Haim M. I. Gevaryahu Memorial Volume_ (eds. Joshua J. Adler and B. Z. Luria; Jerusalem: World Jewish Bible Center, 1990), 53–63.

_____. "Jeremiah and the Break-Away from Authority Preaching." _SEÅ_ 56 (1991), 7–28.

_____. "Rhetorical Structures in Jeremiah 1." _ZAW_ 103 (1991), 193–210.

_____. "Jeremiah (Prophet)," in _ABD_ 3.684–98.

_____. "Jeremiah, Book of," in _ABD_ 3.706–21.

_____. _The Early Career of the Prophet Jeremiah_ (Lewiston, N.Y.: Mellen Biblical Press, 1993).

_____. "Jeremiah 15,15–21 and the Call of Jeremiah." _SJOT_ 9 (1995), 143–55.

_____. "The Inclusio and Other Framing Devices in Deuteronomy I–XXVIII." _VT_ 46 (1996), 296–315.

_____. "Section Markings in Bible Scrolls." _Genizah Fragments_ 32 (1996), 2.

_____. "Scribal Contributions to Old Testament Theology," forthcoming in *Festschrift for Frederick C. Holmgren* (eds. Paul Koptak and Bradley Berg-falk; Chicago: Covenant Publications, 1997).

_____. "Parataxis, Rhetorical Structure and the Dialogue over Sodom in Genesis 18." Forthcoming in JSOTSupp (1997).

MacDonald, J. "Some Distinctive Characteristics of Israelite Spoken Hebrew." *BiOr* 32 (1975), 162–75.

Mack, Burton L. *Rhetoric and the New Testament* (Minneapolis: Fortress Press, 1990).

Malamat, Abraham. "Prophetic Revelations in New Documents from Mari and the Bible," in *Volume du Congrès: Genève, 1965* (VTSupp 15; Leiden: E. J. Brill, 1966), 207–27. Hebrew with English summary: *E. L. Sukenik Memorial Volume* (eds. N. Avigad, et al.; Eretz-Israel 8; Jerusalem: Israel Exploration Society, 1967), 231–40; 75*.

_____. *Mari and the Early Israelite Experience* (Oxford: The British Academy and Oxford University Press, 1989).

Marcus, David. "Animal Similes in Assyrian Royal Inscriptions." *Orientalia* 46 (1977), 86–106.

Marcus, Ralph. "Alphabetic Acrostics in the Hellenistic and Roman Periods." *JNES* 6 (1947), 109–15.

Margalit (Margulis), Baruch. "A New Ugaritic Farce (RS 24.258)." *UF* 2 (1970), 131–38.

_____. "Introduction to Ugaritic Prosody." *UF* 7 (1975), 289–313.

_____. "Alliteration in Ugaritic Poetry: Its Role in Composition and Analysis." *UF* 11 (1979), 537–57.

_____. "Alliteration in Ugaritic Poetry: Its Role in Composition and Analysis (Part II)." *JNSL* 8 (1980), 57–80.

_____. *A Matter of "Life" and "Death": A Study of the Baal-Mot Epic (CTA 4–5–6)* (Neukirchen-Vluyn: Neukirchener Verlag, 1980).

Martin, James D. "The Forensic Background to Jeremiah III 1." *VT* 19 (1969), 82–92.

Massie, John. "The Irony of St. Paul." *The Expositor* 2d Series 8 (1884), 92–107.

Mays, James Luther, and Paul Achtemeier (eds.). *Interpreting the Prophets* (Philadelphia: Fortress Press, 1987).

Mazor, Yair. "Hosea 5:1–3: Between Compositional Rhetoric and Rhetorical Composition." *JSOT* 45 (1989), 115–26.

McCall, Marsh H. Jr. *Ancient Rhetorical Theories of Simile and Comparison* (Cambridge, Mass.: Harvard University Press, 1969).

McCarthy, Dennis J. "Moses' Dealings with Pharaoh: Ex 7,8–10,27." *CBQ* 27 (1965), 336–47.

_____. "The Uses of *weᵉhinnēh* in Biblical Hebrew." *Biblica* 61 (1980), 330–42.

McCartney, Eugene S. "Puns and Plays on Proper Names." *CJ* 14 (1918–19), 343–58.

_____. "Notes on Reading and Praying Audibly." *CP* 43 (1948), 184–87.

Meek, Theophile J. "Was Jeremiah a Priest?" *The Expositor* 8th Series 25 (1923), 215–22.

_____. "The Poetry of Jeremiah." *JQR* New Series 14 (1923–24), 281–91.

_____. "The Structure of Hebrew Poetry." *JR* 9 (1929), 523–50.

Meier, Samuel A. *Speaking of Speaking: Marking Direct Discourse in the Hebrew Bible* (VTSupp 46; Leiden: E. J. Brill, 1992).

Melamed, Ezra Zion. "Break-Up of Stereotype Phrases as an Artistic Device in Biblical Poetry." *ScrHier* 8 (1961), 115–53.

Mendenhall, George E. *Law and Covenant in Israel and the Ancient Near East* (Pittsburgh: Presbyterian Board of Colportage, 1955).

Michaud, J. Fr. (ed.). *Biographie Universelle*, vol. 38 (Graz: Akademische Druck-u. Verlagsanstalt, 1969).

Mielziner, M. "The Talmudic Syllogism or the Inference of Kal Vechomer." *HebRev* 1 (1880–81), 42–53.

_____. "The Talmudic Analogy or the Rules of Gezera Shawa and Heckesh." *HebRev* 2 (1881–82), 79–94.

Miesner, D. R. "Chiasm and the Composition and Message of Paul's Missionary Sermons." Unpublished Th.D. dissertation (Concordia Seminary in Exile, St. Louis, 1974).

Milgrom, Jacob. "The Date of Jeremiah Chapter 2." *JNES* 14 (1955), 65–69.

Millard, Alan R. "The Practice of Writing in Ancient Israel." *BA* 35 (1972), 98–111. Repr. Campbell and Freedman, *The Biblical Archaeologist Reader IV* (1983), 181–95.

_____. "In Praise of Ancient Scribes." *BA* 45 (1982), 143–53.

_____. "An Assessment of the Evidence for Writing in Ancient Israel," in *Biblical Archaeology Today: Proceedings of the International Congress on Biblical Archaeology, April, 1984* (eds. Avraham Biran, *et al.*; Jerusalem: Israel Exploration Society, 1985), 301–12.

Miller, Patrick D. Jr. *Sin and Judgment in the Prophets: A Stylistic and Theological Analysis* (SBLMS 27; Chico, Calif.: Scholars Press, 1982).

Minear, Paul S. "Changes in Metaphor Produce Changes in Thought." *PresO* 165/43 (1983), 6–7.

Mirsky, Aharon. "The Origin of Anadiplosis in Hebrew Literature" [Hebrew with English summary]. *Tarbiz* 28 (1958–59), 171–80, iv*.

_____. "Stylistic Device for Conclusion in Hebrew." *Semitics* 5 (1977), 9–23.

Mitchell, Hinckley G. "The Omission of the Interrogative Particle," in *Old Testament and Semitic Studies in Memory of William Rainey Harper I* (eds. Robert Francis Harper, *et al.*; Chicago: University of Chicago Press, 1908), 115–29.

Mitchell, Margaret M. *Paul and the Rhetoric of Reconciliation: An Exegetical Investigation of the Language and Composition of 1 Corinthians* (Tübingen: J. C. B. Mohr [Paul Siebeck], 1991).

Möller, H. "Strophenbau der Psalmen." *ZAW* 50 (1932), 240–56.

Moffatt, James. "A Rhetorical Figure in the Old Testament III." *ET* 11 (1899–1900), 518–19.

Mohrmann, G. P., *et al.*; (eds.). *Explorations in Rhetorical Criticism* (University Park, Penn.: Pennsylvania State University Press, 1973).

Montague, Gene. "Rhetoric in Literary Criticism." *CCC* 14 (1963), 168–75.

Montefiore, C. G. "A Tentative Catalogue of Biblical Metaphors." *JQR* Old Series 3 (1891), 623–81.

Moor, Johannes C. de. "Narrative Poetry in Canaan." *UF* 20 (1988), 149–71.

Moran, William L. *Adnotationes in libri Deuteronomii capita selecta* (Rome: Pontifical Biblical Institute, 1963).

_____. "Deuteronomy," in *A New Catholic Commentary on Holy Scripture* (ed. Reginald C. Fuller; rev. ed.; Camden, N.J. and London: Thomas Nelson and Sons, 1969), 256–76.

_____. "New Evidence from Mari on the History of Prophecy." *Biblica* 50 (1969), 15–56.

_____. "The Creation of Man in Atrahasis I 192–248." *BASOR* 200 (1970), 48–56.

Morgenstern, Julian. "The Loss of Words at the Ends of Lines in Manuscripts of Biblical Poetry." *HUCA* 25 (1954), 41–83.

Moulton, Richard G. *The Ancient Classical Drama: A Study in Literary Evolution* (Oxford: The Clarendon Press, 1890).

_____. *The Literary Study of the Bible* (New York: D. C. Heath and Co., 1895).

Mowinckel, Sigmund. *Zur Komposition des Buches Jeremia* (Oslo: Jacob Dybwad, 1914).

_____. "Motiver og stilformer i profeten Jeremias diktning." *Edda* 26 (1926), 233–320.

_____. "Die Komposition des deuterojesajanischen Buches." *ZAW* 49 (1931), 87–112; 242–60.

_____. "Jeremiaboken: Innledning," in *Det Gamle Testamente III: De Senere Profeter* (eds. Sigmund Mowinckel, *et al.*; Oslo: H. Aschehoug and Co. [W. Nygaard], 1944), 284–96.

_____. *Prophecy and Tradition* (Oslo: Jacob Dybwad, 1946).

_____. "Literature," in *IDB* K–Q, 139–43.

_____. "Tradition, Oral," in *IDB* R–Z, 683–85.

Müller, D. H. *Die Propheten in ihrer ursprünglichen Form* (Vienna: Alfred Hölder, 1896).

_____. *Komposition und Strophenbau* (Vienna: Alfred Hölder, 1907).

Muilenburg, James. *Specimens of Biblical Literature* (New York: Thomas Y. Crowell Co, 1923).

_____. "Literary Form in the Fourth Gospel." *JBL* 51 (1932), 40–53. Repr. Best, *Hearing and Speaking the Word* (1984), 45–58.

_____. "The Literary Approach: The Old Testament as Hebrew Literature." *JNABI* 1 (1933), 14–22.

_____. "The Literary Character of Isaiah 34." *JBL* 59 (1940), 339–65.

_____. "Psalm 47." *JBL* 63 (1944), 235–56.

_____. "The Poetry of the Old Testament," in *An Introduction to the Revised Standard Version of the Old Testament* (eds. Members of Revision Committee, Luther A. Weigle, Chairman; New York: Thomas Nelson and Sons, 1952), 62–70.

_____. "A Study in Hebrew Rhetoric: Repetition and Style," in *Congress Volume: Copenhagen, 1953* (VTSupp 1; Leiden: E. J. Brill, 1953), 97–111. Repr. Best, *Hearing and Speaking the Word* (1984), 193–207.

_____. "Isaiah," in *IB* 5 (ed. George A. Buttrick; New York: Abingdon Press, 1956), 381–773.

_____. "The Form and Structure of the Covenantal Formulations." *VT* 9 (1959), 347–65. Repr. Noth, *Essays in Honour of Millar Burrows* (1959), 11–20; and Best, *Hearing and Speaking the Word* (1984), 108–26.

_____. "The Gains of Form Criticism in Old Testament Studies." *ET* 71 (1960), 229–33.

_____. "The Linguistic and Rhetorical Usages of the Particle כִּי in the Old Testament." *HUCA* 32 (1961), 135–60. Repr. Best, *Hearing and Speaking the Word* (1984), 208–33.

_____. "Jeremiah the Prophet" in *IDB* E–J, 823–35.

_____. "The Mediators of the Covenant." Unpublished Nils W. Lund Memorial Lectures (North Park Theological Seminary, 1963).

_____. "The Speech of Theophany." *HDivB* 28 (1964), 35–47.

_____. "The 'Office' of the Prophet in Ancient Israel," in *The Bible in Modern Scholarship* (ed. J. Philip Hyatt; Nashville & New York: Abingdon Press, 1965), 74–97. Repr. Best, *Hearing and Speaking the Word* (1984), 127–50.

_____. "A Liturgy on the Triumphs of Yahweh," in *Studia Biblica et Semitica* (Dedicated to Theodoro V. Vriezen; eds. W. C. van Unnik and A. S. van der Woude; Wageningen: H. V. Veenman en Zonen N. V., 1966), 233–51. Repr. Best, *Hearing and Speaking the Word* (1984), 151–69.

_____. "Form Criticism and Beyond." *JBL* 88 (1969), 1–18. Repr. Best, *Hearing and Speaking the Word* (1984), 27–44; and House, *Beyond Form Criticism* (1992), 49–69.

_____. "Baruch the Scribe," in *Proclamation and Presence* (In Honour of G. Henton Davies; eds. John I. Durham and J. R. Porter; Richmond: John Knox Press, 1970), 215–38. Repr. Best, *Hearing and Speaking the Word* (1984), 259–82; also Perdue and Kovacs, *A Prophet to the Nations* (1984), 229–45.

_____. "The Terminology of Adversity in Jeremiah," in *Translating and Understanding the Old Testament* (In Honor of Herbert Gordon May; eds. Harry Thomas Frank and William L. Reed; Nashville and New York: Abingdon Press, 1970), 42–63. Repr. Best, *Hearing and Speaking the Word* (1984), 234–55.

_____. "Poetry," in *EJ* 13.670–81.

Muraoka, Takamitsu. *Emphatic Words and Structures in Biblical Hebrew* (Jerusalem: Magnes Press, The Hebrew University / Leiden: E. J. Brill, 1985).

Myres, John L. "The Last Book of the 'Illiad.'" *JHS* 52 (1932), 264–96.

_____. "The Structure of Stichomythia in Attic Tragedy." *PBA* 34 (1948), 199–231.

_____. "The Pattern of the Odyssey." *JHS* 72 (1952), 1–19.

_____. *Herodotus: Father of History* (Oxford: Clarendon Press, 1953).

Nasuti, Harry P. "A Prophet to the Nations: Diachronic and Synchronic Readings of Jeremiah 1." *HAR* 10 (1986), 249–66.

Natanson, Maurice, and Henry W. Johnstone Jr. (eds.). *Philosophy, Rhetoric, and Argumentation* (University Park, Penn.: Pennsylvania State University Press, 1965).

Nathan, Leonard E. "Conjectures on a Structural Principle of Vedic Poetry." *ComLit* 28 (1976), 122–34.

Nethercut, William R. "Notes on the Structure of Propertius Book IV." *AJP* 89 (1968), 449–64.

Newman, Louis L, and William Popper. *Studies in Biblical Parallelism* (Berkeley: University of California Press, 1918).

Nicholson, E. W. *Preaching to the Exiles: A Study of the Prose Tradition in the Book of Jeremiah* (New York: Schocken Books, 1971).

Nielsen, Eduard. *Oral Tradition* (Chicago: Alec R. Allenson / London: SCM Press, 1954).

Nilsen, Thomas R. (ed.). *Essays on Rhetorical Criticism* (New York: Random House, 1968).

Norden, Eduard. *Die Antike Kunstprosa I–II* (Stuttgart: B. G. Teubner Verlagsgesellschaft, 1958). Originally 1898.

North, C. R. "The Place of Oral Tradition in the Growth of the Old Testament." *ET* 61 (1949–50), 292–96.

Norwood, Gilbert. "Vergil, *GEORGICS* iv, 453–527." *CJ* 36 (1940–41), 354–55.

————. *Pindar* (Berkeley: University of California Press, 1945).

Noth, Martin. "History and the Word of God in the Old Testament." *BJRL* 32 (1950), 194–206.

————— [ed.]. *Essays in Honour of Millar Burrows* (Leiden: E. J. Brill, 1959).

Notopoulos, James A. "Continuity and Interconnexion in Homeric Oral Composition." *TAPA* 82 (1951), 81–101.

Nyberg, H. S. *Studien zum Hoseabuche* (UUÅ 1935: 6; Uppsala: A. B. Lundequistska Bokhandeln, 1935).

Obermann, Julian. "An Antiphonal Psalm from Ras Shamra." *JBL* 55 (1936), 21–44.

O'Brien, John Anthony. *Silent Reading* (New York: Macmillan Co., 1921).

O'Connell, Robert H. "Isaiah xiv 4B–23: Ironic Reversal through Concentric Structure and Mythic Allusion." *VT* 38 (1988), 407–18.

————. "Deuteronomy VIII 1–20: Asymmetrical Concentricity and the Rhetoric of Providence." *VT* 40 (1990), 437–52.

————. *The Rhetoric of the Book of Judges* (VTSupp 63; Leiden: E. J. Brill, 1996).

O'Connor, M. "The Rhetoric of the Kilamuwa Inscription." *BASOR* 226 (1977), 15–29.

————. *Hebrew Verse Structure* (Winona Lake, Ind.: Eisenbrauns, 1980).

Oliver, Robert T. and Marvin G. Bauer (eds.). *Re-establishing the Speech Profession: The First Fifty Years* ([Mineola, N.Y.]: Speech Association of the Eastern States, 1959).

Olrik, Axel. "Episke Love i Folkedigtningen." *DS* 5 (1908), 69–89. German: *ZDA* 51 (1909), 1–12; English: Dundes, *The Study of Folklore* (1965), 129–41.

Oppenheim, A. Leo. "A Note on the Scribes in Mesopotamia," in *Studies in Honor of Benno Landsberger* (Chicago: Oriental Institute of the University of Chicago, 1965), 253–56.

O'Reilly, Leo. "Chiastic Structures in Acts 1–7." *PIBA* 7 (1983) 87–103 + Plate II.

Orlinsky, Harry M. (ed.). *Interpreting the Prophetic Tradition* (Cincinnati: Hebrew Union College Press / New York: KTAV, 1969).

Overholt, Thomas W. "Jeremiah 2 and the Problem of 'Audience Reaction.'" *CBQ* 41 (1979), 262–73.

Pardee, Dennis. *Ugaritic and Hebrew Poetic Parallelism* (VTSupp 39; Leiden: E. J. Brill, 1988).

Parks, E. Patrick. *The Roman Rhetorical Schools as a Preparation for the Courts under the Early Empire* (Baltimore: Johns Hopkins University Press, 1945).

Parry, Milman. "Studies in the Epic Technique of Oral Verse-Making, I: Homer and Homeric Style." *HSCP* 41 (1930), 73–147.

_____. "Studies in the Epic Technique of Oral Verse-Making, II: The Homeric Language as the Language of an Oral Poetry." *HSCP* 43 (1932), 1–50.

Parunak, H. Van Dyke. "Oral Typesetting: Some Uses of Biblical Structure." *Biblica* 62 (1981), 153–68.

Patrick, Dale, and Allen Scult. *Rhetoric and Biblical Interpretation* (Sheffield: Almond Press, 1990).

Paul, Shalom M. "Amos 1:3–2:3: A Concatenous Literary Pattern." *JBL* 90 (1971), 397–403.

Pedersen, Johs. *Israel: Its Life and Culture I–II* (London: Oxford University Press, 1964).

Pelikan, Jaroslav (ed.). *Twentieth Century Theology in the Making I* (trans. R. A. Wilson; London: William Collins / New York: Harper and Row, 1969).

Perdue, Leo G., and Brian W. Kovacs (eds.). *A Prophet to the Nations: Essays in Jeremiah Studies* (Winona Lake, Ind.: Eisenbrauns, 1984).

Perelman, Chaim. "Rhetoric and Philosophy." *PhRh* 1 (1968), 15–24.

_____. "The New Rhetoric: A Theory of Practical Reasoning," in *The Great Ideas Today, 1970* (trans. E. Griffin-Collart and O. Bird; eds. Robert M. Hutchins and Mortimer J. Adler; Chicago: Encyclopaedia Britannica, 1970), 273–312.

_____. "The New Rhetoric and the Rhetoricians: Remembrances and Comments." *QJS* 70 (1984), 188–96.

Perelman, Chaim, and L. Olbrechts-Tyteca. *The New Rhetoric: A Treatise on Argumentation* (trans. John Wilkinson and Purcell Weaver; Notre Dame, Ind.: University of Notre Dame Press, 1969). French: *La nouvelle rhétorique: Traité de l'argumentation I–II* (Paris: Presses Universitaires de France, 1958).

_____. "The New Rhetoric," in *The Prospect of Rhetoric* (trans. E. Griffin-Collart; eds. Lloyd F. Bitzer and Edwin Black; Englewood Cliffs, N.J.: Prentice-Hall, 1971), 115–22.

Pesch R. "Zur konzentrischen Struktur von Jona 1." *Biblica* 47 (1966), 577–81.

Petersen, David L. (ed.). *Prophecy in Israel: Search for an Identity* (Philadelphia: Fortress Press / London: SPCK, 1987).

Peterson, R. G. "Critical Calculations: Measure and Symmetry in Literature." *PMLA* 91 (1976), 367–75.

[Platnauer, Maurice (ed.)]. *Fifty Years (and Twelve) of Classical Scholarship* (Oxford: Basil Blackwell, 1968).

Pogoloff, Stephen M. *Logos and Sophia: The Rhetorical Situation of 1 Corinthians* (SBLDS 134; Atlanta: Scholars Press, 1992).

Popper, William. *Parallelism in Isaiah* (Berkeley: University of California Press, 1923).

_____. "Notes on Parallelism." *HUCA* 2 (1925), 63–85.

Porten, Bezalel. "The Structure and Theme of the Solomon Narrative (I Kings 3–11)." *HUCA* 38 (1967), 93–128.

Porten, Bezalel, and Uriel Rappaport. "Poetic Structure in Genesis IX 7." *VT* 21 (1971), 363–69.

Posner, Ernst. *Archives in the Ancient World* (Cambridge, Mass.: Harvard University Press, 1972).

Poteat, Hubert McNeill. "The Functions of Repetition in Latin Poetry." *The Classical Weekly* 18 (1919), 139–42; 145–50.

Quintilian. *The Institutio Oratoria of Quintilian I–IV* (trans. H. E. Butler; LCL; Cambridge, Mass.: Harvard University Press, 1969).

Rabinowitz, Isaac. "'Word' and Literature in Ancient Israel." *NLH* 4 (1972–73), 119–39.

Rad, Gerhard von. *Studies in Deuteronomy* (trans. David Stalker; London: SCM Press, 1953). German: *Deuteronomium-Studien* (Göttingen: Vandenhoeck & Ruprecht, 1947).

————. "Deuteronomy," in *IDB* A–D, 831–38.

————. *Old Testament Theology II* (trans. D. M. G. Stalker; Edinburgh and London: Oliver and Boyd, 1967).

Radday, Yehuda T. "On Chiasm in Biblical Narrative" [Hebrew]. *BeitM* 20–21 (1964), 48–72.

————. "Chiasm in Samuel." *LB* 9–10 (1971), 21–31.

————. "Chiasm in Tora." *LB* 19 (1972), 12–23.

————. "Chiasmus in Hebrew Biblical Narrative," in J. Welch (ed.), *Chiasmus in Antiquity* (1981), 50–117.

Rainey, Anson F. "The Scribe at Ugarit." *Proceedings of the Israel Academy of Sciences and Humanities III* (Jerusalem: Academy of Sciences and Humanities, 1969), 126–47.

Raitt, Thomas M. "The Prophetic Summons to Repentance." *ZAW* 83 (1971), 30–49.

Ramsey, George W. "Speech-Forms in Hebrew Law and Prophetic Oracles." *JBL* 96 (1977), 45–58.

Rankin, Oliver S. "Alliteration in Hebrew Poetry." *JThS* Old Series 31 (1929–30), 285–91.

Rast, Walter E. *Tradition History and the Old Testament* (Philadelphia: Fortress Press, 1972).

Rendsburg, Gary. "Janus Parallelism in Gen 49:26." *JBL* 99 (1980), 291–93.

————. "The Inclusio in Leviticus xi." *VT* 43 (1993), 418–19.

Renkema, Johan. "The Literary Structure of Lamentations (I)," in *The Structural Analysis of Biblical and Canaanite Poetry* (eds. Willem van der Meer and Johannes de Moor; Sheffield: JSOT Press, 1988), 294–320.

Reumann, John. "St. Paul's Use of Irony." *LQ* 7 (1955), 140–45.

Rice, George E. "The Chiastic Structure to the Central Section of the Epistle to the Hebrews." *AUSS* 19 (1981), 243–46.

Richards, I. A. *The Philosophy of Rhetoric* (London: Oxford University Press, 1936).

Ricoeur, Paul. "Toward a 'Post-Critical Rhetoric'"? Trans. Kathleen McLaughlin. *Pretext* 5 (1984), 9–16.

————. *Time and Narrative I* (trans. Kathleen McLaughlin and David Pellauer; Chicago and London: University of Chicago Press, 1984).

————. *Time and Narrative II* (trans. Kathleen McLaughlin and David Pellauer; Chicago and London: University of Chicago Press, 1985).

————. *Time and Narrative III* (trans. Kathleen Blamey and David Pellauer; Chicago and London: University of Chicago Press, 1988).

Ridderbos, N. H. "The Psalms: Style-Figures and Structure." *OS* 13 (1963), 43–76.

Ridout, George. "Prose Compositional Techniques in the Succession Narrative (2 Sam. 7, 9–20; 1 Kings 1–2)." Unpublished Ph.D. dissertation (Graduate Theological Union, 1971).

Rietzschel, Claus. *Das Problem der Urrolle* (Gütersloh: Gütersloher Verlagshaus, Gerd Mohn, 1966).

Rife, J. Merle. "The Literary Background of Revelation II–III." *JBL* 60 (1941), 179–82.

Ringgren, Helmer. "Oral and Written Transmission in the O.T." *STh* 3 (1949), 34–59.

_____. "The Omitting of *kol* in Hebrew Parallelism." *VT* 32 (1982), 99–103.

Robb, Stephen. "Pre-Inventional Criticism: The Speaking of Douglas Mac-Arthur," in Mohrmann, *et al.*, *Explorations in Rhetorical Criticism* (1973), 178–90.

Robbins, Charles J. "Rhetorical Structure of Philippians 2:6–11." *CBQ* 42 (1980), 73–82.

Roberts, W. Rhys. *Greek Rhetoric and Literary Criticism* (New York: Longmans, Green and Co., 1928).

Robinson, T. H. "The Structure of the Book of Jeremiah." *The Expositor* 8th Series 20 (1920), 17–31.

_____. "Baruch's Roll." *ZAW* 42 (1924), 209–21.

_____. "Some Principles of Hebrew Metrics." *ZAW* 54 (1936), 28–43.

_____. "Anacrusis in Hebrew Poetry," in *Werden und Wesen des Alten Testaments* (BZAW 66; eds. Paul Volz, *et al.*; Berlin: Alfred Töpelmann, 1936), 37–40.

_____. "Higher Criticism and the Prophetic Literature." *ET* 50 (1938–39), 198–202.

_____. *The Poetry of the Old Testament* (London: Duckworth, 1947).

_____. "Basic Principles of Hebrew Poetic Form," in *Festschrift Alfred Bertholet* (eds. Walter Baumgartner, *et al.*; Tübingen: J. C. B. Mohr [Paul Siebeck], 1950), 438–50.

_____. "Hebrew Poetic Form: The English Tradition," in *Congress Volume: Copenhagen, 1953* (VTSupp 1; Leiden: E. J. Brill, 1953), 128–49.

_____. *Prophecy and the Prophets in Ancient Israel* (2d ed.; London: Gerald Duckworth & Co., 1953).

Rofé, Alexander. "Studies on the Composition of the Book of Jeremiah" [Hebrew]. *Tarbiz* 44 (1974–75), 1–29.

_____. "The Arrangement of the Book of Jeremiah." *ZAW* 101 (1989), 390–98.

Rose, Mark. *Shakespearean Design* (Cambridge, Mass.: Belknap and Harvard University Press, 1972).

Ross, David O. Jr. *Style and Tradition in Catullus* (Cambridge, Mass.: Harvard University Press, 1969).

Ross, James F. "The Prophet as Yahweh's Messenger," in Anderson and Harrelson, *Israel's Prophetic Heritage* (1962), 98–107. Repr. Petersen, *Prophecy in Israel* (1987), 112–21.

_____. "Prophecy in Hamath, Israel and Mari." *HThR* 63 (1970), 1–28.

Rossi, Azariah ben Moses de. מאור עינים [*The Light of the Eyes*] (Vienna: Anton Elden v. Schmid Buchdrucker und Buchhändler, 1829). Repr. (Volna: R. M. Romma Press, 1866).

Rowley, H. H. "The Text and Interpretation of Jer. 11:18–12:6." *AJSLL* 42 (1926), 217–27.

_____. "The Nature of Old Testament Prophecy in the Light of Recent Study." *HThR* 38 (1945), 1–38. Repr. Rowley, *The Servant of the Lord and Other Essays* (1952), 91–128.

_____. *The Servant of the Lord and Other Essays on the Old Testament* (London: Lutterworth Press, 1952).

_____. "The Early Prophecies of Jeremiah in Their Setting." *BJRL* 45 (1962–63), 198–234. Repr. Perdue and Kovacs, *A Prophet to the Nations* (1984), 33–61.

Rudd, Niall. "Colonia and Her Bridge: A Note on the Structure of Catullus 17." *TAPA* 90 (1959), 238–42.

Saalschütz, Joseph Levin. *Von der Form der hebräischen Poesie* (Königsberg: August Wilhelm Unzer, 1825). On Azariah de Rossi (pp. 88–113).

Sanders, E. Parish. "Chiasmus and the Translation of *IQHodayot* VII, 26–27." *RQ* 23 (1968), 427–31.

Sappan, R. "Chiasm in Biblical Poetry" [Hebrew with English summary]. *BeitM* 21 (1975–76), 534–39, 623.

Saydon, P. P. "Assonance in Hebrew as a Means of Expressing Emphasis." *Biblica* 36 (1955), 36–50; 287–304.

Schneider, Bernardin. "Katà Pneŭma Àgiōsúnās (Rom. 1,4)." *Biblica* 48 (1967), 359–87.

Schneider, Norbert. *Die rhetorische Eigenart der paulinischen Antithese* (Tübingen: J. C. B. Mohr [Paul Siebeck], 1970).

Schoettgen, Christian. *Horae hebraicae et talmudicae I* (Leipzig and Dresden: Christoph. Hekelii B. Sons, 1733). Dissertatio VI: *De Exergasia Sacra*, 1249–63.

_____. *Horae hebraicae et talmudicae II* (Leipzig und Dresden: Fridericum Hekel, 1742).

Schwartz, Joseph, and John A. Rycenga (eds.). *The Province of Rhetoric* (New York: Ronald Press Co., 1965).

Sebeok, Thomas A. (ed.). *Style in Language* ([Cambridge, Mass.]: MIT Press/ New York: John Wiley & Sons, 1960).

Segert, Stanislav. "Parallelism in Ugaritic Poetry." *JAOS* 103 (1983), 295–306.

Shah, Idries. *Tales of the Dervishes* (New York: E. P. Dutton & Co., 1969).

Sharp, Harry Jr. "Campaign Analysis: Kennedy vs. Big Steel," in Mohrmann, *et al.*, *Explorations in Rhetorical Criticism* (1973), 32–50.

Shea, William H. "The Chiastic Structure of the Song of Songs." *ZAW* 92 (1980), 378–96.

_____. "Chiasm in Theme and by Form in Revelation 18." *AUSS* 20 (1982), 249–56.

_____. "Chiasmus and the Structure of David's Lament." *JBL* 105 (1986), 13–25.

Sievers, Eduard. *Metrische Studien I* (Leipzig: B. G. Teubner, 1901).

Sivan, Daniel, and William Schniedewind. "Letting Your 'Yes' Be 'No' in Ancient Israel: A Study of the Asseverative לא and הֲלֹא" *JSS* 38 (1993), 209–26.

Skutsch, O. "The Structure of the Propertian 'Monobiblos'." *CP* 58 (1963), 238–39.

Sloan, Thomas O. "Restoration of Rhetoric to Literary Study." *ST* 16 (1967), 91–97.

Sloan, Thomas O., and Chaim Perelman. "Rhetoric" in *EncB* 15th edition 15 (1974), 798–805.

Slotki, Israel W. "The Stichometry and Text of the Great Hallel." *JThS* 29 (1928), 255–68.

———. "Forms and Features of Ancient Hebrew Poetry." *JMEOS* 14 (1929), 31–49.

———. "Long and Shorter Versions of Ancient Hebrew Poems." *AJSLL* 50 (1933–34), 15–31.

———. "Antiphony in Ancient Hebrew Poetry." *JQR* 26 (1936), 199–219.

Slusser, Michael. "Reading Silently in Antiquity." *JBL* 111 (1992), 499.

Smit, J. "The Genre of 1 Corinthians 13 in the Light of Classical Rhetoric." *NT* 33 (1991), 193–216.

Smith, Barbara Herrnstein. *Poetic Closure: A Study of How Poems End* (Chicago: University of Chicago Press, 1968).

Smith, C. Alphonso. *Repetition and Parallelism in English Verse* (New York: University Publishing Co., 1894).

Smith, George Adam. *The Early Poetry of Israel in Its Physical and Social Origins* (London: Henry Frowde, Oxford University Press, 1912).

Smith, Henry Preserved. "Old Testament Notes." *JBL* 24 (1905), 30. On "Emphatic" ל and לא.

Smith, John. *The Mystery of Rhetoric Unveiled* (Menston, England: Scholars Press, 1969). Originally 1657.

Smith, P. A. *Rhetoric and Redaction in Trito-Isaiah* (VTSupp 62; Leiden: E. J. Brill, 1995).

Stamps, Dennis L. "Rhetorical Criticism of the New Testament: Ancient and Modern Evaluations of Argumentation," in *Approaches to New Testament Study* (eds. Stanley E. Porter and David Tombs; Sheffield: Sheffield Academic Press, 1995), 129–69.

Stanford, W. Bedell. *Greek Metaphor: Studies in Theory and Practice* (Oxford: Basil Blackwell, 1936).

———. *The Sound of Greek* (Berkeley and Los Angeles: University of California Press, 1967).

Steele, Robert Benson. "Chiasmus in Sallust, Caesar, Tacitus and Justinus." Unpublished Ph.D. dissertation (Johns Hopkins University, 1890).

———. "Anaphora and Chiasmus in Livy." *TAPA* 32 (1901), 154–85.

———. "Chiasmus in the Epistles of Cicero, Seneca, Pliny and Fronto," in *Studies in Honor of Basil L. Gildersleeve* (Baltimore: Johns Hopkins University Press, 1902), 339–52.

Steinmann, Martin Jr. (ed.). *New Rhetorics* (New York: Scribner's, 1967).

Stempvoort, P. A. van "Eine stilistische Lösung einer alten Schwierigkeit in I Thess. 5,23." *NTS* 7 (1961), 262–65.

Sternberg, Meir. "The Bible's Art of Persuasion: Ideology, Rhetoric, and Poetics in Saul's Fall." *HUCA* 54 (1983), 45–82.

———. *The Poetics of Biblical Narrative: Ideological Literature and the Drama of Reading* (Bloomington, Ind.: Indiana University Press, 1985).

Stewart, Charles J. "Historical Survey: Rhetorical Criticism in Twentieth Century America," in Mohrmann, *et al.*, *Explorations in Rhetorical Criticism* (1973), 1–31.

Stewart, Donald C. "Metaphor and Paraphrase." *PhRh* 4 (1971), 111–23.

_____. "The Status of Composition and Rhetoric in American Colleges, 1880–1902: An MLA Perspective." *College English* 47 (1985), 734–46.

Stock, Augustine. "Chiastic Awareness and Education in Antiquity." *BTB* 14 (1984), 23–24.

Storfjell, J. Bjornar. "The Chiastic Structure of Psalm 151." *AUSS* 25 (1987), 97–106.

Streane, A. W. *The Double Text of Jeremiah* (Cambridge: Deighton Bell and Co., 1896).

Talbert, Charles H. "Artistry and Theology: An Analysis of the Architecture of Jn 1,19–5,47." *CBQ* 32 (1970), 341–66.

Talmon, Shemaryahu. "The Presentation of Synchroneity and Simultaneity in Biblical Narrative," in *Studies in Hebrew Narrative Art throughout the Ages* (eds. Joseph Heinemann and Shmuel Werses; Jerusalem: Magnes Press, Hebrew University, 1978), 9–26. Repr. Talmon, *Literary Studies in the Hebrew Bible* (1993), 112–33.

_____. *Literary Studies in the Hebrew Bible* (Jerusalem: Magnes Press, Hebrew University / Leiden: E. J. Brill, 1993).

Thiering, Barbara. "The Poetic Forms of the Hodayot." *JSS* 8 (1963), 189–209.

_____. "Opening and Closing Narratives in the Gospels and Acts." *Abr-Nahrain* 4 (1963–64), 50–55.

_____. "The Acts of the Apostles as Early Christian Art," in *Essays in Honour of Griffithes Wheeler Thatcher* (ed. Evan C. B. MacLaurin; Sydney: Sydney University Press, 1967), 139–89.

Thomas, D. Winton. "A Consideration of Some Unusual Ways of Expressing the Superlative in Hebrew." *VT* 3 (1953), 209–24.

_____. "Some Further Remarks on Unusual Ways of Expressing the Superlative in Hebrew." *VT* 18 (1968), 120–24.

Thomas, Rosalind. *Oral Tradition and Written Record in Classical Athens* (Cambridge: Cambridge University Press, 1989).

Thompson, Wayne N. *The Process of Persuasion: Principles and Readings* (New York: Harper and Row, 1975).

Thomson, George. "Notes on *Prometheus Vinctus.*" *CQ* 23 (1929), 155–63.

Thornton, Agathe H. F. "The Hebrew Conception of Speech as a Creative Energy." *HibJ* 44 (1945–46), 132–34.

Thurén, Lauri. "Vad är retorisk kritik?" *TAik* 96 (1991), 41–45.

Topel, L. John. "A Note on the Methodology of Structural Analysis in Jn 2:23–3:21." *CBQ* 33 (1971), 211–20.

Tov, Emanuel. "The Literary History of the Book of Jeremiah in the Light of Its Textual History," in *Empirical Models for Biblical Criticism* (ed. Jeffrey H. Tigay; Philadelphia: University of Pennsylvania Press, 1985), 211–37.

_____. "The Jeremiah Scrolls from Qumran." *RQ* 54 (1989), 189–206.

_____. "4QJer[c] (4Q72)," in *Tradition of the Text* (Festschrift Dominique Barthélemy; eds. Gerard J. Norton and Stephen Pisano; Freiburg (Switzerland): Freiburg Universitätsverlag / Göttingen: Vandenhoeck & Ruprecht, 1991), 249–76 + plates.

_____. "Three Fragments of Jeremiah from Qumran Cave 4." *RQ* 60 (1992), 531–41.

_____. "4QJer[a]: A Preliminary Edition." *Textus* 17 (1994), 1–41.

Tov, Emanuel (ed.). *The Dead Sea Scrolls on Microfiche* (Leiden: E. J. Brill, [1993]).

Tov, Emanuel, and Stephen J. Pfann (eds.). *The Dead Sea Scrolls on Microfiche: Companion Volume* (Leiden: E. J. Brill, 1993).

Trible, Phyllis. "The Gift of a Poem: A Rhetorical Study of Jeremiah 31:15–22." *ANQ* 17 (1977), 271–80. Repr. Linda Clark, *et al.* (eds.), *Image-Breaking, Image-Building* (New York: Pilgrim Press, 1981), 104–15.

————. *Rhetorical Criticism: Context, Method, and the Book of Jonah* (Minneapolis: Fortress Press, 1994).

Tromp, N. J. "Amos V 1–17: Towards a Stylistic and Rhetorical Analysis." *OS* 23 (1984), 56–84.

Tsumura, D. T. "Literary Insertion (A×B Pattern) in Biblical Hebrew." *VT* 33 (1983), 468–82.

————. "Literary Insertion, A×B Pattern, in Hebrew and Ugaritic." *UF* 18 (1986), 351–61.

Tucker, Gene M. *Form Criticism of the Old Testament* (Philadelphia: Fortress Press, 1971).

————. "Prophetic Speech." *Int* 32 (1978), 31–45. Repr. Mays and Achtemeier, *Interpreting the Prophets* (1987), 27–40.

Untermeyer, Louis. *The Forms of Poetry* (New York: Harcourt Brace & Co., 1926).

Van Grol, H. W. "Paired Tricola in the Psalms, Isaiah and Jeremiah." *JSOT* 25 (1983), 55–73.

Van Iersel, B. M. "Concentric Structures in Mark 1:14–3:35 (4:1) with Some Observations on Method." *BiInt* 3 (1995), 75–98.

Vaux, Roland de. *Ancient Israel: Its Life and Institutions I–II* (trans. John McHugh; New York: McGraw-Hill Book Co. / London: Darton, Longman & Todd, 1965).

————. *Jerusalem and the Prophets* (Cincinnati: Hebrew Union College Press, 1965). Repr. Orlinsky, *Interpreting the Prophetic Tradition* (1969), 277–300.

Vermes, Geza. "The Symbolical Interpretation of *Lebanon* in the Targums: The Origin and Development of an Exegetical Tradition." *JThS* New Series 9 (1958), 1–12.

————. *Scripture and Tradition in Judaism* (Leiden: E. J. Brill, 1961).

Viviano, Pauline A. "2 Kings 17: A Rhetorical and Form-Critical Analysis." *CBQ* 49 (1987), 548–59.

Volz, D. Paul. *Studien zum Text des Jeremia* (BWAT 25; Leipzig: J. C. Hinrichs'sche Buchhandlung, 1920).

Vulpe, Nicola. "Irony and the Unity of the Gilgamesh Epic." *JNES* 53 (1994), 275–83.

de Waard, J. "The Chiastic Structure of Amos V 1–17." *VT* 27 (1977), 170–77.

Walker, H. H., and Nils W. Lund. "The Literary Structure of the Book of Habakkuk." *JBL* 53 (1934), 355–70.

Walsh, Jerome T. "Jonah 2, 3–10: A Rhetorical Critical Study." *Biblica* 63 (1982), 219–29.

————. "Summons to Judgment: A Close Reading of Isaiah xli 1–20." *VT* 43 (1993), 351–71.

Walter, Otis M. "On the Varieties of Rhetorical Criticism," in *Essays on Rhetorical Criticism* (ed. Thomas R. Nilsen; New York: Random House, 1968), 158–72.

Walton, John H. "Vision Narrative Wordplay and Jeremiah XXIV." *VT* 39 (1989), 508–9.

Warner, Martin (ed.). *The Bible as Rhetoric* (London and New York: Routledge, 1990).

Warren, Mervyn A. "A Rhetorical Study of the Preaching of Doctor Martin Luther King Jr., Pastor and Pulpit Orator." Unpublished Ph.D. dissertation (Michigan State University, 1966).

Watson, Duane Frederick. *Invention, Arrangement, and Style: Rhetorical Criticism of Jude and 2 Peter* (SBLDS 104; Atlanta: Scholars Press, 1988).

_____. "Rhetorical Analysis of 3 John: A Study in Epistolary Rhetoric." *CBQ* 51 (1989), 479–501.

_____ (ed.). *Persuasive Artistry: Studies in New Testament Rhetoric in Honor of George A. Kennedy* (Sheffield: Sheffield Academic Press, 1991).

Watson, Duane Frederick, and Alan J. Hauser. *Rhetorical Criticism of the Bible* (Leiden: E. J. Brill, 1994).

Watson, Wilfred G. "Fixed Pairs in Ugaritic and Isaiah." *VT* 22 (1972), 460–68.

_____. "Verse Patterns in Ugaritic, Akkadian and Hebrew Poetry." *UF* 7 (1975), 483–92.

_____. "The Pivot Pattern in Hebrew, Ugaritic and Akkadian Poetry." *ZAW* 88 (1976), 239–53.

_____. "An Unrecognized Hyperbole in *Krt.*" *Orientalia* 48 (1979), 112–17.

_____. "Gender-Matched Synonymous Parallelism in the OT." *JBL* 99 (1980), 321–41.

_____. "Chiastic Patterns in Biblical Hebrew Poetry," in J. Welch, *Chiasmus in Antiquity* (1981), 118–68.

_____. "Reversed Word-Pairs in Ugaritic Poetry." *UF* 13 (1981), 189–92.

_____. "Strophic Chiasmus in Ugaritic Poetry." *UF* 15 (1983), 259–70.

_____. *Classical Hebrew Poetry* (Sheffield: JSOT Press, 1984).

_____. "Further Examples of Semantic-Sonant Chiasmus." *CBQ* 46 (1984), 31–33.

_____. *Traditional Techniques in Classical Hebrew Verse* (Sheffield: Sheffield Academic Press, 1994).

Webster, Edwin C. "A Rhetorical Study of Isaiah 66." *JSOT* 34 (1986), 93–108.

_____. "The Rhetoric of Isaiah 63–65." *JSOT* 47 (1990), 89–102.

Weinberg, Bernard. "Formal Analysis in Poetry and Rhetoric," in *Papers in Rhetoric and Poetic* (ed. Donald C. Bryant; Iowa City: University of Iowa Press, 1965), 36–45.

Weinfeld, Moshe. "Deuteronomy: The Present State of Inquiry." *JBL* 86 (1967), 249–62. Repr. Duane L. Christensen (ed.), *A Song of Power and the Power of Song: Essays on the Book of Deuteronomy* (Sources for Biblical and Theological Study 3; Winona Lake, Ind.: Eisenbrauns, 1993), 21–35.

Weingreen, J. "Oral Torah and Written Records," in *Holy Book and Holy Tradition* (eds. F. F. Bruce and E. G. Rupp; Grand Rapids: Eerdmans Press, 1968), 54–67.

Weippert, Helga. *Die Prosareden des Jeremiabuches* (BZAW 132; Berlin and New York: Walter de Gruyter, 1973).

Weiss, Johannes. "Beiträge zur paulinischen Rhetorik," in *Theologische Studien* (Festschrift für Bernhard Weiss; Göttingen: Vandenhoeck und Ruprecht, 1897), 165–247.

Weiss, Meir. "On the Traces of a Biblical Metaphor" [Hebrew]. *Tarbiz* 34 (1964–65), 211–23; 303–318.

_____. "The Pattern of Numerical Sequence in Amos 1–2." *JBL* 86 (1967), 416–23.

_____. *The Bible and Modern Literary Theory* [Hebrew] (Jerusalem: Bialik Institute, 1967).

_____. "Die Methode der 'Total-Interpretation,'" in *Congress Volume: Uppsala, 1971* (VTSupp 22; Leiden: E. J. Brill, 1972), 88–112.

Weiss, Raphael. "On Chiasmus in the Bible" [Hebrew]. *BeitM* 13 (1962), 46–51.

Welch, Adam C. "A Problem in Jeremiah." *ET* 26 (1914–15), 429–30.

_____. *Jeremiah: His Time and His Work* (Oxford: Oxford University Press / London: Humphrey Milford, 1928). Repr. (Westport, Conn: Greenwood Press, 1980).

_____. *The Work of the Chronicler* (London: British Academy and Oxford University Press, 1939).

Welch, John W. "Chiasmus in Ugaritic." *UF* 6 (1974), 421–36.

_____ (ed.). *Chiasmus in Antiquity* (Hildesheim: Gerstenberg Verlag, 1981).

_____. "Chiasmus in the New Testament," in J. Welch, *Chiasmus in Antiquity* (1981), 211–49.

Wellhausen, Julius. *Prolegomena to the History of Ancient Israel* (Cleveland: Meridian Books / New York: World Publishing Co, 1965). German: *Prolegomena zur Geschichte Israels* (2d ed.; Berlin: George Reimer, 1883). Originally 1878.

_____. *Die kleinen Propheten übersetz und erklärt* (3d ed.; Berlin: Georg Reimer, 1898).

Wenham, David. "The Structure of Matthew XIII." *NTS* 25 (1979), 516–22.

Wenham, Gordon J. "Bᵉtûlāh 'A Girl of Marriageable Age'." *VT* 22 (1972), 326–48.

_____. "The Coherence of the Flood Narrative." *VT* 28 (1978), 336–48.

Wenham, Gordon J., and J. G. McConville. "Drafting Techniques in Some Deuteronomic Laws." *VT* 30 (1980), 248–52.

Westermann, Claus. "The Way of the Promise through the Old Testament," in *The Old Testament and Christian Faith* (ed. Bernhard W. Anderson; New York/Evanston: Harper and Row, 1963), 200–224.

_____. *Basic Forms of Prophetic Speech* (trans. Hugh Clayton White; Philadelphia: Westminster Press, 1967).

_____. *Prophetic Oracles of Salvation in the Old Testament* (trans. Keith Crim; Louisville: Westminster / John Knox Press, 1991).

Wette, Wilhelm de. *A Critical and Historical Introduction to the Canonical Scriptures of the Old Testament II* (3d ed.; trans. and enlarged Theodore Parker; Boston: Little, Brown and Co., 1858). German: *Beiträge zur Einleitung in das Alte Testament II: Kritik des israelitischen Geschichte* (Halle: Schimmelpfennig und Compagnie, 1807).

Whitekettle, Richard. "Leviticus 15.18 Reconsidered: Chiasm, Spatial Structure and the Body." *JSOT* 49 (1991), 31–45.

Whitman, Cedric H. *Homer and the Heroic Tradition* (Cambridge, Mass.: Harvard University Press, 1958; 1967).

Wichelns, Herbert A. "The Literary Criticism of Oratory," in Drummond, *Studies in Rhetoric and Public Speaking in Honor of James Albert Winans* (1925), 181–216. Repr. Bryant, *The Rhetorical Idiom* (1958), 5–42.

_____ (ed.). *Studies in Speech and Drama* (In Honor of Alexander M. Drummond; Ithaca, N.Y.: Cornell University Press, 1944).

_____. "Some Differences between Literary Criticism and Rhetorical Criticism," in Howes, *Historical Studies of Rhetoric and Rhetoricians* (1961), 217–24.

Widengren, G. *Literary and Psychological Aspects of the Hebrew Prophets* (UUÅ 1948:10; Uppsala: Lundequistska Bokhandeln, 1948).

_____. "Oral Tradition and Written Literature among the Hebrews in the Light of Arabic Evidence, with Special Regard to Prose Narratives." *AcOr* 23 (1959), 201–62.

Wiklander, Bertil. *Prophecy as Literature: A Text-Linguistic and Rhetorical Approach to Isaiah 2–4* (Uppsala: CWK Gleerup, 1984).

Wild, Laura H. *A Literary Guide to the Bible* (New York and London: Harper and Bros., 1922).

Wilder, Amos N. *The Language of the Gospel: Early Christian Rhetoric* (New York: Harper and Row, 1964).

_____. "The Rhetoric of Ancient and Modern Apocalyptic." *Int* 25 (1971), 436–53.

Wilke, Christian Gottlob. *Die neutestamentliche Rhetorik* (Dresden und Leipzig: Arnoldische Buchhandlung, 1843).

Williams, Michael J. "An Investigation of the Legitimacy of Source Distinctions for the Prose Material in Jeremiah." *JBL* 112 (1993), 193–210.

Williams, Ronald J. "Writing and Writing Materials," in *IDB* R–Z, 909–21.

_____. "Scribal Training in Ancient Egypt." *JAOS* 92 (1972), 214–21.

Willis, John T. "The Structure of Micah 3–5 and the Function of Micah 5:9–14 in the Book." *ZAW* 81 (1969), 191–214.

_____. "The Juxtaposition of Synonymous and Chiastic Parallelism in Tricola in Old Testament Hebrew Psalm Poetry." *VT* 29 (1979), 465–80.

_____. "Dialogue between Prophet and Audience as a Rhetorical Device in the Book of Jeremiah." *JSOT* 33 (1985), 63–82.

Wilson, John F. "Fifty Years of Rhetorical Criticism by Laymen," in Oliver and Bauer, *Re-establishing the Speech Profession: The First Fifty Years* (1959), 8–11.

Winans, J. A. "The Need for Research." *QJS* 1 (1915), 17–23.

Wohlberg, Joseph. "The Structure of the Laodamia Simile in Catullus 68b." *CP* 50 (1955), 42–46.

Wright, Addison G. "Structure of the Book of Wisdom." *Biblica* 48 (1967), 165–84.

Wright, G. Ernest. "Deuteronomy," in *IB* 2 (ed. George A. Buttrick; New York: Abingdon Press, 1953), 311–537.

_____. "The Lawsuit of God: A Form-Critical Study of Deuteronomy 32," in Anderson and Harrelson, *Israel's Prophetic Heritage* (1962), 26–67.

Wuellner, Wilhelm. "Paul's Rhetoric of Argumentation in Romans: An Alternative to the Donfried-Karris Debate over Romans." *CBQ* 38 (1976), 330–51.

_____. "Where Is Rhetorical Criticism Taking Us?" *CBQ* 49 (1987), 448–63.

Yaron, Reuven. "On Divorce in Old Testament Times." *RIDA* 3d Series 4 (1957), 117–28.

_____. "A Royal Divorce at Ugarit." *Orientalia* 32 (1963), 21–31.

_____. "The Restoration of Marriage." *JJS* 17 (1966), 1–11.

Yates, Francis A. *The Art of Memory* (Chicago: University of Chicago Press, 1966).

Yellin, David. "The Use of Ellipsis in 'Second Isaiah.'" *JPOS* 1 (1920–21), 132–37.

Yoder, Perry B. "A–B Pairs and Oral Composition in Hebrew Poetry." *VT* 21 (1971), 470–89.

Young, Richard E., and Alton Becker. "Toward a Modern Theory of Rhetoric: A Tagmemic Contribution," in Steinmann, *New Rhetorics* (1967), 77–107.

Zalcman, Lawrence. "Ambiguity and Assonance at Zephaniah ii 4." *VT* 36 (1986), 365–71.

Zeitlin, Solomon. "Hillel and the Hermeneutic Rules." *JQR* 54 (1963–64), 161–73.

Zevit, Ziony. "Roman Jakobson, Psycholinguistics, and Biblical Poetry." *JBL* 109 (1990), 385–401.

Zimmerli, Walther. "Prophetic Proclamation and Reinterpretation," in *Tradition and Theology in the Old Testament* (ed. and trans. Douglas A. Knight; London: SPCK, 1977), 69–100.

_____. "Visionary Experience in Jeremiah," in *Israel's Prophetic Tradition* (eds. Richard Coggins, *et al.*; Cambridge: Cambridge University Press, 1982), 95–118.

Index of Authors

Index of Scripture

New Testament and Deuterocanonical Literature

Luke
  1:47   158

Acts
  2:17–18   122 n. 79

2 Maccabees
  4:26   133
  4:38   133
  5:9–10   133
  8:33   133

  9:5–6   133
  13:3–8   133

Sirach
  3:16   161